The Ozone Layer

The Ozone Layer provides the first thorough and accessible history of stratospheric ozone, from the discovery of ozone in the nineteenth century to current investigations of the Antarctic ozone hole. Drawing directly on the extensive scientific literature, Christie uses the story of ozone as a case study for examining fundamental issues relating to the collection and evaluation of evidence, the conduct of scientific debate and the construction of scientific consensus. By linking key debates in the philosophy of science to an example of real-world science the author not only provides an excellent introduction to the philosophy of science but also challenges many of its preconceptions. This accessible book will interest students and academics concerned with the history, philosophy and sociology of science, as well as having general appeal on this topic of contemporary relevance and concern.

MAUREEN CHRISTIE is Lecturer in Philosophy of Science at the University of Melbourne, Australia.

The Ozone Layer

A Philosophy of Science Perspective

Maureen Christie

University of Melbourne

CAMBRIDGE
UNIVERSITY PRESS

PUBLISHED BY THE PRESS SYNDICATE OF THE UNIVERSITY OF CAMBRIDGE
The Pitt Building, Trumpington Street, Cambridge, United Kingdom

CAMBRIDGE UNIVERSITY PRESS
The Edinburgh Building, Cambridge CB2 2RU, UK
40 West 20th Street, New York, NY 10011–4211, USA
10 Stamford Road, Oakleigh, Melbourne 3166, Australia
Ruiz de Alarcón 13, 28014 Madrid, Spain
Dock House, The Waterfront, Cape Town 8001, South Africa

http://www.cambridge.org

First published 2001

Printed in the United Kingdom at the University Press, Cambridge

Typeface Plantin 10/12   *System* QuarkXPress™   [SE]

A catalogue record for this book is available from the British Library

Library of Congress Cataloguing in Publication data
Christie, Maureen
The Ozone Layer: a philosophy of science perspective / Maureen Christie.
    p. cm.
Includes bibliographical references and index.
ISBN 0 521 65072 0 (hardback); 0 521 65908 6 (paperback)
1. Ozone layer. 2. Science–Philosophy. I. Title.
QC881.2.O9 C48 2001
551.51′42–dc21   00 036295

ISBN 0 521 65072 0 hardback
ISBN 0 521 65908 6 paperback

To the memory of Mary Agnes Christie
(14 February 1911 – 17 October 1996)

Contents

Figures

Abbreviations

AAOE   Airborne Antarctic Ozone Experiment. A suite of experiments
        in the form of observations from two high-flying aircraft in the
        Antarctic region in August/September 1987.

AEC   Atomic Energy Commission. US government agency.

AES   Atmospheric Environment Service. Canadian government
        agency.

bpi   bits per inch. A measure of how densely data is recorded on
        magnetic tape.

CFC   chlorinated fluorocarbon. One of a series of artificial and
or cfc unreactive chemical substances, first developed as refrigerants
        in the 1930s, and later in wide industrial and domestic use.

DU   Dobson unit. A measure of the integrated ozone concentration
        up a vertical column of the atmosphere. 100 DU corresponds
        to a layer of pure ozone gas 1 mm thick at 1 atmosphere pres-
        sure and 0°C.

EBCDIC a protocol for binary coding of data, current in the 1960s and
        1970s.

ENSO   El Niño Southern Oscillation. A climatic phenomenon affect-
        ing mainly the Southern Pacific region, where a pool of warm
        water develops off the Western coast of South America, and
        disrupts normal climate patterns.

IDL   Interactive Data Language. A software system used by NASA
        in analysing satellite data.

IGY   International Geophysical Year. A period in 1957 and 1958 set
        aside by UNESCO for a special international effort in geo-
        physics research.

NAS   National Academy of Sciences. US organisation.

NASA   National Aeronautics and Space Administration. US govern-
        ment agency.

nm   nanometres. 1 nanometre is a millionth of a millimetre. The
        unit is commonly used for the wavelength of visibile light (range
        to 700 nm) and ultraviolet light (range about 50 to 400 nm).

NOAA   National Oceanic and Atmospheric Administration. US government agency.

NOx   A term used by atmospheric scientists for the total atmospheric content of all of the reactive oxides of nitrogen, that is all nitrogen oxides except for nitrous oxide, N_2O.

NOZE   National Ozone Experiment. Two US scientific expeditions to Antarctic, specifically set up to conduct a number of upper atmosphere observations in August 1986 and August 1987.

ppbw and variants   parts per billion by weight. The fourth letter may also be a 'v' for parts by volume. The third may alternatively be 'm' for million, or 't' for trillion. The billion and trillion are American billions and trillions, 10^9 and 10^{12} respectively.

QBO   Quasi-biennial oscillation. A semi-regular climatic pattern seen in changing direction of the prevailing airflow at the equator. The pattern repeats with a period ranging from about 24 to 32 months.

SBUV   Solar back-scattered ultraviolet. A satellite-based series of instrumental observations which provides ozone data.

SST   Supersonic Transport. A term for the various projects seeking to produce supersonic passenger aircraft.

STP   Standard temperature and pressure. Because gases are very compressible, concentrations depend sensitively on temperature and pressure conditions. Gas properties are often converted to STP – the properties the gas would have at 0°C and 1 atmosphere pressure.

TOMS   Total ozone monitoring spectrometer. A satellite-based series of instrumental observations of ozone data.

UT   Universal Time. Typically measured in seconds after midnight Greenwich Mean Time, or as a simple alternative to GMT.

UV   Ultraviolet. Refers to light whose wavelength is shorter than visible light. Often divided for medical purposes into UV-C, UV-B, and UV-A in order of shortening wavelength, and increasing danger from bodily exposure to the radiation.

VAX   A mainframe computer dating from the early 1970s.

WMO   World Meteorological Organisation. A United Nations agency.

WODC   World Ozone Data Centre. The world repository for ozone data. Hosted by the Canadian Atmospheric Environment Centre at Downsview, Ontario, under a WMO United Nations charter. It has now become WOUDC: World Ozone and Ultraviolet Data Centre.

Preface

When choosing a topic for my doctoral studies in the History and Philosophy of Science, I wanted to do something that was important to our understanding of the way science works. I was also anxious to avoid the musty and much-travelled corridors of European science of a century or more ago. It was important to me that my topic should have strong relevance to today.

I became interested in stratospheric ozone, CFCs, and the Antarctic ozone hole when my husband John, who is a chemist, outlined a new course of lectures he was preparing. I asked him if I could sit in on his lectures. As the course unfolded I became enthralled with the topic. I hope that in presenting this very rich history of stratospheric ozone, and the scientific investigation of the Antarctic ozone hole in this way, and relating it to some consideration of how scientists collect and evaluate evidence, I will have provided material of great interest and value for all who read these pages.

This book is an extension of the work in my doctoral thesis. I am greatly indebted to my husband, Dr John R. Christie, for his help, support, encouragement and for his long-suffering patience. As a scientist himself, he has been a very wonderful resource and this book would never have been written without his help. I would like to thank him for the many hours he gave me and for the very many valuable discussions we have had. He has made many valuable contributions towards getting this book together, which should not be overlooked. They included helping me with the knobs and whistles on our computer software, and, more importantly, invaluable help with, and contribution to, the more technical aspects of the chemical discussions.

I would also like to thank Dr Neil Thomason. Neil supervised my doctoral work. He also took much of the initiative in getting my work brought to the notice of the publishers. He catapulted me into taking effective steps to produce this volume, by arranging an interview for me with Catherine Max (formerly of Cambridge University Press). I would also like to thank Catherine who did much to encourage me. She was always very positive and enthusiastic. All the staff at HPS Department at the University of Melbourne have also been very supportive.

I would like to thank several scientists who granted me some of their very precious time and who were all very generous to me. They include Jonathan Shanklin from the British Antarctic Survey, Dr David Tarasick, from Environment Canada, Dr Susan Solomon, NOAA, Boulder, Dr Adrian Tuck, NOAA, Boulder, Professor Harold Johnston and his wife Mary Ella, of Berkeley, Dr Charles Jackman and Dr Rich McPeters, both of NASA Goddard Space Flight Centre.

I would like to thank my extended family, Peter and Suzie, Wendy and John, Phil and Karen, and Steve. I would especially like to thank my five lovely grandchildren, Tristan Richards, Orien Richards, Shannon Richards, Danielle Barker and Jocelyn Barker. They provided a much needed source of joy and distraction.

And last but not least: the book has been dedicated to the memory of my very lovely mother-in-law and special friend, Agnes Christie. She was a great source of encouragement not only to me, but to all who knew her. I undertook university studies as a mature age student and Agnes was so supportive, and very proud of me. She passed away just six months prior to the completion of my doctoral work.

1   Introduction

This book tells the story of scientific understanding of the stratospheric ozone layer. It is certainly not the first work to be written on this subject! But the approach here is somewhat different. We are looking at the story of a series of scientific investigations. And we are looking at them from the point of view of evidence: what conclusions were drawn, and when? How were experiments designed to try to sort out the different possibilities? What happened to cause scientific opinion on certain issues to change? The first part of the book sets out the history, with these sorts of issues in focus.

This then sets the basis for the second part. Philosophers of science have tried to analyse the way that science is conducted. They have written about the way that theories are devised, become consensually accepted, and then may be revised or even overthrown in the light of new evidence. The history of stratospheric ozone is full of unusual twists and changes. So in this work it is used as a case study: an example we can use to examine how some philosophical accounts of evidence in science might compare with the actual conduct of modern science. The example even suggests some new aspects that differ from the philosophers' accounts.

Does that mean that this is a work without a clear focus? A book that is trying to tackle two quite separate issues, rather than concentrating on one of them? I would certainly hope not. The aim is rather to achieve a sort of two-way feedback that enriches both themes. On the one hand, the philosophical issues can be more clearly brought out when they are related to a real and interesting case in near-current science. The relevance of the several philosophical accounts, and the problems with them, are exposed in a different way when they are applied to actual scientific practice rather than idealised science, and to recent science rather than the science of the past. And on the other hand, looking at the history of a series of scientific investigations from the point of view of collection and presentation of evidence, can provide novel and interesting insights. These insights differ from, and are perhaps complementary to those which are obtained when the history is analysed primarily in terms of

1

political and social issues, a more typical perspective in modern history writing. Examination of the history informs the philosophical analysis; an understanding of the philosophical issues enriches the history.

The main source of material for the analysis of the investigation is the primary scientific literature. The history that is presented and discussed here is the 'official' scientific development of the subject, as presented in numerous peer-reviewed scientific papers.

There is a rationale for approaching the history in this particular way. The philosophical questions that I address later, relate to the basis for evaluation of the evidence, and the justification of the theoretical framework. To examine these issues, it is fair to consider the evidence as presented, at the various stages of the unfolding story. Exploring the accident of the detail of the way the evidence was actually collected, or the way theoretical insights were actually gleaned, might produce rather a different picture. On that account science might appear rather less like a rational enterprise. This approach to the history and sociology of science is an important undertaking in its own right. But I see it as largely irrelevant to the specific issues that are being addressed here. The questions of importance to this discussion relate not to whether new evidence or insight was collected as the result of a rational approach, but rather to whether the construction that is put together in reporting the evidence or insight, after the fact, provides a convincing justification.

Some who have written on issues like this have been largely concerned with questions of vested interest and hidden motive. These might certainly colour the way in which a scientific investigation proceeds. Certain projects may receive funding, which others are denied. A group of scientists might be sensitive to the interests of sponsors and 'put a spin' on their published findings. But similar factors apply in any situation where evidence is presented and conclusions drawn from it. What really matters is whether the evidence leads convincingly or compellingly to the conclusions that are drawn. Scientists do not work in a social and political vacuum. There are certainly possibilities that vested interests, improper motives, or pre-conceived ideas might lead some lines of enquiry to be pursued and others neglected. In extreme cases, evidence may be suppressed, distorted, or fabricated. The concern of others with these issues is a legitimate one, even in examining a scientific investigation. But they are not the main concern of this work. Vested interests may indeed have played a major role in some aspects of the ozone investigations. The issues will be indicated, but any deep analysis left to others.

There is an important problem with trying to use the record of the primary scientific literature as an historical source in this way. It is incomplete. It is incomplete in a systematic way, and in a way that is sometimes

– fortunately rarely – misleading. A scientific paper sometimes contains errors that escape the notice of the referees. Simple miscalculations or transcriptions are of course corrected in errata published by the relevant journal. But there are also significant errors of experimental design or interpretation that arise from time to time. A publication which corrects such an error is often, and justifiably seen as an insubstantial and derivative piece of work, and editors are understandably reluctant to publish such snippets. So in discussion with leading scientists you might hear that 'that paper was flawed', 'that paper was not widely accepted at the time', 'that paper has been discredited', or even that 'the referees really should not have accepted that paper'. And they can point out the flaws to justify such statements. Although the refutations are well known to, and circulate widely within the specialist scientific community, many do not appear in the primary scientific literature, nor even in the review literature.

This underlines the importance of discussions with scientists, and of some of the informal material, in helping to provide a balanced picture.

There is a debate in the Philosophy of Science about the relationships between philosophy, history and science. One view is that philosophers should stand apart from science in prescribing the epistemic standards that science ought to adopt, and the methodologies that are appropriate to this task. They can thereby become an independent arbiter of the performance of scientists. The other view is that philosophers should discern and describe the epistemic standards and methodologies that scientists claim to adopt or actually adopt. By doing this, a more accurate picture of what science actually is emerges, but the philosophers leave themselves with no basis from which to criticise.

Both of these attitudes toward the philosophy of science are fraught with peril.

If we take the first attitude, we are immediately faced with all of the traditional philosophical problems of world view. Should a philosophy of science be based on a realist or an anti-realist ontology? Or can it somehow embrace both? Can parameters be devised for rational scientific methodology while sceptical arguments about the impossibility of any sort of knowledge remain largely unassailable? A path must be traced through these minefields before the specific questions and problems that affect scientific enquiry can be addressed.

Then, even if we succeed in this part of the enterprise, there is a second and much more practical area of difficulty. The demands of logical and philosophical rigour will have constrained the idealised methodology we describe into an artificial enterprise that will probably bear little relationship to the way science is actually conducted. And the work will probably strike few chords with scientists, be of little practical use to the scientific community, and have little practical influence. It is important to stress that this is not necessarily the case. Popper's work, which falls squarely into this mould, has had a huge influence among scientists, and strongly colours the way that they describe and discuss their methodology. But there is plenty of evidence that it does not fit very well with the actual methodology that is adopted in modern science. We will be looking at some of this evidence in later chapters of this book.

The alternative approach is for philosophers rather to recognise that modern science is a huge and relatively successful enterprise that has largely set its own rules and methodologies, and to adopt the task of collecting, describing, systematising, and possibly rationalising the methods that are used and that have been successful. The problem here is that the philosopher who adopts this approach seems to be left without means of handling the traditional philosophical imperatives such as rationality and justification. If the focus is on what science *is*, without a clear model of what science *ought to be*, there is no means of distinguishing good science from bad science. And perhaps the only issue on which there is general agreement among scientists, philosophers of science, historians of science, sociologists of science, and science educators, is that some scientific investigations involve good science and some involve bad science.

Kuhn's account of Scientific Revolutions and Lakatos' account of Research Programmes are among the influential works that can be seen to come from this perspective. The main claim in these works is to describe the actual conduct of science, and there is little in the way of value judgements to enable us to recognise 'good' science. A notion of 'fruitfulness' as a measure of a paradigm or a research programme does emerge: this does seem to be a case of the end justifying the means. Generally these works are less recognised than Popper's by working scientists, and regarded with more hostility.

The approach of this book is to be generally descriptive rather than prescriptive of modern science. But I have tried to maintain some basis for rational examination and judgement. I believe that it is possible to maintain a significant basis for legitimate critical analysis of scientific arguments, and to distinguish good science from bad science, without having to be prescriptive of any ontological or methodological basis. It arises simply from a requirement of legitimate evaluation of the evidence, in the same way that disputes about matters of fact might be resolved in a court of law. The science is clearly flawed, for example, if a particular result is claimed as an entailment of a particular theory, and it can be demonstrated that it is not! Grounds for criticism of the performance of science also remain when it can be shown that parts of the edifice of science rest on improper bases, for example cultural prejudice, political influence of a few leading scientists, fabricated evidence, or the like. There is, in my view, a fundamental requirement that elements of the corpus of scientific knowledge should ultimately be grounded and justified in a reasonable interpretation of observational or experimental evidence. There may also be room for criticism elsewhere in the gap between scientists' claims and performance.

This, then, is the basis on which I have conducted the research that underlies this book. The primary scientific literature which forms the basis for my discussion is supplemented only to a small extent. There are occasional passing references to non-scientific works discussing aspects of the ozone investigation. There have been several books and papers written about the ozone investigation from journalistic, political, or sociological points of view. These secondary sources have been freely drawn on as required to illustrate various points. They are of very widely varying quality, and have not been treated as authoritative sources. This book does not pretend to cater for those whose main interests are in political or sociological questions; these other works should be approached directly.

I include references to scientific reviews and published reminiscences. It would be inconceivable to tackle a project like this without reference to the several reports of the Ozone Trends Panel, for example, or to the Nobel lectures of Molina and Rowland.

I also refer to some unpublished material, some email and usenet news-group communications from individual scientists. I conducted a series of interviews in April and May 1996 with a number of scientists who were involved in the investigation in different ways, about their views and their reminiscences. This less formal material is used primarily for illustration, rather than as a central basis for any of my arguments. Much of it has contributed to my own background understanding of the issues, and has perhaps influenced the writing in ways that are not and cannot be directly attributed.

The main focus of this book, then, is on a series of scientific investigations which took place quite recently: between about 1970 and 1994.

In 1987, the governments of many nations agreed to limit, and eventually to phase out the widespread domestic and industrial use of chlorinated fluorocarbons (the Montréal Protocol). This was because of scientific suspicion that continued use of these compounds posed a real threat to the structure of the upper atmosphere. In particular they are supposed to be involved as precursors to chemicals which deplete ozone levels in the stratosphere. Significant loss of ozone from the stratosphere would allow damaging ultraviolet radiation, presently absorbed by ozone, to penetrate to the earth's surface. Because of the potential seriousness of this problem, regulating authorities adopted a standard of caution, and acted before the scientific issues had really been decided. Action on this scale against industrial products, particularly ones which have no direct toxic, carcinogenic, explosive, or corrosive effects, is quite unprecedented.

The background to this decision goes back to the discovery of ozone 160 years ago, and the gradual discovery and investigation of its presence and role in the stratosphere between about 1880 and 1970.

Chlorinated fluorocarbons were developed as refrigerants in the 1930s. They had remarkable properties which led to their being enthusiastically adopted for various applications during the four subsequent decades.

Then, as environmental awareness became an important issue during the 1970s, there were warnings about possible damage to the ozone layer as a result of human activity. First, there was the problem of high-flying planes, and then a warning about inert chlorine-containing compounds.

The last part of the story centres around the discovery and subsequent investigation of the Antarctic ozone hole, which occurred at much the same time as the negotiations that led to the Montréal Protocol. A scientific consensus about the general basis of the phenomenon was achieved in the late 1980s, and about its detailed mechanism in the early 1990s. But there are remaining problems and uncertainties, and stratospheric ozone remains an active area of current scientific research.

Part I

History of the understanding of stratospheric ozone

2   Stratospheric ozone before 1960

Ozone, O_3, is a highly reactive form of oxygen, which is found in trace quantities both in the natural stratosphere (15–50 km altitude), and in polluted surface air. It was discovered and characterised in 1839 by Schönbein. It cannot easily be prepared pure, but can readily be obtained in quantities up to 50 per cent by passing an electric spark discharge through normal oxygen. Ozone is much more reactive than normal molecular oxygen, and is also very toxic.

The presence of ozone in the upper atmosphere was first recognised by Cornu in 1879 and Hartley in 1880. Its particular role in shielding the earth's surface from solar ultraviolet light with wavelength between 220 and 320 nm then became apparent. Meyer (1903) made careful laboratory measurements of the ozone absorption spectrum. Fabry and Buisson (1912) were able to use these results to deduce the amount of ozone present in the atmosphere from a detailed analysis of the solar spectrum. It was not hard for the scientists to deduce that gases in the earth's atmosphere must be responsible for any missing frequencies observed in the spectrum of sunlight. To produce an absorption in the solar spectrum, a molecule must be somewhere on the path of the light from the sun to the earth's surface. The solar atmosphere is much too hot for any molecules to be present, let alone a relatively unstable one like ozone. There is ample other evidence that interplanetary space is much too empty to be a location for the required quantity of ozone. Therefore the ozone is somewhere in the earth's atmosphere.

Fabry and Buisson (1921) returned to the problem later, having produced a spectrograph better designed for measuring ozone absorption. They measured ozone levels over Marseilles several times a day for fourteen consecutive days in early summer. Their measurements appear to have been quite accurate. They concluded that the thickness of the ozone layer was about 3 mm at STP. That is, if all of the ozone in a column above the observer were warmed to 0°C, and compressed to a partial pressure of 1 atmosphere, it would form a layer 3 mm thick. In current units, this amounts to 300 Dobson units, very much in line with more recent measurements. They also found that ozone levels showed a small but significant irregular variability with time of day, and from day to day.

Measurements taken at Oxford by Dobson and Harrison in autumn 1924 and spring 1925 showed that springtime levels were much higher than autumn, and also showed much greater short term irregular variability than the Marseilles results had (Dobson and Harrison, 1926). Over the course of the next few years they were able to establish a regular annual pattern which reached a minimum in autumn, and a maximum in spring. They were also able to demonstrate a close correlation between ozone measurements and surface air pressure, with high pressure corresponding to low stratospheric ozone (Dobson, 1968b).

Discovery of these variations in ozone with season and weather conditions was of great interest to meteorologists and atmospheric physicists. It immediately raised the problem of discovering a mechanistic link, and a direction of causality between the phenomena. Also, the correlation with surface weather conditions meant that ozone monitoring held some promise as an extra piece of evidence that might become useful in weather forecasting.

The discoveries also stimulated an interest in the wider investigation of regional distribution of stratospheric ozone. Already, ozone levels had been found to vary from place to place, from season to season, and with weather patterns. Systematic collection of much more data was seen as a necessary prelude to any deeper theoretical understanding of a possible connection between ozone levels and climate, weather patterns, or air circulation.

Some effort was made to obtain regular readings from a series of observing stations with wide geographic distribution. The first attempt in 1926 involved measurements with matched and carefully calibrated instruments from stations at Oxford, Shetland Islands, Ireland, Germany, Sweden, Switzerland, and Chile. In 1928 these instruments were moved to give worldwide coverage. The new network included Oxford, Switzerland, California, Egypt, India, and New Zealand. An attempt to set up an instrument in the Antarctic at this stage, in the care of an Italian team, ended in disaster. The Dobson spectrometer finished up at the bottom of the Southern Ocean (Dobson, 1968b).

Between 1928 and 1956 a lot of painstaking work was conducted. The main achievements could be classified in the following areas:
1. The need for a global network of ozone monitoring stations was recognised, and protocols were devised to try to ensure that observations from different stations would be directly comparable.
2. Techniques and instrumentation were greatly refined. Initially the spectra taken had to be from direct sunlight (or, with much less accu-

racy, from moonlight). Methods were developed initially for clear zenith sky, and then for cloudy zenith sky. A comprehensive monitoring network needs methods that will work on cloudy days, or the data from some locations will be very sparse indeed.

3. New techniques were developed to give information about the vertical distribution of ozone. The only information available from a conventional ozone spectrometer is the amount of ozone in the line between the instrument and the sun. This can be readily and accurately converted to 'total column ozone' – that is the total amount of ozone in a vertical column directly above the observer. But there are effects arising from light scattering in the upper atmosphere that can be exploited. Sunlight travels directly from sun to instrument. Skylight travels along one line from the sun to a scattering centre, and another from scattering centre to instrument. Tiny differences between sunlight and skylight spectra can provide information about differences in the amount of ozone along the two paths. If the distribution of scattering centres is known or can be safely assumed, then this data can be transformed to calculate varying distributions of ozone with height. The results are very approximate. But ground-based instruments can provide some vertical distribution information. Development of methods suitable for balloon-borne experiments was a separate aspect of this work. At that time, balloon-borne instruments were the only practical means of directly probing the stratosphere. Attempts to measure ozone in aircraft in 1952 had mixed success – they did indicate (as expected) that ozone levels were very low throughout the troposphere, and started to increase rapidly above the tropopause. But the altitude of the ozone layer was well above the operating height of the aircraft. Very little ozone could be measured at altitudes the aeroplane was capable of reaching.

4. Gradually a picture was built up of the annual and short term variation patterns for stratospheric ozone. A strong correlation of the short term variations with surface weather patterns was established. Some theoretical explanations for these variations and connections were starting to emerge. The situation was seen almost entirely in circulation terms, with low column ozone levels associated with upwelling of ozone-poor tropospheric air, and higher levels associated with downward air movements in the stratosphere.

5. The group of scientists with an interest in stratospheric ozone monitoring gradually increased. The International Ozone Commission was set up in 1948, and atmospheric ozone was one of the major issues addressed in planning the International Geophysical Year (IGY) programme for 1957–8. Unlike most years, the IGY lasted for eighteen

months. At that time the number of ozone monitoring stations increased greatly. Responsibility for collection and publication of data from the worldwide network of ozone monitoring stations was transferred from Oxford to the Canadian Meteorological Service, operating under a World Meteorological Organisation (WMO) charter. Unfortunately, a significantly large proportion of the ozone monitoring stations only operated for a few years after the IGY.

In 1957 and 1958, the first measurements of ozone from the British station at Halley Bay in Antarctica were obtained. These showed a pattern which was different from the pattern normally obtained in Northern polar regions, and in temperate regions in both hemispheres. Instead of a fairly regular annual oscillation, with an autumn minimum and spring maximum, the ozone levels remained fairly close to the autumn level throughout winter and early spring. They then rose rather suddenly to a peak in late spring, and slowly declined, as expected, through the summer.

This effect was known as the 'Southern anomaly' and was placed alongside similar anomalous patterns which were obtained from several other specific regions of the world.

Unlike Svålbard (Spitzbergen) and Alaska, inland Northern Canada shows a pattern similar to the Antarctic pattern, but with the springtime rise occurring significantly earlier in the spring season, and at a more variable time. Northern India shows consistently lower ozone levels than other regions at similar latitudes. These other anomalies were known to Dobson when he described the 'Southern anomaly'.

The discussion so far has centred very much on the physics and meteorology of stratospheric ozone. But there was a separate series of chemical issues that called for investigation. Why is ozone present in the atmosphere at all? What chemical reactions account for its presence, but restrict the amount to trace levels? Why is ozone distributed so that its presence is largely restricted to a 'layer' between 15 and 50 km in altitude, rather than, say, being uniformly distributed throughout the atmosphere? Physics and meteorology deal with air circulation, but circulation alone cannot discriminate between chemical species in order to concentrate a particular chemical in a particular region. Any major variation of chemical composition in different regions of the atmosphere requires a chemical explanation.

In 1930, Sydney Chapman published the first moderately successful attempt to provide an explanation of ozone chemistry in the stratosphere (Chapman, 1930a, 1930b). His scheme, which ruled unchallenged until around 1970, and continued to form the basis for later theories, involved four main reactions.

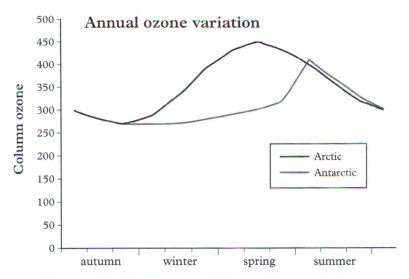

Figure 2.1 The 'Southern anomaly' in annual ozone variation.

A chemical 'explanation' of this sort typically involves accounting for chemical change in a system by identifying a set of 'elementary' reaction processes. Variations in the concentrations of various substances in the system are rationalised in terms of the rate behaviour of these elementary reactions.

For purposes of explanation, the reactions are introduced in an order different from that in Chapman's papers. The first two reactions involve a simple recycling of ozone. No chemical consequences follow from the successive occurrence of these two reactions.

$$O_3 + \text{light (wavelength 220--320nm)} \rightarrow O_2 + O \qquad (1)$$

$$O_2 + O + M \rightarrow O_3 + M \qquad (2)$$

In the first, ozone is destroyed, and ultraviolet light is absorbed. In the second reaction, the ozone is regenerated whenever the atomic oxygen produced in the first reaction becomes involved in a three-body collision with molecular oxygen. It does not matter what the third body is. 'M' is simply a symbol representing any other molecule that happens to be present to act as an energy sink (it will usually be molecular nitrogen, N_2, simply because of its 78 per cent abundance). Heat is generated in this second reaction. The overall effect of these two reactions is thus removal of much of the ultraviolet component of sunlight, and injection of heat into the upper stratosphere.

Chapman added two other reactions to these. The first is necessary to explain how any 'odd oxygen' (a term which embraces atomic oxygen and ozone, while excluding normal molecular oxygen) comes to be present at all. Molecular oxygen can also break down in ultraviolet light, but the wavelength must be much shorter, and it usually occurs much higher in the atmosphere.

$$O_2 + \text{light (wavelength 120–210nm)} \rightarrow O + O \tag{3}$$

Finally, this reaction needs to be balanced with a reaction that can actually remove odd oxygen from the system. Reactions (1) and (2) conserve odd oxygen, and without such a balancing reaction, the concentration of odd oxygen species would simply build up without limit. Chapman's choice for such a reaction was:

$$O_3 + O \rightarrow 2\,O_2 \tag{4}$$

Chapman was able to use his scheme to provide a qualitative explanation of much of the behaviour of stratospheric ozone.

The scheme explained why ozone was only present between 15 and 50 km of altitude in any quantity. At lower levels the ultraviolet light that drives the system has all been filtered out, so reaction (3) cannot proceed. At higher levels, the three-body collisions necessary to produce ozone are too infrequent because of the extremely low air pressure. The frequency of three-body collisions is a very sensitive function of pressure, and the rapid fall-off of pressure with increasing height in the atmosphere ensures that this frequency is a very sensitive function of altitude. Above 60 km, three-body collisions are so rare that most of the 'odd oxygen' present is in the form of atomic oxygen, O, rather than ozone, O_3. In effect, the rate of reaction (2) falls to a very small value. No ozone is produced unless reaction (3) is followed by reaction (2); reactions (1) and (4) remove ozone to provide the balance which ensures a small and fairly steady concentration.

The cycle of reactions (1) and (2) explained why the upper stratosphere is heated. Ultraviolet light with 220 to 320 nm wavelength is filtered out at this level by reaction (1). The energy of this light goes instead into heating the gases involved in the three-body collision of reaction (2). Air temperatures around 50 km are similar to those at ground level, as a result of this warming, while those at 15–20 km are very much lower.

But when quantitative detail was added, Chapman's scheme had some problems. The ozone levels predicted using Chapman's model with the best available rate data for the elementary reactions involved were much higher than those actually observed. They were roughly double.

The problem may have been with inaccurate values for the rate constants. Reactions (1) and (2) simply determine the rate at which light is converted into heat; they do not affect the total amount of ozone present. There is little real uncertainty about the rate of reaction (3), because it is directly connected with light absorption, and can be studied by measuring the efficiency of this light absorption, rather than by measuring the concentrations of chemical species which might be involved in other reactions. So the only likely candidate for an inaccurate rate constant that could reconcile Chapman's model with the system was reaction (4). This was recognised as a very difficult reaction to study in the laboratory, but the consensus was that the error in the recognised value would be around 20 per cent. An error of up to 50 per cent might be plausible, but the factor of 5 required to reconcile Chapman's scheme was not (Wayne, 1991, pp. 123–5).[1]

Another plausible explanation of the discrepancy was that other reactions, not included in Chapman's scheme, were also playing a significant part in ozone chemistry. Modification of Chapman's scheme with the inclusion of extra reactions was called for. Reactions which supplemented reaction (4) in removing odd oxygen would be more directly effective than others in accounting for the discrepancy between model and observation.

A convenient but limited analogy can be drawn with a bathtub, with 'odd oxygen' for the water. Reaction (3) is working like a tap that is constantly pouring water in, and reaction (4) is like the plug hole that is constantly letting water out again. The water will eventually find a steady level in the tub. But when we calculate this steady level using the known water flow and size of plug hole, we deduce that the steady water level ought to be twice as high as it actually is. We are quite sure that we have the correct value of water flow, and fairly sure about the size of the plug hole. We might have a plug hole that is a bit larger than we thought, but not five times as large. The most likely other explanation is that there is a large leak in the tub, i.e. an alternative plug hole.

When scientists are faced with a situation like this, where a theory provides some good qualitative explanations, but falls down in quantitative detail, they usually accept that it has some basic soundness. They typically use it as a basis and seek to modify it, rather than abandoning it and looking for an alternative. Scientists usually prefer to describe Chapman's theory as 'correct but incomplete'. With some important misgivings and reservations we will go along with this description.[2]

Interestingly, the particular problem of how to modify Chapman's scheme to produce a better account of observed ozone levels in the stratosphere was largely put aside, and left unresolved for several decades! The search for an improvement was either not strenuously pursued, or it was completely fruitless. The question was not addressed again in detail in any significant published scientific work until after 1960.

Why was an anomaly like this allowed to persist? Why was it not dealt with? The answer seems to have been that although physicists and meteorologists were very interested in stratospheric ozone, the small community of atmospheric chemists was concentrating almost exclusively on air pollution issues close to ground level. There simply does not seem to have been much work done on stratospheric chemistry between 1930 and the 1960s.

NOTES

1 Although the predicted ozone concentration is only out by a little more than a factor of 2, the change in this rate constant needs a larger factor of about 5 to produce the correct ozone levels. There is an approximate square root ratio: a factor of 5 increase in this rate constant produces roughly a factor of $\sqrt{5}$ decrease in the ozone level.
2 The case of Chapman raises an interesting tension between the attitudes of the scientist and the logician. I have been taken to task by at least one scientist for not being sufficiently laudatory about Chapman's work. His claim, in which he is not alone, is that Chapman's theory is correct, but incomplete. I feel that it would be more accurate to say that his theory is wrong because it is incomplete. Chapman identified four or arguably five reactions which might account for the chemistry of the ozone layer. All of his reactions are included in the modern scheme of over a dozen reactions that have been identified and used to present a quantitatively successful theory. Three of them are clearly the most important reactions in the whole scheme.

So, from the point of view of the scientist, Chapman's theory was correct in that it correctly identified five of the reactions important in stratospheric ozone chemistry, including the three most important ones. It contained no incorrect or unimportant reactions. And it formed the basis around which the "correct" modern theory could be built.

But a philosopher of science cannot regard any theory as correct if it has entailments or consequences that are not borne out by observation. Chapman's theory made a clear prediction of stratospheric ozone levels that were roughly twice the levels that were actually observed. It therefore had clear empirical failings, and in this sense it was 'falsified' or 'wrong'.

Regardless of whether it is described as 'right' or 'wrong', what is quite clear is that Chapman's work was a brilliant and definitive theoretical insight, that provided a sound basis for later efforts.

We will meet exactly the same problem again later in this story, in assessing the contribution of Molina and Rowland.

3   Chlorinated fluorocarbons

The most common form of refrigeration technology is based on the fact that when a liquid is forced to evaporate, it removes a large amount of heat from its immediate surroundings. The technology therefore relies on a gas which is fairly readily condensed by cooling or compression – a normal boiling point somewhere in the range from about 0°C to -50°C is preferred. Differences in other physical quantities then distinguish some such substances as good refrigerants or bad refrigerants.

But the physical properties are not the whole story. There are also chemical requirements. A substance cannot be used as a refrigerant unless it is chemically robust and stable. The refrigerant is cycled through a closed loop with two heat exchangers. In one it evaporates, and heat is removed from the interior of the refrigerator. In the other it is re-condensed by compression and the heat is emitted from the coolant loop into the room external to the refrigerator. There are moving parts that require lubrication, so the refrigerant must either itself have some lubricant properties, or be chemically compatible with separate lubricant substances that must be added. It is also desirable that a refrigerant does *not* constitute a toxic, corrosive, fire, or explosive hazard.

There are very few substances with boiling points in the range from -50°C to 0°C. The number of such substances that are chemically robust and were generally available during the 1920s was fewer than 10. All were either highly toxic, or highly flammable, or both. In the early days of refrigeration, the gas of choice for most applications was ammonia. Although ammonia is quite toxic, it has two advantages in that regard. It is an extremely pungent gas, so that if it were to leak, anyone in the vicinity would be rapidly aware of the fact. And it has a very high affinity for water, so that it can be rapidly and efficiently removed by water spraying. Ammonia is only very slightly corrosive. Although it is usually regarded as non-flammable, it can burn in certain circumstances, and was implicated in a few explosions at refrigeration plants. Several other gases were either used on a smaller scale, or investigated for possible use.

Sulfur dioxide is similar to ammonia in its toxicity, pungency, and high affinity for water. It is completely non-flammable, but very much more corrosive than ammonia. Methyl chloride and methyl bromide are actually less toxic than ammonia or sulfur dioxide, but far more insidious: they have only slight odours, and are oily substances that do not mix with water. Carbon dioxide is of much lower toxicity, and is non-corrosive and non-flammable. But its normal evaporation point is at -78°C, and it condenses to a solid rather than a liquid. The only way it could be used as a refrigerant in a conventional system would be if the coolant loop were to operate at a pressure of several atmospheres, where the boiling point would be higher, and liquid carbon dioxide would form. This adds significant cost and complication. Butane and propane have low toxicity, but high flammability, and have fairly poor refrigerant properties. It is not surprising then, that right from the early days of refrigeration, there was an active search for better alternatives.

The family of substances known as chlorinated fluorocarbons (CFCs) was discovered and patented for refrigerant purposes in the early 1930s.

The abstract of the paper containing the initial announcement (Midgley and Henne, 1930, p. 542) is written in these terms:

Irrespective of otherwise satisfactory engineering and thermodynamic properties, all refrigerating agents previously used have been either inflammable, toxic, or both.

This paper covers a new class of refrigerating agents – organic substances containing fluorine. Some of them are surprisingly non-toxic. Dichlorodifluoromethane is less toxic than carbon dioxide, as non-inflammable as carbon tetrachloride, and very satisfactory from every other standpoint.

CFCs were marketed under the trade name Freon (® Du Pont). Freons are usually regarded as synthetic compounds, which do not occur in the natural environment. (There are, however, claims published in the scientific literature that they do occur naturally[1]). With the use of chlorinated fluorocarbon refrigerants, refrigeration and the associated technologies made great advances, and the manner in which food could be stored, presented and marketed was revolutionised.

CFCs were first investigated by Thomas Midgley Jr in 1930. Midgley was a gifted industrial chemist who worked for General Motors. He had been set the task of finding and developing a new non-toxic, non-inflammable and inexpensive refrigerant for Frigidaire (the refrigeration division of General Motors). Midgley began with a systematic review and survey of all possible compounds. He worked his way through the periodic table. Many elements could be rapidly eliminated, because their volatile compounds were all too unstable or too toxic. Very few compounds fell into a suitable boiling point range.

He paused when he came to fluorine compounds. The prevailing view of the time was that all fluorine compounds were toxic. But Midgley reasoned that some classes of fluorine compounds would not necessarily show the extreme reactivity of fluorine itself, and hoped to find compounds that were not only unreactive, but might also be non-toxic. He initially was led to investigate these compounds by a misprinted boiling point. He seriously considered carbon tetrafluoride, whose boiling point was listed in the International Critical Tables as -15°C, and which appeared to be fairly unreactive. As he soon discovered, the actual boiling point is more like -128°C. But his attention had been directed to fluorine compounds as a result. This was serendipitous.

His whole approach was speculative and exploratory (Midgley, 1937, p. 244):

Plottings of boiling points, hunting for data, corrections, slide rules, log paper, eraser dirt, pencil shavings, and all the rest of the paraphernalia that takes the place of tea leaves and crystal spheres in the life of the scientific clairvoyant, were brought into play.

The first material that Midgley decided to investigate was dichlorodifluoromethane (CCl_2F_2). This compound had been made previously. The recipe required a reaction between carbon tetrachloride and antimony trifluoride. The former reagent was readily available, but antimony trifluoride was rarely made or used at the time. Midgley was only able to locate and obtain five 1 oz bottles of the material. With his co-workers Albert Henne and Robert MacNary, Midgley used one of these bottles to make a few grams of dichlorodifluoromethane. The product was placed under a bell jar with a guinea pig. The guinea pig survived. The scientists were delighted. But when the procedure was repeated using the second bottle of antimony fluoride, the guinea pig died. When they made the third batch, the scientists smelled the product, and recognised the odour of phosgene ($COCl_2$). This is an extremely poisonous, volatile substance which had been used as a war gas in the 1914–19 war. It was possible to remove the phosgene from the product with a simple caustic wash, and it then appeared to be safe. Four of the five bottles of antimony fluoride had been contaminated with a salt that caused lethal amounts of phosgene to be produced as a by-product of the reaction. Serendipity once more! But for the misprint, it is quite unlikely that fluorine compounds would have been chosen for investigation. Had the first guinea pig died, the investigation would probably have stopped then and there (as Midgley later admitted). Fluorine compounds were, after all, known to be highly toxic (Midgley, 1937, p. 244).

Of five bottles marked "antimony trifluoride," one had really contained good material. We had chosen that one by accident for our first trial. Had we chosen any one of the other four, the animal would have died, as expected by everyone else in the world except ourselves. I believe we would have given up what would then have seemed a "bum hunch".

Before a new material is adopted for industrial use, or indeed, for any use that might involve the exposure of workers or the general public to the material, it clearly must be checked out for possible hazards. Rigorous testing and investigation of a new material is therefore always carried out. This was the case even back in the 1930s, though the standards and procedures of those days were quite different, and generally less stringent than those of today.

Midgley and his colleagues undertook a series of experiments to test the effects of dichlorodifluoromethane on guinea pigs, dogs, and monkeys. These toxicity tests were quite bizarre, by today's standards. The animals were put in rooms where they had to breathe an atmosphere of air to which a set proportion of dichlorodifluoromethane had been added. Some of these tests lasted for days. It was only when the proportion of dichlorodifluoromethane exceeded 20 per cent that the animals started to show respiratory and nervous symptoms. But they soon recovered when put back into normal atmosphere, and showed no later ill-effects. But the protocols for toxicity testing demanded that the scientists find the size of the lethal dose for inhalation. So an admixture of 80 per cent dichlorodifluoromethane with 20 per cent air was tried. The guinea pigs went to sleep almost immediately, dying in ten minutes or so if the exposure was continued, or recovering completely if allowed to resume breathing normal atmosphere before death.

It then occurred to the scientists that there was small wonder to this result. The animals were dying, not from exposure to dichlorodifluoromethane, but from a simple lack of oxygen. The atmosphere they were breathing was only 20 per cent air, and air contains only 20 per cent oxygen. The animals were trying to breathe an atmosphere with only 4 per cent oxygen! So the protocols were changed. For the higher exposures, the dichlorodifluoromethane was mixed with pure oxygen rather than with air, so as to maintain roughly the same amount of oxygen as in normal air. An exposure to 80 per cent dichlorodifluoromethane and 20 per cent oxygen typically did not result in the death of a guinea pig until after sixty to ninety minutes. It had proved almost impossible to find a toxic dose for exposure to dichlorodifluoromethane.

Midgley was a little bit of a showman. How do you demonstrate to the public that dichlorodifluoromethane is neither toxic nor flammable? On one public occasion, Midgley deeply inhaled some, and then proceeded to breathe out a lighted candle. In this way he sorted out both issues with a single blow!

Dichlorodifluoromethane was shown to meet all of the required criteria for a good and safe refrigerant. Moreover, it could be produced very economically. Right from the outset, it clearly filled a particular technological niche. It was so satisfactory on all counts that it rapidly became the dominant refrigerant, at least in domestic refrigeration. But its particularly impressive safety record strongly suggested other applications for it and for the other closely related CFC compounds. The development of CFCs revolutionised refrigeration. But beyond that, CFCs were widely used as propellants in aerosol spray cans, and as blowing agents for foams and foam plastics. They also found application as solvents, lubricants, and dry-cleaning agents. They were the perfect chemicals. They were non-reactive (inert), non-toxic, non-flammable and, as an extra bonus, they were cheap to make on an industrial scale.

In the 1960s and the early 1970s there was a great increase in both scientific and public awareness of environmental and ecological issues. Industrial use of chemicals came under fresh scrutiny. New techniques allowed detection of trace levels of toxic chemicals. In some instances they were found in unexpected places. For example, DDT was found in Antarctic ice. Organochlorine pesticides had been widely used around the world for many years, and there had been huge benefits. DDT was a major weapon in the fight against malaria, a fight that is still far from won. Organochlorine pesticides were important in controlling crop pests, thus preventing widespread famine. It would be a great mistake to think of them as all bad. But it had been found that they did tend to pass up the food chain, accumulating in the fatty tissue of birds and mammals. And it was also discovered that they could affect calcium metabolism in these creatures. Residues of organochlorines are often very persistent in the environment. Controls and limitations on their use were necessary. Like these organochlorine pesticides, CFCs are unreactive, and tend to accumulate in the environment. But CFCs differed from the pesticides in that they were remarkably non-toxic, did not enter the food chain, and no other adverse effects of their presence were known.

CFCs continued in widespread industrial use, and they were even held up as exemplary industrial chemicals. In the early 1970s per capita consumption of CFCs ranged from about 30 gram in most third world countries to about 1 kg in the USA and Australia.

NOTES

1 The claim is made by G.W. Gribble, in a letter to *Chemistry & Industry*, 6 Jun 1994, p. 390.

It relates to emission of CFCs in the gaseous effluent from volcanic fumaroles in Central America and on the Kamchatka Peninsula, Eastern Siberia. On the one hand it is not totally implausible that CFCs might be synthesised naturally in the interaction of a fluoride-rich magma with a carboniferous sediment bed; on the other, it also seems a real possibility that the observations might have been artifacts caused by contamination in the sampling procedure. Stoiber *et al.*, ((1971) *Bull. Geol. Soc. Am.* 82 2299–304), who detected CFCs in measuring trace gases from the Santiaguito volcano in Guatemala, mention the possibility of contamination from their use of mineral acids, but provide justification for dismissing it. The Kamchatka work is more difficult to trace. The local scientists studying effluents from the Kamchatka volcanoes describe their field sampler as a ceramic tube . . . "connected to a series of gas absorbers by teflon and rubber links" (Taran *et al.*, (1991) *J. Volc. Geotherm. Res.* 46 255–63). Trace levels of CFCs could easily be provided by the interaction of teflon with very hot HCl (J.R. Christie, private communication).

4   The Supersonic Transport (SST) debate

The first supersonic manned flights occurred in the years immediately following the Second World War. The first that was officially recognised and recorded took place during 1955. By 1962 the technology had reached the stage where the use of supersonic aircraft for passenger transportation had become a serious possibility. A joint announcement was made by the British and French authorities that they would co-operate in the development of a new supersonic aircraft designed for commercial passenger transportation. There soon followed similar announcements of American and Soviet projects to develop fleets of supersonic passenger airliners. Almost from the very start, these programmes ran into difficulties with design problems and cost overruns. As the programmes slowly got underway, and public awareness of the issues increased, two sets of environmental concerns came to the fore.

The more obvious and more spectacular issue was the problem of the shock wave or 'sonic boom' that is always associated with an object moving through the air at supersonic speeds. This produces an effect like a loud thunderclap on the ground when the aeroplane passes over, and under certain circumstances it could crack windows or knock small ornaments or crockery from shelves. It soon became apparent that aircraft would have to maintain sub-sonic speeds when travelling over populated land areas. Even so, a series of concerns were strongly expressed in various forums. Some of the more interesting were that sonic booms would stop Cornish cows from producing milk, or that they would break the eggs of sea-birds nesting on remote rocky islands in the Atlantic.

The second issue was a more subtle one. It had become apparent that the optimum operating heights for supersonic airliners of the type that were being designed would be much higher than those used by conventional sub-sonic passenger aircraft.

The lower region of the atmosphere, the troposphere, extends to about 12 km height in temperate regions. It contains about 90 per cent of the total mass of the atmosphere, and is thoroughly and rapidly mixed by the turbulence associated with weather systems. The top of the troposphere is defined by a temperature minimum, known as the tropopause. Above the tropopause lies the stratosphere, which extends to a height of about 50 km. Only about 10 per cent of the atmosphere is contained in the stratosphere. There is little transfer of air between troposphere and stratosphere, and vertical mixing within the stratosphere is much slower and less efficient than in the troposphere. Conventional large passenger airliners typically operate at altitudes close to the tropopause; it was planned that the super-sonic airliners would operate in the stratosphere. This meant that their exhaust would be injected into a reservoir of air that was both much smaller and much less well-mixed than the tropospheric reservoir which received the exhaust of conventional aircraft. There were concerns about the introduction of foreign materials into the rather delicate environment of the stratosphere.

In the United States, the pressures of these concerns came together in a 'Climatic Impact Assessment Program' initiated by the US congress in 1971. The results of this inquiry, together with questionable commercial viability, led to the withdrawal of US government support, and the col-lapse of the American project.

The Russian and the Anglo-French projects limped ahead. They even-tually came to fruition when first the Anglo-French Concorde, and shortly afterward the Russian Tupolev Tu-144 were unveiled.

The Concorde operated for many years, though on a very much smaller scale than was originally projected. The Tupolev Tu-144 was taken out of service, but currently a joint US/Russian venture is seeking to restore it with some design modifications.

The first serious scientific concerns about damage to the stratospheric environment were expressed in the late 1960s. It was thought that ice condensation from the aircraft exhaust stream might lead to great increases in stratospheric aerosol levels. When normal aviation fuel is burnt, about 1.2 kg of ice is produced for each kg of fuel consumed. The stratosphere is normally a very dry place, with very low water vapour concentrations, and ice clouds are not usually present. The initial concern was that increased aerosol levels in the stratosphere would decrease the amount of sunshine reaching the earth's surface, leading to significant surface climatic changes. These suggestions were speculative, and not closely followed up.

Halstead Harrison (1970) turned attention to the possible effects of water injection on ozone, rather than climate. In his model calculations he showed firstly that the exhaust of a fleet of supersonic aircraft operating in the stratosphere would add significantly to the low water levels present in the natural stratosphere, and secondly that any such increase in water levels would be followed by a decrease in stratospheric ozone. For each 3 per cent increase in water vapour, a 1 per cent decrease in ozone levels would follow.

There had been some progress made during the 1960s in improvement on the Chapman model of stratospheric ozone chemistry. Hunt (1966a; 1966b) developed a model based on a suggestion by Hampson (1964) that water vapour might have an important role in ozone chemistry. Reactions involving the hydroxyl (OH) and hydroperoxy (H_2O_2) radicals along with water and atomic hydrogen were added to Chapman's scheme. Later, Leovy (1969) presented a detailed series of calculations with a slightly simplified form of Hunt's scheme, and showed that it could provide a good match with observed ozone levels and distributions for the region between 15 km and 60 km altitude, provided that rate constant values for several of the reactions were chosen carefully. Unlike the Chapman mechanism, the Hunt-Leovy mechanism could be reconciled with the observed stratospheric ozone levels, but only if rate constant values were chosen at the extremes of the uncertainty limits, rather than as most probable values. The conclusion was that water, even at the low concentrations naturally present in the stratosphere, did play an important part in stratospheric ozone chemistry.

The details of the chemical scheme of the model Harrison used are not explicitly presented in his paper (Harrison, 1970); it is clear that a Hunt/Leovy scheme including the effects of hydrogen-containing radicals on ozone was used. What is not clear is the extent to which his modelling tried to allow for changes in circulation or radiation patterns consequent on water increase.

At the end of the 1960s, new values were obtained for several of the important rates in the hydrogen/oxygen reaction schemes. The most important was a large increase in the rate of collisional quenching of singlet atomic oxygen. With this new value, it became clear that the Hunt/Leovy additions to Chapman's reaction scheme could only make a minor contribution to ozone removal, and that they could not successfully account for stratospheric ozone levels.

Harold Johnston (1971a, 1971b) then pointed out the likelihood that nitrogen oxides from aircraft exhaust might play a more significant role in ozone depletion than water vapour. The reactions

$$NO + O_3 \rightarrow NO_2 + O_2 \tag{5}$$

$$NO_2 + O \rightarrow NO + O_2 \tag{6}$$

form a 'catalytic chain' reaction system, in which a single molecule of nitric oxide (NO) can destroy many molecules of odd oxygen because of the way in which it is recycled by the reaction system. Note that the net effect of adding together reactions (5) and (6) is exactly the same as the odd oxygen removal mechanism in Chapman's scheme:

$$O_3 + O \rightarrow 2\,O_2 \tag{4}$$

Although these reactions were well known, and had been studied in the laboratory, their possible role in stratospheric ozone chemistry had largely been overlooked.[1] Crutzen had published a paper the previous year examining the role of nitrogen oxides in stratospheric chemistry (Crutzen, 1970), and Johnston's suggestion was largely based on this work. Nitric oxide is formed in significant quantities as a by-product of fuel combustion in an internal combustion engine whenever the ignition temperature is sufficiently high. A mixture of oxygen and nitrogen gas (i.e. air) reacts to form about 1 per cent of nitric oxide whenever its temperature is taken above about 2200°C. It is therefore present in aircraft exhaust. Because the reactions in which nitric oxide is involved with ozone are a chain reaction, it does not matter too much that nitric oxide is present in the exhaust at much lower concentrations than water – it might nevertheless be just as effective in destroying ozone, or even more so.

Ian Clark (1974) uses an analysis of the SST debate as the vehicle for an essay on the role of 'expert advice' in modern issues of public policy. At the time he wrote he had little benefit of hindsight. He stresses the speculative nature and variable quality of many of the 'expert' submissions to the debate. One of his claims is particularly telling:

The conference devoted to the Study of Critical Environmental Problems held in 1970, which was attended by chemists and meteorologists who were unfamiliar with the stratosphere, concluded that NOx emissions from the SST could be ignored. When the question of stratospheric ozone had gained sufficient publicity to make the real experts familiar with the problem, a meeting of well-chosen experts held in March 1971 grasped the problem almost immediately: the depletion of ozone from NOx catalysis would be the major stratospheric hazard from the SST.

Even after reading this passage many times, I am not sure how much tongue-in-cheek sarcasm is intended.

The next major development was an important argument against the likely impact of nitrogen oxides from SSTs (Goldsmith et al., 1973). They pointed out that extensive atmospheric nuclear testing between 1957 and 1963 had occurred at a time when stratospheric ozone levels were regularly monitored around the world. The products of the nuclear detonation would have included a large nitrogen oxide input directly into the stratosphere. (Air was heated to well over the required 2200°C, and the blast plumes often extended to great heights). The data, plotted as a time series, showed absolutely no correlation of significance between ozone levels and atmospheric nuclear detonations. Even a large fleet of supersonic transport aircraft (SSTs) would not produce an NOx^2 input to match that of the nuclear tests of 1961–2. There must therefore be some fallacy in the argument that stratospheric ozone levels would respond in a sensitive fashion to anthropogenic NOx inputs.

Around 1974–5 it became clear that the reason for limited stratospheric response to anthropogenic NOx was the presence of a much higher level of natural NOx in the lower stratosphere than had previously been supposed.

During the late 1960s Paul Crutzen had been working on the chemistry of nitrous oxide, N_2O, in the atmosphere. Nitrous oxide is produced by soil bacteria in relatively small quantities, and it escapes to the atmosphere. Because it is quite unreactive, it has a long atmospheric lifetime of about ten years, and so it can build up to significant levels. Nitrous oxide is present in the lower atmosphere at a level about 300 parts per billion. It is rapidly destroyed when it rises to a height in the stratosphere where it can encounter some of the ultraviolet sunlight that is filtered out by ozone.

Crutzen (1970, 1971) discussed a possible role for nitrous oxide and the reactive nitrogen oxides in the natural ozone chemistry of the stratosphere. He suggested that the main source of stratospheric nitric oxide might be as a product of the known reaction of nitrous oxide with singlet atomic oxygen:[3]

$$N_2O + O\ (^1D) \rightarrow 2\,NO \tag{7}$$

Johnston (1972) estimated on the basis of this chemistry that the anthropogenic input of nitric oxide from SST exhaust would, by the mid 1980s, be of similar magnitude to the supposed natural input. The estimate was, of course, based on the projection of much larger operating fleets of SSTs than actually eventuated.

The currently accepted view is that natural NOx levels in the stratosphere are right at the upper end of Crutzen's original estimated range. Natural odd oxygen removal from the stratosphere occurs roughly 60 per cent via the NOx catalytic cycle, 20 per cent via the direct Chapman mechanism, and the remaining 20 per cent via four other catalytic cycles similar to the NOx cycle, but involving other catalysts. These include the hydroxyl and hydroperoxy radical reactions in the Hunt/Leovy scheme, a hydrogen atom reaction not included in the Hunt scheme, and the natural chlorine cycle, of which a great deal more will be said later.

So injection of NOx into the stratosphere by aircraft exhaust, instead of providing a major new insult to the ozone chemistry occurring in the stratosphere as Johnston had feared, would rather be producing a small increase in the levels of NOx that were already, naturally present, and a slight enhancement of what was already the major natural ozone removal mechanism.

The other factor that led to the decline (not really a resolution) of the SST debate was a major reduction in the scale of the project. Economic factors meant eventually that a fleet of fewer than 30 SSTs would be operating at about mach 2.2, rather than the 300 SSTs operating at mach 3 which had originally been projected. This amounted to a very much smaller environmental impact.

In spite of this rather tame conclusion to the debate, it is clear that the SST debate was an important vehicle for focusing the attention of scientists, administrators and the general public on the delicate nature of the stratospheric ozone shield. It also seems to have provided some of the impetus for new research in stratospheric chemistry that enabled scientists to clear up the long-standing anomalies and inconsistencies in the understanding of stratospheric ozone chemistry that had been based on the Chapman model.

NOTES

1 The earliest suggestion of a natural nitrogen oxide cycle in the lower stratosphere was made by Hampson(1966).
2 NOx is an abbreviation used by atmospheric chemists for reference to the reactive oxides of nitrogen as a whole. In most situations NOx consists mainly of nitric oxide, NO, and nitrogen dioxide, NO_2, with much smaller amounts of NO_3, N_2O_3, N_2O_4, and N_2O_5. All of these species can be rapidly interconverted by reaction with other substances naturally present in the atmosphere. NOx does *not* include nitrous oxide, N_2O, the one oxide of nitrogen that is very unreactive in the normal atmospheric environment.
3 'singlet' atomic oxygen, O (^{1}D), is a high energy, but long-lived variety of the oxygen atom in which all electrons are supposed to be paired. Normal atomic oxygen is supposed to have its eight electrons arranged in three pairs, with two unpaired single electrons left over. Although the paired form has higher energy, the pair is not easily uncoupled in collisions with other atoms or molecules. 'singlet' atomic oxygen sometimes forms when ozone is broken up by ultraviolet light – about 10 per cent of ozone dissociations, but the fraction does vary with the ultraviolet wavelength. It has different reactions to normal atomic oxygen, and is generally somewhat more reactive.

5   Molina and Rowland: chlorine enters the story

In 1971, a suggestion was made in a letter to *Nature* that CFCs could be used as markers for wind patterns and currents (Lovelock, 1971). James Lovelock had been involved with the development of the electron capture detector for use in gas chromatography. This provided a very sensitive means of detecting minute amounts of certain gases, but mainly only those that contain fluorine or chlorine. These gases could be detected and measured even when their mixing ratio was only a few parts per trillion. In exploring possible applications, Lovelock had made some observations on surface air in rural Ireland. An increase in CFC levels up to 20-fold occurred when the wind blew from the direction of continental Europe rather than from the North Atlantic Ocean. His suggestion was that air parcels which had come from industrial or heavily populated areas of Western Europe contained high levels of unreactive CFC gases, while those that had Arctic or oceanic origins had much lower levels.

This letter caught the attention of Professor Sherwood Rowland. His main interest was not in Lovelock's suggestion about monitoring air circulation patterns. He was more concerned about the fact that there was a measurable and not insignificant level of CFCs in the atmosphere – even in unpolluted atmosphere from the Arctic Sea. He included in his research grant application to the US Atomic Energy Commission a proposal to investigate the way that CFCs cycled through the atmosphere. He was interested in particular to find out their eventual fate. What natural systems were removing them from the atmosphere? Lovelock had initially estimated an average residence time of about one year for dichlorodifluoromethane in the atmosphere.

Mario Molina was at that time just starting as a post-doctoral researcher in Rowland's laboratory. Rowland offered him the choice of several projects to work on, and Molina chose the investigation of natural cycling of CFCs. He commenced his work in 1973.

A few things rapidly became apparent. The first was that Lovelock's estimate of atmospheric lifetime had not been particularly accurate, and that actual lifetimes for the commonly used CFCs were more like thirty to fifty years.

The second was that none of the natural systems that are usually associated with the removal of trace species from the atmosphere were particularly effective at getting rid of CFCs. They were not taken up in any significant quantities by plants. Nor were they dissolved into rain water or the oceans. They were not chemically transformed by reaction with species like ozone molecules or hydroxyl radicals in the atmosphere. And there was no indication that they could be effectively processed in any way by soil microorganisms. That left only one possible removal mechanism. Any molecule can be broken into smaller fragments if it absorbs energy from sufficiently short wavelength ultraviolet radiation. In the case of CFCs, the ozone layer filters out all of the wavelengths that might break up the molecules. But if they were to travel to 15 km altitude and higher, they would start to rise above some of the ozone. Then some of the ultraviolet light that could break the molecules down into smaller fragments would not be so effectively blocked. The molecules would be broken into very reactive free radicals by any of this light that got through.

Molina and Rowland's programme of investigation and calculation led them to the conclusion that most of the CFCs in the atmosphere would eventually be removed as a result of being broken up by sunlight in the stratosphere. All other mechanisms could only account for 50 per cent of the removal at the very most, and more probably for 20 per cent or less.

They further considered the nature and the chemical behaviour of the fragments that would be produced, and did some preliminary calculations with a computer model. The results convinced them to publish a warning that CFCs might pose a more serious threat to stratospheric ozone than supersonic aircraft (Molina & Rowland, 1974). The timing of their announcement matched the effective waning of the SST debate, and carried forward some of its momentum.

Rowland and Molina's argument was that atomic chlorine can catalytically decompose ozone in a chain reaction analogous to, but at least five times more efficient than the nitrogen oxide cycle. The reactions involved are:

$$Cl + O_3 \rightarrow ClO + O_2 \tag{8}$$

$$ClO + O \rightarrow Cl + O_2 \tag{9}$$

These reactions are exact analogues of the NOx reactions (5) and (6) discussed in the last chapter. Again, a single chlorine atom can destroy many molecules of ozone because of the way it is recycled in these reactions.

Again, the net effect of the two reactions added together is the same as Chapman's odd oxygen removal reaction (4).[1]

The argument is particularly clearly set out in a later *New Scientist* article by Rowland (1975).

1. The molecules CCl_3F and CCl_2F_2 are essentially inert toward environmental reactions in the lower atmosphere and are accumulating there.
. . .

2. Both chlorofluoromethane gases rise into the stratosphere and are decomposed at altitudes between roughly 15 and 40 km.
. . .

3. CCl_3F and CCl_2F_2 are decomposed by ultraviolet radiation in the 190–215 nm band, with the release of Cl atoms.
. . .

4. The important chemical reactions for chlorine in the stratosphere are those summarized in the diagram:

$$HCl \; \underset{CH_4,\, H_2}{\overset{OH}{\rightleftarrows}} \; Cl \; \underset{O,\, NO}{\overset{O_3}{\rightleftarrows}} \; ClO$$

. . .

5. Gaseous HCl is the predominant chlorine-containing decomposition product at most stratospheric altitudes, but increases in mixing ratio with increasing altitude.
. . .

6. No quantitatively important stratospheric chlorine chemistry has been omitted.

The evidence they were able to muster for their theory was very indirect. Rowland writes:

In early 1974 no successful measurement of any chlorine-containing compounds had been reported in the stratosphere, and relatively few in the troposphere. Some of the other input into the original theory was also based on a minimum of evidence, although Dr Molina and I felt that it was adequate.

Both of these reactions (8) and (9) had been investigated previously in a laboratory setting, and the known rates suggested an efficiency roughly five times that of the NOx cycle – that is, one atom of chlorine would have roughly the same ozone-depleting potential as five molecules of nitric oxide.

It was known from laboratory studies and theoretical considerations that ultraviolet light of wavelength between 190 and 215 nm was capable of decomposing CFC molecules to produce atomic chlorine. This particular wavelength region is a significant one. Wavelengths below 190 nm are strongly absorbed by molecular oxygen, but in this region the absorption of molecular oxygen is weak. Similarly, ozone absorbs strongly above 215 nm, but only weakly between 190 and 215 nm. So there is a little gap in the atmospheric absorption spectrum, where UV light can penetrate deeper into the atmosphere. A significant amount of this light is available above about 20 km altitude. The neighbouring wavelength regions below 190 nm and above 215 nm are strongly absorbed by oxygen or ozone. They are effectively completely filtered out by 150 km or 50 km altitude respectively.

A global inventory calculation based on Lovelock's background CFC measurements and other similar determinations showed that something like 90 per cent of the CCl_3F *ever manufactured* until 1972 was resident in the lower atmosphere in 1972. There was clearly no natural removal process of significance. Weather circulation mixes gases very thoroughly through the troposphere (even very heavy gases), and so a slow transfer to the stratosphere is inevitable when the tropospheric concentration has built up.

So the story was that tropospheric accumulation of CFCs is followed by leakage to the stratosphere. There, these compounds are exposed to ultraviolet light at wavelengths that will cause their photochemical decomposition. One of the fragments of this decomposition is atomic chlorine, which in turn can catalytically decompose ozone.

But one more strand is needed to establish the argument. It must be shown that CFC decomposition produces *significant* amounts of atomic chlorine, and that natural sources of chlorine do not dominate. This evidence was provided during 1975 with at least two independent measurements of the vertical distribution of HCl in the stratosphere (Lazrus *et al.*, 1975; Farmer *et al.*, 1975).

The fact that HCl mixing ratios[2] *increase with increasing altitude* is only consistent with a source of active chlorine at or above the upper part of the stratosphere. The main natural chlorine sources – volcanic effluent and salt spray – are already in an active form, and if the main origin of stratospheric active chlorine were via upward transport from these sources, HCl would be most abundant at the bottom of the stratosphere. The inverse mixing ratio profile requires an inactive chlorine-containing molecule to migrate upward through the stratosphere, not reacting to produce HCl until it reaches a high altitude. CFCs clearly fit this requirement. Methyl chloride is the only significant natural source of *inactive* chlorine that might behave in this way. Unlike CFCs, it has significant tropospheric sinks, so that most of it is destroyed before it can reach the stratosphere.[3]

But the argument about HCl distribution is based on a one-dimensional view of stratospheric circulation. Because the stratosphere has a temperature inversion (warmer at the top) it is generally vertically stable, and not turbulent like the lower atmosphere with its winds and weather systems. But there is a strong and consistent circulation pattern in the stratosphere (well known to meteorologists at the time) where tropical air is carried upward, and then moves to higher latitudes where it descends again (see, e.g., Dobson, 1968a, pp. 126–8). Any tropospheric pollutant which does manage to enter the stratosphere from the equatorial troposphere might well be carried high into the stratosphere before moving to higher latitudes and descending again. A mid-latitude assay of that material might then find that its concentration increased with height, even though it had entered the stratosphere from the bottom. Only a tropical assay would be bound to show the expected decrease with altitude. This particular point of Rowland's argument was not as strong as it seemed. Measurements of the stratospheric distribution of HCl at several different latitudes would have been required to make it secure.

With the wisdom of hindsight, Rowland's last point (that no quantitatively important stratospheric chlorine chemistry had been omitted from their considerations) sounds rather optimistic. Certainly, it proved to be the weak link in the chain of argument.

Molina and Rowland's warning was thus primarily a theoretically based speculation, involving the drawing together of indirect evidence from diverse areas. The argument appears to be soundly and cleverly constructed. But while their conclusions are clearly indicated by deduction from the indirect evidence, there was no direct empirical evidence to support them.

In the years immediately following Rowland's paper, searches for evidence of ozone depletion were fairly inconclusive; the results typically pointed to a depletion around 1 per cent, but estimated error ±2 per cent. There is a great deal of difficulty in determining the level of depletion, or even defining what is meant by it. The problem is that many other factors affect ozone levels. Variations in ozone level of magnitude similar to, or slightly greater than that predicted for chlorine-mediated depletion, occur in correlation with a number of regular and irregular natural cycles. The seasonal cycle, the quasi-biennial oscillation (QBO),[4] the cycle of solar activity,[5] the El Niño Southern Oscillation (ENSO),[6] and the general level of volcanic activity around the world, all produce correlations of this sort. For some of these factors, ozone increases or decreases uniformly on a global basis; other factors affect different regions differently. Some of the correlations were well understood and quantified; others were much less so. The prediction of chlorine-mediated depletion was ceteris paribus, and this must introduce a certain vagueness in a complex system of this sort, while some other factors are not thoroughly understood.

In 1988, the NASA Ozone Trends Panel report indicated a measured decline in ozone levels in the North temperate regions of about 1.7 per cent ±0.7 per cent (standard error) between 1969 and 1986, which is just marginally significant (NASA, 1988, p. 40).

The report was based on a careful and critical analysis of data from numerous ground-based stations in this region, and a strenuous attempt to statistically remove the influence of other factors. A similar analysis was not attempted for tropical regions, nor for the Southern Hemisphere, where monitoring stations were not so numerous.

The data were carefully corrected to allow for two regular natural cycles which affect ozone levels. The solar cycle, which repeats with a period of about eleven years, causes a variation in high latitude ozone levels of about 2 per cent. The quasi-biennial oscillation cycle is less regular. Ozone variations of about 2 per cent – in different directions at different places – are also associated with this cycle!

The influence of the El Niño Southern Oscillation and the pattern of significant volcanic eruptions were also considered by the panel to be important, but these factors are more irregular, and their influences less well understood. A global ozone depletion was confirmed, but it could only just be distinguished in 1988. Until then, the evidence was suggestive, but inconclusive.

Molina's original computer modelling suggested that anthropogenic inputs of inert chlorine compounds may have caused current depletions of about 5 per cent, and would cause eventual depletions around 13 per cent, relative to 'natural' levels. But it had been a one-dimensional model – that is, it had considered variations of concentration only with altitude, and had therefore necessarily taken a very naïve view of circulation factors. Over the following few years, the models were made more sophisticated. Several new discoveries in stratospheric chlorine/ozone chemistry that were made during this period had significant effects on the projections. Most notable was the discovery of the role of chlorine nitrate, $ClONO_2$, as a significant reservoir of stratospheric chlorine. This substance formed in three body collisions involving ClO and NO_2, and thus limited the length of both the chlorine and NOx catalytic chains.[7] And also during this period enormous strides were made in computer technology, which allowed serious two-dimensional models of both circulation and chemistry to be developed for the first time. This allowed better account to be taken of circulation effects and latitude variations. Predictions of expected amounts of ozone depletion varied widely during the period, but eventually seemed to settle down to a figure around half of Molina's original prediction.

This had the advantage of being very much in line with what limited indications were available from the observational evidence. But it had the 'disadvantage' of making the problem appear to be only a minor one, probably of little significance. Many in the scientific community ceased to regard anthropogenic ozone depletion as a major concern. The National Research Council reported in these terms in 1984. Susan Solomon (1988, p. 131) recalls in her review:

Indeed, by about 1984, concern over the possible depletion of the ozone layer had certainly reached a minimum in comparison to earlier years.

In the early 1980s, there was clearly no scientific consensus supporting the Molina and Rowland thesis that stratospheric ozone was likely to be significantly depleted by anthropogenic chlorine compounds. The observational data indicated some ozone depletion, but did not show depletion at a statistically significant level. Many natural factors were known or thought to contribute to ozone variability, and in many cases the detail of the operation of these factors was poorly understood. The only areas of agreement were that much was uncertain, and that if there was an effect it was still very small – much less than 5 per cent.

The debate on the possible role of CFCs in ozone depletion had been prominent in the news media and among the general public throughout this time. Right from the very start, Molina and Rowland had taken the social policy implications of their findings very seriously, and had ensured that the news media were informed about their work and its possible ramifications. There were strong vested interests involved in the public debate – not least those of the companies who manufactured CFCs, or used them in their products. There was also a fairly natural political division, with environmentalists tending to maximise the possible dangers of CFC usage, and conservatives tending to discount them.

By the early 1980s, a popular political lobby seeking to have CFCs banned had become well established, particularly in the United States. It had been based on Molina and Rowland's original warning, and amplified by seizing on the aerosol spray can as the ultimate symbol of the unnecessary product, and of rampant and irresponsible consumerism. The finer nuances of the scientific debate did not appear to have any great effect on the momentum of this movement. A few American states passed legislation restricting the use of CFCs at a very early stage. The political conferences and the groundwork that eventually led to the Montréal Protocol were already well under way by 1984 in spite of the lack of scientific consensus, or even direct scientific evidence (Benedick, 1991, pp. 14–18).

The issue of vested interest, and the way it can feed back into the science, is a complex one, and one that will not be addressed in detail in this book. The issues, including the role of DuPont that is briefly outlined below, are much more fully discussed by Benedick (1991) and Litfin (1994) among others. There is no evidence that issues of politics and vested interest produced gross distortions in the science in this case.

A particularly interesting aspect is the way that vested interest worked with the DuPont chemical company. Initially, their public statements and attitudes were (understandably) aimed at minimising and downplaying the likely dangers of their products. But then, as Molina and Rowland's work gained wider acceptance, and as moves to restrict CFCs in various ways started to be adopted by several American states, the company put a large effort into research and development of work-arounds and alternatives. The company adopted and publicly proclaimed a policy that it would abandon manufacture and use of CFCs if the scientific evidence that they caused significant ozone depletion became sufficiently strong. But they had commercial interests to protect. At this stage, their main concern was that the American government should work hard to ensure that any measures restricting CFC usage were internationally uniform, so that their foreign competitors should not gain a competitive edge. Eventually the company came out in enthusiastic support of international restrictions. This may have been partly because they felt that they were several years ahead of their competitors along the path towards developing substitutes.

There is a very complex feedback between commercial vested interest, scientific research, and public perception and debate. Each clearly has a strong influence on the others. It does not seem likely that any of the three controls the others. The interplay needs to be carefully considered.

NOTES

1 The possible involvement of these two reactions in stratospheric chemistry had first been suggested a few months earlier in a paper by Stolarski and Cicerone (1974). They had been working at the Goddard Space Flight Centre of NASA, and their particular interest was in possible effects on stratospheric chemistry of exhaust from the space shuttle (which contained a lot of HCl).
2 The 'mixing ratio' of a gas in an air sample is its proportion of the total by volume, by partial pressure, or by number of molecules; these three scales agree. Proportion by weight is different. (See, for example, Wayne, 1991, p. 1).
3 Any hydrogen-containing organochlorine or organofluorine compound reacts readily with hydroxyl radicals in the troposphere. Initially, organic free radicals are produced. These readily and rapidly react further to form soluble substances, which are readily 'rained out'. The extreme chemical inertness of CFCs is a property only of such substances as have no hydrogen in the molecule.
4 The QBO is an oscillating change in the pattern of the prevailing winds around

the earth. It has a slightly irregular period, ranging from about twenty-four to thirty-two months.

5 There is an eleven-year cycle in the pattern of solar activity, which shows up in sunspot numbers, slight changes in radiation, and the frequency of solar storms which bombard the earth with high energy particles.

6 The ENSO is a change in prevailing circulation patterns in the entire South Pacific region, occasioned by an irregular variation in the ocean currents off the Pacific coast of South America, which correlates with rainfall levels and storm frequencies in Eastern Australia and the Pacific Islands.

7 The length of a catalytic chain is the average number of times that a catalyst molecule is recycled before something else happens to it. Thus, in this case, it also corresponds to the number of ozone molecules destroyed per chlorine atom or nitric oxide molecule that gets involved.

6 Too much of a good thing? Crucial data backlog in the Antarctic ozone hole discovery

The next major development in the story took place in 1985, when the discovery of the Antarctic ozone hole was announced. This did not happen until about eight years after the effect first appeared. It was a surprise announcement from a group that had been involved in the routine collection of data from a British Antarctic station for many years. Those involved with more sophisticated satellite-based ozone monitoring experiments had missed the effect completely, though they were able to find it in their data once the British announcement had been made. We will examine the rather surprising delay in discovery by the British team, and failure to discover by the NASA team.

In 1985, a letter was published in *Nature*, which dramatically changed the course of scientific investigations of stratospheric ozone (Farman *et al.*, 1985). A team of scientists from the British Antarctic Survey reported a very large seasonal fall in column ozone values measured over their station at Halley Bay in Antarctica. Every year in September and October, ozone levels were falling significantly – typically by about 25 per cent, but sometimes by as much as 60 per cent.

The decline had started around 1976. Nineteen years of carefully collected data between 1957 and 1975 showed no such effect. But in the eight years from 1977 to 1984 the effect was clearly apparent, and seemed to be increasing. By about mid-November each year, the levels were returning to normal.

The background to, and the context of this announcement is important. Ozone is a trace gas in the atmosphere. Even in the stratosphere, where it is at its most concentrated, it forms only a few parts per million of the local atmospheric composition. But it has two vital functions. It is almost solely responsible for filtering out a large wavelength band of ultraviolet solar radiation – radiation that would be lethal to creatures on the earth's surface if it were to arrive here at its full intensity. This radiation also greatly warms the upper stratosphere, which is an important part of the mechanism of the weather systems of the earth's atmosphere.

Concerns of various sorts had already been expressed about possible human influences on stratospheric ozone levels. The first debate, discussed in Chapter 4, related to oxides of nitrogen and water vapour from the exhaust of high-flying aircraft. This was later followed by a carefully formulated and widely publicised argument that inert chlorine-containing compounds might significantly deplete stratospheric ozone (see Chapter 5). By 1985, the concerns about nitrogen oxides had largely been laid to rest. Current analyses based on improved understandings of the chemistry of stratospheric ozone suggested a much smaller influence of NOx in ozone depletion than the original estimates. And operating fleets of supersonic passenger aircraft were much smaller than had at first been expected. Inert chlorine compounds were still taken seriously as a potential threat to the ozone layer. Statistical evidence was starting to emerge that a small global ozone depletion could be discerned from the background of many other factors that affect ozone levels, both globally and locally (NASA, 1988).

One of the side-effects of these concerns was an increased monitoring of ozone levels around the world. A worldwide network of over 200 ground stations had been monitoring ozone levels in various locations since the International Geophysical Year in 1957–8. But not all of them had operated continuously. Many stations had large gaps in the historical data record, while others had produced data which did not appear to be totally reliable. Operating a Dobson spectrophotometer is a technically demanding task, and the instruments require regular rather expensive recalibration, which was often overlooked. Many new stations joined the network in the 1970s and 1980s, while some existing ones improved their data collection regimes. In addition, instruments designed to obtain data about stratospheric ozone were included on the American weather satellites.

From the mid 1970s, then, there was intense worldwide scientific interest in stratospheric ozone, and several monitoring programmes were in operation. A large ozone depletion had been occurring on a regular annual basis since 1977. It was more than ten times larger than the global depletion that the statistical modellers were trying to unravel from other effects, though it was both local and seasonal. It is most surprising in these circumstances that the effect should not be announced until 1985. Why had nobody else noticed the effect? Why had Farman's team taken so long to make the announcement?

There were other reasons why the announcement was quite surprising and shocking to the atmospheric science community.

The effect was quite different in size and character from anything that had been expected. The work of Molina and Rowland had led scientists to look thoroughly for a global ozone decrease somewhere in the region of

1 per cent to 5 per cent. The results of the search had been suggestive of a small depletion, but had thus far come short of a convincing trend in terms of statistical significance. Here was a series of observations which included depletions of up to 60 per cent, but only in a very specific geographical location, and only for a month or two each year.

The effect appeared to start quite suddenly around 1976. But there was no clear evidence of any climatic change at that time that could have explained it. Alternatively, it was difficult to see why, if a build-up of chlorine compounds was indeed responsible, it should trigger a sudden change in this way, rather than bring on a gradual change.

All of the indications from what was then known of stratospheric ozone chemistry, were that any chemically mediated unusual effect ought to occur in equatorial regions. There, a nearly vertical sun would provide the ultraviolet radiation required to drive the photochemical reactions that lead to ozone loss. And these are also the regions where the normal stratospheric circulation patterns would carry pollutants entering from the troposphere high into the stratosphere where there is less atmospheric shielding. Plenty of light in the crucial 190–215 nm wavelength region would be available to break up molecules of CFCs and other substances. The equatorial stratosphere is where any chemically-based ozone depletion would have been expected. The polar skies, especially in springtime when the sun is very low in the sky, had been thought of as a fairly inert reservoir as far as chemical reactions were concerned. Very little ultraviolet light is available.

It is clear that even the British group themselves were very surprised by their results.

The British Antarctic station at Halley Bay has maintained one of the most complete records of local stratospheric column ozone since 1956. Consistently low values for ozone in September and October were first noticed in 1981. The following year's readings were even lower, and confirmed the trend. At the time, there was a backlog of data for about six years from 1974 to 1979/80. The raw readings had been taken at Halley Bay, but the data had not been entered into the computer at BAS HQ Cambridge and 'reduced', i.e. interpreted as ozone column thicknesses. Jonathan Shanklin was involved with entering and interpreting this data backlog during the early 1980s (Shanklin, private communication). Thus it was not until about 1983 that fully analysed data from 1974 to 1979/80 became available to the British team.

Springtime in the Antarctic stratosphere is a time of unstable circulation conditions as a transition occurs from the stable winter polar vortex to a rather different summer circulation pattern. Farman in particular was not easily convinced that there was any great significance to springtime ozone levels. He thought, in line with most circulation-oriented scientists at the time, that almost any ozone level might occur during this unstable period, and that low levels could easily be accounted for by chance admixtures of ozone-poor tropospheric air.

In prior publications, Farman had analysed ozone data from both Halley Bay and another British Antarctic station at Argentine Islands (Farman, 1977; Farman & Hamilton, 1975). He had shown that readings in late winter and spring exhibited a large variability, whereas those in late summer and autumn were remarkably stable. He had argued that *autumn* ozone levels measured at Antarctic stations could be a very sensitive measure of global ozone trends, because they would avoid the variation due to the quasi-biennial oscillation that would be shown at lower latitudes.

Thus, when Farman was first presented by his junior colleagues with evidence of low springtime ozone levels at Halley Bay, he was not convinced that they were significant. A year later confirmation of the trend was provided, and shortly after that the data from the years of analysis backlog became available, and a very clear picture started to emerge. Springtime ozone levels at Halley Bay had been more or less consistent until 1976, but from then onward they showed a marked, continuing, and increasing decline.

There were still at least two problems, however, that needed to be cleared up. The likely explanation of any unexplained and inexplicable variation in measured ozone levels has always been an instrumental artefact. The way the instruments are used to obtain the data means that any of a number of factors might cause their calibration to drift off, or some other instrumental problem that might not be readily apparent. In this particular case, it was a little difficult to understand why an instrument might fail for six to eight weeks each spring, but produce normal results during the summer and autumn. Nevertheless, there was a need to demonstrate that an instrumental artefact was not involved. During the summer, a different spectrometer was taken down to Halley Bay, and the instrument that had been there returned to Cambridge for recalibration and checking. The following spring, similar results were obtained on the second instrument.

This activity is obliquely referred to in the publication (Farman *et al.*, 1985, p. 207):

There was a changeover of spectrophotometers at the station in January 1982; the replacement instrument had been calibrated against the UK Meteorological Office standard in June 1981. Thus, two spectrophotometers have shown October values of total O_3 to be much lower than March values, a feature entirely lacking in the 1957–73 data set.

The passage continues, suggesting and dismissing a few other ways in which the results might be artefactual.

The second issue that really troubled the team was why nobody else had noticed the trend they were observing. On the face of it, there should have been about six other sets of data collected from Antarctic stations that might have shown something similar. But all of these could be fairly readily dismissed.

There are some general problems with the data set from the network of ground-based ozone monitoring stations. They were very clearly expressed to me by a scientist from the Canadian Atmospheric Environment Service (Tarasick, private interview, 1996):

There is a fairly large variation of quality of data from the individual stations. There certainly is a large variation in how data is submitted to us. Some stations are very good about it, some stations are very lax, and some don't submit at all. There are of course differences because of weather conditions. You don't get reliable total ozone data when it's cloudy of course. There is a lot of variation if you look at the station record, simply because many stations have started operating, stopped operating, started operating. That's usually dependent on funds and on operators. Many stations are run by University personnel, or others who are dependent on funding, and dependent on time. Sometimes the person retires, and they have no one else to run it, so they shut down the station. Or a technician's funding dries up, and the technician goes somewhere else. So we have lots of cases where there are records for, say, two years, then a break of ten years, and then it gets started again . . .

Quality also depends – some of the operators are extremely knowledgeable and extremely careful, and calibrate their instruments regularly. Some are very careful, but cannot afford to get their instruments calibrated.

The Canadian Atmospheric Environment Service at Toronto acts under a World Meteorological Organization (WMO) charter to distribute and archive the data collected by the network of ground-based ozone monitoring stations. This operation is now known as the World Ozone and Ultraviolet Radiation Data Centre. Part of its purpose has been described in the following terms:

The early examination of measurements by researchers in addition to those responsible for the measurements is a valuable form of quality control that can lead to improvements in measurement and analysis techniques. The WODC, therefore, encourages originators to make their data so available. Research is also facilitated by providing uniform sets of ozone data which can be easily used by the scientific community. This is done by maintaining an up-to-date well-qualified archive which involves applying simple quality control procedures, organizing the data logically, and providing value-added output products such as time series and maps of ozone data. (AES, 1998)

The primary responsibility for data quality remains with the originating stations, however. Comprehensive central review of data quality is prevented by lack of resources. One could reasonably suppose that political sensitivities might also be a factor.

Most of the other ground stations that might have collected data to complement the Halley Bay findings were at sub-Antarctic rather than truly Antarctic latitudes. Others, for a variety of reasons, had not been systematically collecting data at the right times. The American base at the South Pole had its own special problem, which is discussed later in this chapter.

There was a more serious problem than the lack of confirmation from other ground-based ozone monitoring stations. NASA had been collecting a systematic set of ozone data from weather satellites in polar orbits during the relevant period. If the effect had been genuine, it did not seem likely that such a satellite survey would have missed it.

Jonathan Shanklin wrote a letter to the group at NASA whom he believed to be involved with the analysis of the satellite ozone data, seeking to discuss the anomalous Halley Bay results:

Actually I did write to two groups involved with satellite measurements of ozone prior to the publication of our paper in *Nature*. Perhaps fortunately one group did not respond and the other forwarded my letter to a third group as they were no longer working in the field. (Shanklin, 1996)

When asked why he had used the term 'fortunately' in describing the lack of response, Shanklin tersely replied that their group might have been beaten to publication if the satellite scientists had looked closely at his message.

By late 1984, the British Antarctic Survey team were fully convinced that the effect was a genuine one, and prepared their publication. The announcement eventually appeared more than three years after they had first noticed the effect, and perhaps five years after the effect ought to have been noticed if ozone levels had, in fact, been carefully watched throughout the period.

The next question, then, is why the ozone hole had not been noticed by the scientists working with the satellite data. There were two different satellite-borne ozone monitoring systems in place during the relevant period. SBUV (surface backscattered ultraviolet) and TOMS (total ozone monitoring spectrometer) operated between October 1978 and February 1987. Both programmes were under the control of scientists from the NASA Goddard Space Flight Center. TOMS provided a global survey of total column ozone levels. SBUV produced a data set for a more sparse location sampling regime, that contained additional information about the vertical distribution of ozone within the column. Several other satellite experiments that provided information about ozone vertical distribution operated for shorter periods during 1979 to 1984.

One year after the British announcement of anomalously low ozone levels in the Antarctic spring, a publication by the NASA scientists confirmed the observation, and reassured that it was a genuine phenomenon that affected the whole Antarctic area (Stolarski et al., 1986). The advantages of satellite observation for global ozone monitoring were re-iterated. Satellite observations could confirm that the phenomenon was general over the Antarctic area. They could even map its extent. This does represent a significant advance over results, however diligently obtained, from a single ground station. But there was no explanation of why the scientists working with the satellite data had failed to discover the phenomenon.

The prevalent story circulating about the NASA non-discovery of the ozone hole concerns an automatic computer routine that 'threw out' anomalous ozone values in the data work-up. For example, Benedick (1991, p. 19) reports that:

Interestingly, it was discovered that U.S. measuring satellites had not previously signaled the critical trend because their computers had been programmed automatically to reject ozone losses of this magnitude as anomalies far beyond the error range of existing predictive models.

and attributes this to personal discussions with F.S. Rowland, R.T. Watson, and R. Cicerone.

It is, however, quite clear that this could not have been done by the satellite computers involved in data acquisition. If it had, the anomalous data involved could not have been archived and retrievable for the later analysis by Stolarski's team. If there was any truth in this story (and it seems there is not), the 'rejection' must have been done in some subsequent data work-up on a ground-based computer.

Rich McPeters, head of the ozone processing team at the NASA Goddard Space Flight Centre, denies the story of data being rejected by a computer algorithm (McPeters, 1997):

This myth was the result of a statement made by my colleague, Dr Richard Stolarski, in reply to an interview on the Science program Nova . . . Dr Stolarski was not directly involved in ozone processing at that time and his answer was not correct . . . Our software is designed so that data are never just thrown out. Rather, questionable data are "flagged" as not being of best quality . . . ozone amounts less than 180 DU were flagged as possibly being in error.

McPeters' side of the story is published elsewhere (Pukelsheim, 1990).

By mid 1984, the NASA team were independently aware of low Antarctic ozone levels in the satellite data, as the result of frequent triggering of the <180 DU low ozone flag during the Southern autumn of 1983. These low levels were investigated.

This was noticed in our quality control screening as a sudden increase in flags for ozone too low. Since this could have been the result of an instrument problem, we compared our measurements with the only Dobson ground station data then available, that from the Amundsen-Scott station at the South Pole. . . . Unfortunately, because of an error, the South Pole Dobson station was reporting ozone values of 300 DU when our satellite instrument was reporting less than 180 DU. (McPeters, 1997)

Apparently, the instrument at the South Pole had been set to the wrong wavelengths for ozone measurements, and data from October to December 1983 were later found to be 'erroneous and uncorrectable'. A purely speculative possibility is that an operator at the South Pole may have noticed a series of 'ridiculous' ozone levels coming in, misread the manual, and mistakenly re-adjusted the wavelength settings!

As a result of this conflict between satellite and ground station data, the attention of the satellite team had been directed to a possible instrument malfunction rather than a genuine ozone depletion until after the British announcement had appeared.

But even accepting this story as completely accurate, we are not really presented with a convincing explanation for the failure of the NASA team to discover the Antarctic ozone hole. The hole was particularly deep and extensive in the 1983 season, leading to frequent triggering of the low ozone flag, and the start of a NASA investigation. But 'normal' column ozone values are between 300 and 400 DU, while the low ozone flag is not triggered until the ozone falls below 180 DU. There is a large region for 'low' ozone concentrations to fall below 300 DU and above 180 DU. A significantly low average ozone level over the Antarctic could have been found (indeed, can be found – see NASA, 1988, p. 91) in the TOMS data for any spring season from 1977 to 1984. Individual ozone levels in these seasons may seldom fall below 180 DU (the triggering level), but the majority of them must fall in the 180 to 300 DU range. The ground-based data from Halley Bay makes this clear (see figure 6.2). Anomalously low springtime ozone levels in the Antarctic had clearly been present in the TOMS data set for several years of non-discovery.

There is thus no satisfactory story of why NASA scientists did not notice the low ozone levels. It could be that the explanation is quite mundane. NASA was at that time subject to funding and program cuts. The scientists involved in the ozone program had other priorities and preoccupations. It seems that they were simply unable to deal efficiently with the analysis of the vast amounts of data that their ozone-monitoring program was generating. Without the cue to look specifically at Antarctic values in September/October, the team simply did not notice the anomaly. It is doubtful that anybody at NASA had actually ever had a close look at the relevant data.

Once Farman's announcement had been made, roughly coinciding with the time that the NASA team convinced themselves that their 1983 data showed genuine low ozone levels rather than instrumental artefacts, the NASA scientists were able to make a major contribution to the unfolding investigation. Their data, unlike any of the ground station data, were able to give a global picture, as opposed to a time series at a fixed geographic point. They also were not affected by adverse surface weather conditions, and had some advantages over ground stations in obtaining vertical profiles of ozone distribution.

It was the American NASA satellite team that coined the phrase 'The Antarctic Ozone Hole' – this was a very effective and evocative term that played a large part in the press and public discussion of the phenomenon, though it caused some of the scientists involved concern because the picture it provided was not a very accurate one. The British conceded that their paper received a lot more attention because of this than it might otherwise have done (Shanklin, private communication, 1996). They complained, on the other hand, that the use of 'Antarctic Ozone Hole' to describe the phenomenon was a bit misleading. There was really a depletion of ozone rather than an actual hole in the ozone layer (Stratospheric Ozone Review Group, 1988, p. 6). Since the mid 1990s, this fine distinction has no longer been relevant. There is now, by mid October each year, an almost total removal of ozone between 15 and 25 km altitude throughout the Antarctic.

Suggestions have been published in various places that the British Antarctic Survey discovery of the Antarctic ozone hole has been wrongly attributed. They will be considered here, almost parenthetically to the main argument. Two of the suggestions need not be taken seriously. The first is the suggestion that the Antarctic ozone hole had been discovered by Dobson, when he visited the Antarctic in 1956/1957. Dobson described a phenomenon which he labelled as the 'Southern anomaly' in ozone concentrations.

In the temperate zones of both hemispheres, monthly ozone levels show a simple annual variation with a maximum in springtime, and a minimum in the autumn. Spitzbergen, in the Arctic, showed a similar trend, except for a slightly larger annual variation, and the questionable quality of data from the winter season. But in the Antarctic, the measurements in early spring were similar to autumn levels, and it was not until November that ozone levels rose to a rather sharp maximum. But there was no 'hole', and even the idea of regarding Spitzbergen data as the

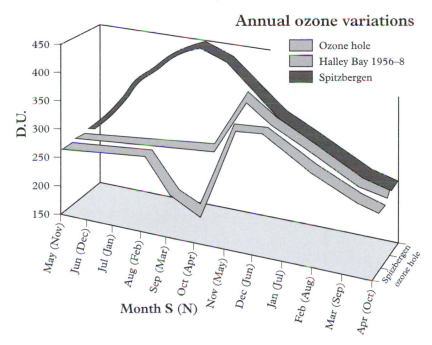

Figure 6.1 Differences between the Southern anomaly and the Antarctic ozone hole (diagrammatic).

'norm' from which Antarctic readings 'deviated' shows a certain Northern Hemisphere chauvinism in attitude. The 'ozone hole' shows up in quite a different way. Early spring levels in the Antarctic since 1977 have been significantly and increasingly lower than the autumn minimum. A graph of October average ozone levels at Halley Bay (see figure 6.2) shows steady behaviour from 1957 until 1975, followed by a steep and increasing decline from 1977.

A different claim of a major Antarctic ozone depletion in 1958 arises from a re-analysis of some data collected from the French Antarctic station at Dumont d'Urville (Rigaud & Leroy, 1990). This claim has been criticised and refuted (Newman, 1994). There is a very large scatter in the original data. The ozone measurements were not made with a Dobson spectrophotometer, but by an alternative method, involving spectra collected on photographic plates in a grating spectrograph. Such methods always rely on exposures judged so that analysis can be carried out in the fairly narrow range where photographic image density varies linearly and sensitively with light intensity. The crucial spectra on which the argument

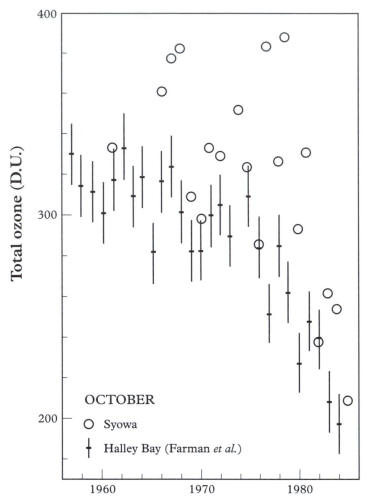

Figure 6.2 Comparison of Halley Bay and Syowa data for springtime ozone.
Reproduced from S. Chubachi & R. Kajiwara, *Geophys. Res. Lett.* (1986) **13**, 1197. © 1986, American Geophysical Union.

is based are taken using moonlight, blue sky, or even starlight as the light source. Faint light sources introduce additional difficulties and unreliability into the measurements. Data from other Antarctic and sub-Antarctic stations for the same period in 1958 give no indication of any similar anomaly. The present consensus of atmospheric scientists is put very succinctly in the 1994 WMO report:

A single report of extremely low Antarctic winter ozone in one location in 1958 by an unproven technique has been shown to be completely inconsistent with the measurements depicted here and with all credible measurements of total ozone. (WMO, 1994, p. xxxi)

The more serious challenge to the British Antarctic Survey claim to discovery of the Antarctic phenomenon arises from conference papers and publications by a Japanese group from the Antarctic station at Syowa.

One year earlier than the British announcement, Chubachi announced at a conference that ozone readings were anomalously low at the Syowa station during September and October 1982 (Chubachi, 1994). This has led to some suggestion, particularly outside the mainstream scientific literature, that the Japanese group ought to be given priority in attributing the discovery of the Antarctic ozone hole. I would argue that this would be unjust, for the following reasons.

Firstly, the title of Chubachi's paper is 'Preliminary Result of Ozone Observation at Syowa Station from February 1982 to January 1983'. This indicates two things. A 'Preliminary Result' means that the data is to be subjected to further and deeper analysis before it is to be taken too seriously. And the data under discussion are from a single year. At best, what is being talked about is a single unusual season. There is nothing in the scope of the paper, nor in Chubachi's results *at that time* to indicate an ongoing new phenomenon.

Secondly, the quality of the Japanese data did not provide evidence of nearly the same strength as the British data. In figure 6.2 the Japanese scientists superimpose their results on those of the British team (reproduced from their earlier publication). The British data show nineteen years of results (1957–75) with October mean values between 280 and 335 DU, a few transition years, and five years of results for 1980–4 with October means between 200 and 250 DU. Error bars, representing intra-monthly standard deviations in the data, are set at around ±15 DU. The Japanese data have several missed seasons. Sixteen data points representing years between 1961 and 1981 show October means liberally scattered between 280 and 390 DU, and no error bars to indicate intra-monthly variation. The 1982 reading of about 240 DU is accompanied by points at 260, 255, and 210 respectively for the years 1983–5. Chubachi may have had the 1983 data at the conference, and may even have informally referred to them. But the last two points clearly postdated his 1984 paper. The much larger scatter of data from the Japanese observations does not necessarily indicate less careful technique. It may simply be indicative of a more unsettled and variable climate at Syowa than at Halley Bay. Ozone levels vary significantly with surface weather conditions. Syowa is in fact at much lower latitude than Halley Bay – 69°S as against 76°S. This puts it almost on the typical edge of the Antarctic vortex. It would move in and out of the Antarctic circulation system frequently. Halley Bay, being further South, would be consistently situated within the vortex.

The point of comparison is not concerned with scientific technique or accuracy, but with statistics. The Halley Bay readings more than doubled the historical range, and showed a consistent trend over five to eight years. They are to be taken much more seriously as evidence than a single year's observation which only extended the historical range by less than 50 per cent.

These, then, are the reasons why I would argue that the discovery of the Antarctic ozone hole is indeed properly attributed to the British Antarctic Survey team of Farman, Gardiner, and Shanklin.

The fact that the discovery took so long needs further consideration. For any scientific investigation, it is usual to suppose that the more relevant data are available, the better the basis for theorising and understanding the behaviour of a natural system. But in this history we see, both with the British Antarctic Survey investigation, and more importantly with the NASA satellite monitoring programme, that the large volume of data collected proved in some ways to be a major hindrance to an important scientific discovery.

The first problem was that the data collection exercise in each case was seen as routine, and not likely to lead to any scientific results of great interest.

The British Antarctic Survey at Halley Bay had been very meticulous in collecting a continuous record of column ozone measurements, involving many instrument readings each day, right from the time when Dobson established the instrument there in 1956. But the data analysis that followed the collection was given a low priority. It is easy to understand why. For two decades, all that the record showed was a pattern of fairly random and meaningless hourly and daily change superimposed on a regular seasonal variation.

The data analysis started to fall behind under the pressure of other, more obviously important tasks. Shanklin (private interview, 1996) reminisces:

And we had got a data gap between about 1972 and 1980 – not quite that long, it was about five to seven years data gap. We had been collecting observations, but they hadn't been reduced. They had just been sitting there. One of my jobs when I first joined the survey was to supervise getting it typed on computer and produce a data correlation on that.

This data backlog actually spanned the years when the ozone hole first appeared.

But the lapse in analysis at BAS pales into insignificance alongside the data backlog at NASA. The TOMS data set consists of some 50 million ozone readings per year. In the late 1970s and early 1980s, computer technology was in a state where collection of data on this magnitude was not difficult, convenient storage was something of a problem, and retrieval and analysis of data on this scale had lagged behind. This particularly applied to graphical presentation – the ozone maps that began to appear later in the 1980s – and to pattern recognition. Analysis of a large data set was easily achievable in terms of some preconceived idea of its information content. But work on the problem of getting computer programmes to look at the data in a general way and pick out the unexpected pattern had not then progressed very far. McPeters(1997) comments as follows:

I tend to forget how much computer systems and the way we work have changed just in the last ten years. In 1985 production was on an IBM 360–95, disk storage was dear, and the production system was entirely tape-based, with intermediate results being written to tape, etc. We thought we were at the cutting edge in being able to produce data a mere 10 months after it was taken. The final products were distributed on 6250 bpi tapes – in IBM EBCDIC binary – by the NSSDC (National Space Science Data Center) at Goddard . . .

As for maps – there was very little imaging software available. We studied the low values by paging through thick printouts and looking at numbers. In 1986 Rich Stolarski did some of the first TOMS images by taking colored pens and coloring-in contour plots. Mark Schoeberl looked at them and said that he could do better than that – and proceeded to write the first mapping routines for IDL to do the images directly. (He gave his routines to the people at IDL and they are now incorporated into the language.) Mark next coupled the map routines to an automatic camera to do the first ozone hole movies (which ate up lots of VAX time).

The scientists at NASA had enthusiastically and efficiently arranged for the data to be collected by the satellite-borne experiments, and had put considerable effort into ironing out instrumental problems, and accurately calibrating the data against that obtained from ground stations. The actual data were archived on magnetic tape, and circulated by NASA to other scientists who specifically wanted to use them. But within NASA there had not been a project that had ever taken a general look at the data in a way that might have picked up the strong pattern – a seasonal and regional trend, whose magnitude was quite significant even in the years before 1983, when frequent tripping of the 'low ozone' flag alerted the scientists to the effect.

So there was much the same picture as at the British Antarctic Survey, only on a much larger scale. NASA scientists were doing a thorough job of *collecting* the data required to monitor stratospheric ozone around the globe, but no-one was really *looking at* the data that were being collected – at least not from the right point of view.

Again, the reason is not too difficult to understand. The data set was large, rich, and regarded as routine. Nobody was really expecting anything untoward. The data could be, and were being used in various projects relating to stratospheric circulation, and the like. There was no specific interest in Antarctic data, because no model, neither chemistry-based nor circulation-based, had at that stage indicated the likelihood of anything particularly interesting or unusual happening in the Antarctic. The sheer size and inaccessibility of the data set was of itself a disincentive for anyone to simply examine it with a more general and speculative approach. The magnitude of the task was too great for any analysis other than one arising from a preconceived view.

This case, then, seems to be a very clear instance where the collection of too much data actually proved to be a hindrance to making a scientific discovery. It is possibly an historical accident. In the case of the satellite data, the timing of the events is crucial. A decade earlier, the data could not have been collected on quite this magnitude. A decade later, and advances in graphical presentation of computer data, and in the pattern recognition problem in artificial intelligence, would have made this type of data backlog much less likely in a 'state of the art' scientific investigation.

7 Antarctic ozone hole – theories and investigations

At the time of its discovery, the springtime Antarctic ozone depletion was an unexpected phenomenon that had no obvious explanation. A new problem had been set for theoretical science: the task of finding an explanation that fitted with the observational evidence, and that could be integrated into the body of what was already known about ozone and the stratosphere. Rapidly, a number of speculative hypotheses were put forward.

In the paper announcing the original discovery (Farman *et al.*, 1985), the effect was attributed to rising levels of inert chlorine compounds in the atmosphere. This in turn was linked to the widespread and increasing production and use of CFCs. The authors pointed to a correlation between CFC mixing ratios in the atmosphere at ground level, and Antarctic ozone levels in the stratosphere, both in spring and in autumn.

But models of stratospheric chemistry had always shown that any chlorine-mediated ozone depletion would be most significant at high altitudes in the tropical stratosphere. An Antarctic anomaly could not be produced within the normal framework of reactions used for stratospheric chlorine/ozone chemistry. It was clear that any attempt to explain the phenomenon would need to be based on the inclusion of some new chemical reactions in the system.

Farman's proposal was a very minor amendment to Molina and Rowland's assessment of stratospheric chemistry to include one extra crucial reaction:

$$ClO + NO \rightarrow NO_2 + Cl \tag{10}$$

He thought that this particular reaction could provide an explanation because it is unusual in showing an inverse temperature dependence. Unlike almost every other chemical reaction, this one is faster at lower temperatures (Farman *et al.* p. 209). This might allow overall ozone loss to be faster and more efficient at lower temperatures as well, because it provides an alternative pathway at very low temperatures for regenerating the atomic chlorine that can destroy ozone. So Farman attributed ozone loss in the Antarctic to changes in the normal gas phase chemistry arising from the operation of this reaction in the extreme low temperatures of the springtime stratosphere.

The CFC/ozone correlation drawn out by Farman and his colleagues was not a particularly close one. It provided only the flimsiest of circumstantial evidence for the involvement of chlorine chemistry in the ozone depletion phenomenon. Moreover their reaction model was seriously flawed. Others (Solomon *et al.*, 1986; McElroy *et al.*, 1986) were able to show that Farman's scheme could not account for major depletion of Antarctic ozone, nor for the very rapid changes in ozone level associated with the annual formation and repair of the ozone hole. The new reaction ran only slightly faster at lower temperatures, and there was some error in Farman's modelling. While the scheme might account for a small ozone depletion, it was most improbable that it could produce a depletion as large as had been observed, and quite certain that it could not produce the rapid onset of the phenomenon (a time scale of a week or two at most was needed). Something more drastic was required.

Thus, while Farman, Gardiner, and Shanklin's announcement and their experimental results were taken seriously, their attribution of cause was far from convincing. The suggestion that CFCs were likely to be responsible for the phenomenon was seriously taken up, but those who did so admitted that some 'new chemistry' would be required.

A number of alternative suggestions as to the cause of the Antarctic depletion phenomenon followed quite quickly in the wake of the announcement. They can conveniently be divided into three main families. In the first group of hypotheses, the phenomenon is attributed to chlorine chemistry. Different approaches to the detailed chemical mechanism distinguish these theories from one another.

There are two main problems for any explanation in terms of chlorine chemistry. The first is that the region where the phenomenon occurs is isolated from any source of far ultraviolet light. Atomic oxygen is therefore absent.

For the normal chlorine cycle

$$Cl + O_3 \rightarrow ClO + O_2 \tag{8}$$

$$ClO + O \rightarrow Cl + O_2 \tag{9}$$

atomic oxygen is required to keep the chain going. It is usually obtained from the break-up of ozone in UV light:

$$O_3 + \text{light (wavelength 220–320nm)} \rightarrow O_2 + O \tag{1}$$

When ultraviolet light is absent, some alternative to at least reaction (9) is needed.

Farman's attempt fits and illustrates this requirement:

$$Cl + O_3 \rightarrow ClO + O_2 \tag{8}$$

$$ClO + NO \rightarrow Cl + NO_2 \tag{10}$$

is a catalytic cycle that seems to get around the problem. But Farman had overlooked the fact that this still requires either a vast independent source of nitric oxide (NO), or

$$NO_2 + O \rightarrow NO + O_2 \tag{6}$$

to complete the chain. This is a large part of the reason why Farman's scheme could not really work properly, especially at the lower altitudes where the actual depletion was occurring.

The second main problem for a chemical approach is to provide an explanation of why the phenomenon is *restricted to* the Antarctic. An alternative cycle that avoids the use of atomic oxygen could affect ozone levels anywhere in the stratosphere unless it has some other attribute that only allows it to work in the Antarctic. Again, Farman's idea of a reaction with inverse temperature dependence runs along the right lines, but is not nearly drastic enough. His crucial reaction runs only slightly faster as temperature decreases – certainly not enough that a depletion phenomenon could change from its dramatic scale in the Antarctic to being undetectable in the Arctic,[1] over a temperature change of 5° or so.

Others who put forward theories based on chlorine chemistry recognised a possible role for chemical reactions at ice crystal surfaces (Molina *et al.*, 1987; Solomon *et al.*, 1986). Rowland and Molina had originally considered only gas phase reactions. The stratosphere is a very dry place. Normally clouds do not form. But in the polar night in the Antarctic it gets cold enough for cloud formation in the lower stratosphere. Polar stratospheric clouds are made up of ice crystals which contain both water and nitric acid. They are often referred to as 'mother of pearl' clouds, and are said to be very beautiful. Once formed, these clouds persist until after springtime sunrise. Polar stratospheric clouds also form in the Arctic. But a slightly different circulation pattern there causes the Northern polar vortex to be less stable and less cold. The Northern clouds form in smaller numbers, and usually disperse before springtime. Here at least was a significant and relevant difference between Arctic and Antarctic that might be used in an explanation of the phenomenon.

Opponents of the approach based on chlorine chemistry spoke, with some justification, of the need for 'unusual and speculative chemistry' in producing an explanation along these lines (Stolarski & Schoeberl, 1986).

The second family of theories (Mahlman *et al.*, 1986; Tung *et al.*, 1986) attributed the phenomenon not to any chemical effects at all, but rather to air circulation patterns. Air bodies from the stratosphere and the troposphere do not normally mix much at all. Such mixing as there is, is mainly due to tropospheric air rising episodically into the stratosphere in equatorial regions, and stratospheric air returning to the troposphere at high latitudes.

The main feature of stratospheric circulation is two large fairly stable cells, one in each hemisphere. In each cell, equatorial air is carried high, and moves to higher latitudes before returning to the lower stratosphere, and back toward the equator in the lower stratosphere. In addition there is a special circulation pattern set up in the polar winter. In both the troposphere and the stratosphere, a vortex is set up, keeping the polar air isolated from the rest of the world's air as it circulates around the winter pole. This pattern occurs in both hemispheres, but the Antarctic vortex is more intense and stable.

The circulation-based theories of the Antarctic phenomenon considered the role of the polar vortex in the mixing of tropospheric and stratospheric air. They focused particularly on the early spring period when the returning sunlight started to warm the air mass and cause the break-up of the polar vortex. Tropospheric air contains comparatively little ozone. If there were a net upwelling of tropospheric air into the lower stratosphere during this period, then that could explain the apparent ozone depletion in this particular region. Moreover, it would also mean that what was being observed was more likely to be a redistribution of ozone than an actual depletion. If this were really the basis of the phenomenon, then it was likely (but not necessarily the case) that the stratosphere in the sub-Antarctic regions was actually being temporarily enriched in ozone during the depletion phenomenon. Ozone-rich stratospheric air would have to be pushed aside from the polar region to the sub-Antarctic. There were two main questions that the circulation theories had to address. Could evidence – either from modelling or from direct observation – be collected to confirm tropospheric upwelling at the appropriate times and places? And could an explanation be found for why this pattern had suddenly started in the mid-1970s, when it had not been present previously?

A third group of theories started from this last point (Callis & Natarajan, 1986). Oxides of nitrogen are produced in very large amounts in the extreme upper atmosphere (around 200 km altitude) by particles emitted from the sun during solar storms. Moreover the earth's magnetic field concentrates these charged solar particles strongly into the polar regions. It is therefore in polar regions that these particles will collide with nitrogen and oxygen molecules, and trigger a series of reactions leading to

NOx formation. Downward transport of nitrogen oxides, coupled with the isolation of the air parcel within the Antarctic vortex, could lead to a very large build-up of stratospheric NOx during the polar night. This could, in turn, lead to ozone depletion in this region through the normal NOx cycle (reactions 6 and 7) with the return of the sunlight. The period from 1975 to 1980 was a period of rapidly increasing solar activity, building up to a particularly strong sunspot maximum, which fitted in with the observed initial formation and build-up of the ozone hole from 1976 onward.

There were several difficulties for this theory. The first is the poor quality of the correlation. Ozone measurements had been systematically taken from ground stations in the Antarctic since 1957. No anomalous ozone depletions were observed in the data for the two previous solar maxima in the 1957–75 period. These solar maxima were, it was argued, less strong than the 1980 maximum. But the complete absence of any indication of modulation of the ozone levels in phase with the sunspot cycle in the earlier period made the explanation seem a little implausible.

Then there is the difficulty of the quantity of nitrogen oxides required. The atmospheric pressure at the altitudes where the nitrogen oxides were supposed to be formed is at least a thousand-fold smaller than that in the stratosphere. It seemed unlikely that the build-up of nitrogen oxides could be sufficient, even if the downward transport were quite efficient, and horizontal transport did not interfere.

And finally, the normal nitrogen oxide cycle in the springtime Antarctic stratosphere was in trouble for the same reasons that the normal chlorine cycle was: there is insufficient ultraviolet light to generate the atomic oxygen required to complete the chain.

Discovery of the ozone hole had caught the world's attention. The previous concern about stratospheric ozone depletion was amplified with hard evidence of spectacularly low ozone levels to provide a focus. But the evidence had been found in an unexpected form, and in an unexpected place, and it was clear that the new phenomenon was not understood properly.

For the international conferences working on agreements to limit the use of CFCs, it may have provided an extra impetus to help conclude negotiations. In Rowland's view:

Subsequent developments in that remote geographical region have undoubtedly played an important role in stimulating international discussion of possible regulations for restriction of future emissions of CFCs. . . . While the Montreal Protocol was specifically and repeatedly stated not to be dependent upon the observations over Antarctica, it is also certainly true that none of the delegates in Montreal was unaware of the latter's existence. (Rowland, 1988)

Benedick, who was himself involved in the negotiation, argues otherwise. Too little was known at that stage about the phenomenon or its significance. Would its effects remain local and seasonal, or could they be the precursor to a more general ozone loss? There was even considerable scepticism about whether the phenomenon was genuine, and extensive doubt that CFCs had anything to do with it.

A year later Rowland appeared to believe that the Antarctic revelation was the "driving force" behind the negotiations. Other observers have also ascribed the success at Montreal to the "dread factor" of Antarctica. But for those closest to the process, these judgements seem more a product of hindsight, overlooking how little was known about this phenomenon during the negotiations. (Benedick, 1991, pp. 19–20)

By 1986 the keyword for the scientific investigations was uncertainty. Government planning authorities and international negotiators were working on the limitation of CFCs. They needed definite and authoritative answers from the scientists, and the scientists were not yet in a position to provide them. The negotiators had reached a point where they could no longer wait for scientific certainty and decided that they should take active steps forward. At an international workshop in Leesburg, Virginia, they adopted the idea of an 'Interim Protocol'.

This concept implied that participating governments need not wait until they agreed on a definitive solution to the CFC problem. Rather, a treaty could be designed that would provide for periodic reassessments of the evolving science and that would contain built-in mechanisms for revising the controls if necessary. (Benedick, 1991, pp. 49–50)

Nevertheless, there remained considerable pressure on the scientists to arrive quickly at a much better understanding of the Antarctic phenomenon, and of the influence of anthropogenic chlorine compounds on stratospheric ozone more generally. In the medium term, there were important public policy questions that hinged on the scientific conclusion. Had the ozone hole arisen as a result of the widespread use of CFCs and similar compounds? Or was it due to a natural change in some pattern of air circulation, or of solar interaction with the upper atmosphere? In the latter case CFCs were innocent of responsibility at least for the ozone hole.

In 1986, a team of American scientists led by Dr Susan Solomon travelled to Antarctica to set up experiments and take measurements aimed at providing a better characterisation of the Antarctic phenomenon. The project was known as NOZE-1 (National Ozone Experiment, #1).

Susan Solomon's recollection (personal interview, 1996) is that:

At the time we went, there was even some doubt about whether the ozone hole was real, whether Farman was correct. We certainly didn't know what time of year it developed, and in fact one of the key points in the dynamics theories was the idea that maybe the ozone actually goes away in the middle of the winter.

The scientists were able to monitor ozone levels from the end of August through the depletion period. Rather than relying totally on Dobson UV spectrometry, they used four very different methods. In the ultimate analysis, the ozone data obtained from these four different techniques agreed. They thus established that the ozone depletion started in late August, and that it was a genuine phenomenon. The argument that Farman's low values might have been caused by volcanic aerosols, or some artefactual interference, was effectively rebutted.

One contribution I think that is perhaps overlooked in NOZE-1 is the simple fact that we measured the ozone. We showed that four instruments of very different methods got the same answer. And we showed that the ozone goes away in September. Because there were even questions about whether the Dobsons were being affected by El Chichon aerosols or something. (S. Solomon, private interview 1996)

The other important aspect of the ozone measurements was that accurate vertical profiles of the ozone distribution were obtained. These showed that on establishment of the depletion phenomenon, ozone was being removed selectively between about 12 and 25 km altitude. This counted against the solar cycle theory, which would have suggested a depletion starting in the upper stratosphere, and the circulation theories, which would have suggested a total disruption of the lower part of the vertical profile with upwelling tropospheric air.

Levels of nitrogen dioxide were measured which were extremely low. This was a confirmation of similar results which had been obtained by a group of New Zealand scientists (McKenzie & Johnston, 1984). Observation of low levels of nitrogen dioxide could fairly be regarded as a classical falsification of the solar cycle theories.

Abnormally high levels of chlorine dioxide were also measured (S. Solomon et al., 1987). These data provided strong but not conclusive evidence of the involvement of chlorine chemistry in the Antarctic ozone depletion phenomenon.

There was also a series of measurements that showed high chlorine monoxide (P. Solomon et al., 1987; not a relative of S. Solomon). But there were serious doubts about the validity of this result. Ironically, one of the factors behind this doubt was that the instrument ought at the same time to have detected nitrous oxide, and no nitrous oxide was observed. Part of the reason was that nitrous oxide levels in the polar stratospheric vortex are unexpectedly low.[2] This was not recognised at the time. In later investigations, abnormally low nitrous oxide levels were confirmed, and formed an important part of the evidence against the circulation-based theories of Antarctic ozone depletion. But there was a widespread feeling in the atmospheric science community that there were other problems of method and inconsistency in the published data of P. Solomon *et al.*

Involvement of chlorine chemistry was strongly, but not conclusively indicated by the NOZE experiments.

The scientists were much better informed about the nature of the Antarctic depletion phenomenon after NOZE-1, but still not in a position to give definitive answers. The measurements in NOZE-1 had largely been based on remote rather than direct sensing (though some balloon-borne observations were involved). And the measurements had mainly been directed at concentrations of chemical substances, and confirmation or falsification of the chlorine theory. More measurements of circulation and related effects were needed to test the account of the circulation-based theories.

In 1987 an experiment was set up which involved a large team of scientists from various disciplines, including those most readily associated with each of the rival theories (Kerr, 1987). It was an international effort, on a fairly large scale. The US National Aeronautics and Space Administration (NASA) co-ordinated a project involving 150 scientists and their associated support personnel. They represented nineteen different agencies, and four countries. A total of $US 10 million was provided by the US government and these agencies. Two aeroplanes, carrying a wide range of scientific instruments, were used to make detailed observations in various parts of the Antarctic stratosphere over a six-week period in 1987 that started prior to the beginning of the depletion phenomenon, and extended to the time of maximum depletion. One of the aircraft was capable of flying at unusually high altitude. The airborne observations were matched by the intensive collection of ground-based data at a series of Antarctic stations (NOZE-2), and near simultaneous satellite observations. The project was called the Airborne Antarctic Ozone Experiment (AAOE).[3]

The launching of an effort on this scale indicates clearly that the scientists were anxious to obtain definite answers. There was also a political driving force – the planning authorities were anxious for some sort of scientific certainty to base their policies on.

The aircraft were based near Punta Areñas, in far Southern Chile. About a dozen flights were made by each plane between mid-August and the end of September. The aircraft had different capabilities: the DC8 had a long operating range and was capable of flying in darkness. The ER2 could operate at unusually high altitude, so that it could take measurements directly within the stratosphere. But it had a shorter range, and much more stringent take-off and landing requirements – that is, it was more easily grounded by bad weather conditions. Return flights were made roughly along the meridian towards the pole, with the aircraft turning back when cold or darkness dictated (Tuck *et al.*, 1989).

About a dozen different measuring instruments were installed on each plane. Eleven questions had been identified for which answers were particularly sought. The instruments were chosen and experiments designed with a view to obtaining these answers. Most of the measurements were aimed at collecting data which might count as evidence for or against the rival theories currently under consideration, but there was also an element of general collection of in situ data that would provide a better characterisation of the phenomenon in case none of the current theories remained viable (Tuck, private interview, 1996).

Of the many results obtained from the AAOE, the one that has been regarded as the most influential was the observation of abnormally high levels of ClO radicals in close spatial and temporal correlation with regions of ozone loss.

Two figures are reproduced here from the original paper (Anderson *et al.*, 1989). The first, which encapsulates the famous 'smoking gun' result,[4] is obtained from data collected on the ER2 flight of 16 September, when the ozone depletion was well established. The horizontal axis of the plot is a latitude axis, but also represents flight time as the flight followed a Southward course after reaching stratospheric altitude near Punta Areñas. Mixing ratios of ozone and ClO are plotted on two separate vertical scales (ozone levels are always much higher than ClO).

The left hand part of the plot shows a sub-Antarctic region outside the polar vortex, where ClO levels – the dark curve – are around 50 parts per trillion (i.e. parts in 10^{12}), and ozone levels – the broken curve – are normal at around 2.4 parts per million. At the right side of the plot, inside the polar vortex, ClO levels have risen 20-fold to around 1100 parts per trillion, and ozone levels have fallen by about 60 per cent to 1.0 parts per million. But the most dramatic part of the plot is the transition region between, where irregular peaks and troughs in the two plots match one another precisely in perfect anti-correlation: ozone depletion occurs at precisely the same locations as ClO enhancement! One of the scientists involved in the project is reported to have remarked on seeing this result: 'These measurements are better than a "smoking gun" – this is more like seeing the guy pull the trigger!' (Silver & de Fries, 1990, p. 109).

But this is only one of many figures from that particular paper. Equally of interest in providing a diagnosis of what is happening is a similar graph from an earlier flight in the series. The plot from 23 August shows a similar but smaller rise in ClO, but without the corresponding ozone depletion so well established. A less significant depletion, around 15 to 20 per cent can arguably be seen in the transition region, but not within the vortex itself.

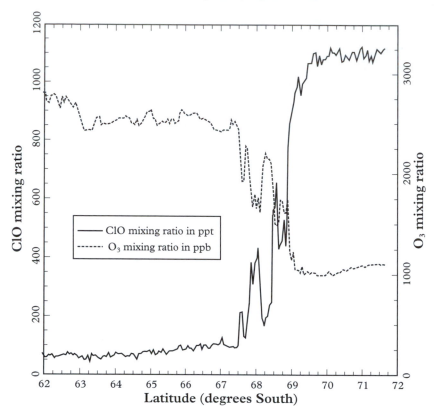

Figure 7.1 The 'smoking gun' result from the AAOE.
Reproduced from Anderson *et al.*, *J. Geophys. Res.* **94** (1989), Fig. 14,
p. 11474. © American Geophysical Union.

The interpretation that fits this data must run somewhat as follows:

> In early spring, some chemical reactions occur that lead to the
> generation of atomic chlorine in the polar vortex, which can then
> react to produce chlorine monoxide via the familiar reaction

$$Cl + O_3 \rightarrow ClO + O_2 \qquad (8)$$

Because no further reaction channel is available which might use up the
ClO, this species simply accumulates in the local stratosphere. Because
the chlorine species are so much less abundant than ozone (i.e. by a factor
of close to 1000 even when ClO is at elevated levels), the one ozone molecule that is destroyed per ClO radical generated does not constitute a
significant ozone depletion (one part per thousand at most).

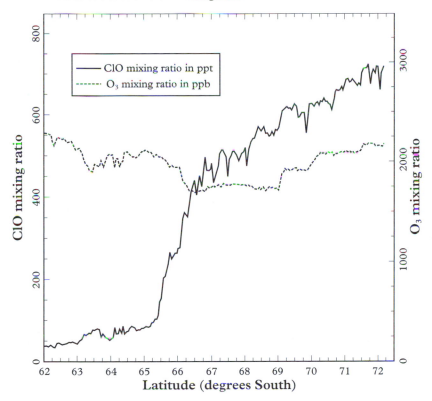

Figure 7.2 An ozone/ClO correlation from earlier in the season. Reproduced from Anderson *et al.*, *J. Geophys. Res.* **94** (1989), Fig. 2, p. 11467. © American Geophysical Union.

Hence greatly elevated ClO, without much effect on ozone levels.

Between August and mid September, another reaction channel must open up which somehow regenerates atomic chlorine from ClO. When this happens, a chain can be set up whereby the recycling of atomic chlorine can eventually lead to massive ozone depletion. The fact that ClO levels remain high, even increasing, is strongly suggestive, though not definitive of a mechanism involving two ClO radicals reacting together. The chain is probably quite a slow one. The ozone depletion lags well behind the ClO increase, and takes several weeks to become established. The timing is clearly indicative of some photochemistry in the new channel – the returning sunlight is the obvious factor that might trigger its onset at precisely that time.

These particular results, then, provided such strong direct evidence for the involvement of chlorine chemistry in the observed ozone depletion that little ground remained for continuing to pursue the circulation or solar cycle theories. The philosophical and evidential issues are discussed in later chapters. It is a matter of historical record that the alternative theories were all but abandoned immediately these results became available.

Sharon Roan's evaluation (1989, pp. 219–20) is that:

At a conference in West Berlin during the first week of November, several of the proponents of the dynamic theories tried to salvage what they could of their arguments. But, one by one the theories were dismissed. The evidence for chlorine was overwhelming. . . . The following week, at a meeting of the Ozone Trends Panel in Switzerland, the debate had come to an end. There was now detailed evidence of the presence of chlorine chemicals at work in the stratosphere.

There were many other successful experiments in the AAOE, and a very wide range of useful and informative data were collected. Two other results are worthy of brief mention here.

Measurements of NOx indicated that nitric oxide and nitrogen dioxide levels were unusually low in the chemically perturbed region in the polar vortex. For the first time these measurements could be supplemented with nitric acid measurements that showed that the removal of these species was associated with their uptake into the polar stratospheric clouds as nitric acid. This was a strong confirmation of earlier evidence of NOx depletion. It counted very strongly against solar cycle theories, which, in their original form, relied on a NOx build-up. It also helped to explain how ClO levels could build up so high without being removed as chlorine nitrate, $ClONO_2$.

Measurements of nitrous oxide, N_2O, also showed abnormally low levels. Nitrous oxide is quite different to other oxides of nitrogen in being relatively unreactive in the atmospheric situation. It cannot easily be transformed to nitric acid, or even to other oxides of nitrogen. It does, however, absorb ultraviolet light in the same wavelength range as ozone does, decomposing when it does so.

Nitrous oxide is relatively abundant as a trace gas in the troposphere, at a level around 300 parts per billion. But as it starts to rise above the ozone shield it encounters the ultraviolet light that can decompose it. Nitrous oxide levels fall rapidly with altitude through the stratosphere, from about 300 parts per billion at 15 km to values that are too small to measure around 40 km. This fact, coupled with its non-participation in other chemical reaction schemes, enables it to be used as a tracer in studies of stratospheric circulation. When significantly low levels of nitrous oxide were measured in the polar vortex at about 15 km altitude in the lower stratosphere, it clearly indicated that this parcel of air had recently arrived there from above 30 km (Loewenstein et al., 1989).

This very clear evidence that air was descending so strongly in the polar vortex provided an exact contradiction of the supposed upwelling postulated in the circulation theories.

NOTES

1 At that time, there was no evidence of a similar phenomenon in the Arctic. In more recent spring seasons, some significant Arctic ozone depletion has been occurring, but not nearly on the same scale as in the Antarctic (WMO 1994, p. 3.3).

2 Even so the nitrous oxide level should not have been below the limits of detection of Phillip Solomon's apparatus. This work is still regarded as largely unsound by many of the atmospheric scientists.

3 The planning details and results of the AAOE are published in a series of papers in two special issues of the *Journal of Geophysical Research*: *J. Geophys. Res.* **94** (1989), No. D9, pp. 11181–737, and No. D14, pp. 16437–854.

4 The 'smoking gun' refers not to the shape of the curves as plotted, nor to a quirk of the experimental apparatus or the aircraft! It is a reference to the mythology of the American West, where the sheriff comes upon a recently dead body in the street. He looks up to see in the porch of a nearby building a man holding a handgun, with smoke still rising from the muzzle. In the present case the imprint of the same detailed pattern on the ClO curve as is seen in the ozone depletion, points clearly to ClO as the culprit.

8   Completing the picture: from AAOE to 1994

The data from the AAOE provided a strong direct confirmation of the chlorine theories generally, as opposed to circulation or solar cycle theories. Important parts of the story had been correctly anticipated by some of the chlorine theories: the involvement of reactions at ice-crystal surfaces, dimerisation of ClO (i.e. $ClO + ClO \rightarrow ClOOCl$), dissociation of Cl_2 and HOCl by visible light, and the involvement of bromine species (though only as a minor contributor; not as the main channel).[1] A large degree of consensus was reached among the community of atmospheric scientists, and some closure of many of the aspects of the problem. A fairly clear course was mapped out for further investigation, and resolution of the fine details of mechanism. This was largely achieved in the few years immediately following the AAOE.

The 1994 WMO report addresses the issues in a rather more confident tone than the earlier reports: the emphasis changed from outlining the large uncertainties that still needed to be resolved, to discussing fine details of the modelling, comparing models, and pointing out problems with some input parameter values, or gaps in the observational data set. Likely future implications of various public policy scenarios were modelled and presented with greater certainty and authority.

But the tone of confidence in the report does not run very deep. Examples of remaining problems with the detail of the currently accepted mechanisms are not hard to find.

In the summary of the chapter on stratospheric ozone modelling, for instance, it is said that:

The model-simulated ozone concentration in the upper stratosphere is typically 20 per cent smaller than the observed values, a problem that has been identified previously. This suggests that there is a problem with our understanding of the photochemistry in that region. (WMO 1994, p. 6.1)

The eleventh chapter of the report deals with likely future effects of emissions from aircraft on stratospheric chemistry. After twenty-five pages of describing models and understandings, and presenting and discussing simulation results, it concludes with the rather poignant passage:

Early assessments of the impact of aircraft on the stratosphere varied enormously with time as understanding slowly improved. Our understanding of the lower stratosphere/upper troposphere region is still far from complete and surprises can still be anticipated,[2] which may either result in greater or lesser aircraft effects on the atmosphere. (WMO, 1994, p. 11.26)

In June 1991, there was a major volcanic eruption of Mt Pinatubo in the Philippines. Large quantities of material were thrown as high as the stratosphere. When this happens, the coarser particles precipitate out of the stratosphere within a week or two, and a mid-range fraction of particles over the course of about six months. But there is also a very significant fraction of very fine particles that precipitate downward very slowly indeed. In the tropics, these particles are carried upward to the upper stratospheric regions with the stratospheric circulation, and are joined by others that are borne on the upwelling currents from the tropical upper troposphere into the stratosphere. After the eruption of Pinatubo, the amount of aerosol particles in the upper stratosphere took half a year to reach a maximum, and persisted at a higher than normal level for two to three years (WMO, 1994, p. 4.19).

The increase in stratospheric aerosol following an eruption of this type and magnitude can affect the stratosphere in several distinct but interacting ways. The particles can absorb, reflect, or scatter light. Areas underneath aerosol clouds receive lower amounts of solar radiation as a result. Aerosol clouds can be locally heated, while shielded areas are cooled. This can cause changes in the normal temperature and circulation patterns in the stratosphere. Ultraviolet light is scattered particularly effectively by small aerosol particles. Less ultraviolet light enters the shielded area, reducing the incidence of some of the photochemical reactions that are important in normal stratospheric chemistry. And the aerosol particles themselves can provide catalytic surfaces, where special chemical reactions might occur, similar to those that take place on ice crystal surfaces. So there is the possibility of some anomalous chemistry, similar to that believed responsible for the ozone hole.

Modelling the effect of volcanic aerosols on stratospheric ozone chemistry was a significant and largely unconquered research problem in the early 1990s. The 1994 WMO report reviews both then current understandings of mechanism (Ch. 4.3) and modelling results (Ch. 6.3.3).

Meanwhile, the eruption interfered with statistical analysis. Measured ozone losses increased slightly faster between 1991 and 1994 than they had in the previous decade. But major volcanic eruptions are unique and irregular rather than cyclic occurrences. Because of that, there is no statistically valid way to apportion blame for ozone loss between consequences of the eruptions, the use of inert chlorine compounds, and other factors (WMO, 1994, p. 1.4).

Earlier projections of the future levels of stratospheric chlorine had shown that the Montreal agreement would not be sufficient to actually reduce the size of the problem. Stricter protocols were adopted at a conference in Copenhagen in 1992. A projection based on total compliance with these stricter protocols suggested that tropospheric levels of the inert chlorine-containing gases should peak around 1994, with stratospheric chlorine levels peaking around the turn of the century, and then starting a slow decline over the next 200 years or so. Measurements of source gases in the troposphere showed that there had been good compliance with the protocols, and by 1994 levels of most of the important gases were increasing at less than half the rates that they had been five years earlier. Nevertheless the levels were still increasing, and only one significant species, carbon tetrachloride, had actually started to show a global decline (WMO, 1994, p. xiii; Cunnold et al., 1994). The extent of the annual Antarctic ozone phenomenon was continuing to increase, both in area and duration. Indications of significant Arctic ozone depletion were also emerging.

It was fully expected that stratospheric chlorine trends would lag behind those in the troposphere by about five to seven years. Even so, there was room for disquiet that phenomena that were supposed to be peaking within a few years were still showing such a strongly increasing trend.

Disquiet was also starting to emerge about exemptions from the protocols sought by some nations (Hadfield, 1994), and about a possible 'black market' where CFCs might be illegally manufactured and 'dressed up' as recycled product (D. MacKenzie, 1994).

Finally, there was increasing concern in the early 1990s about the possibly severe consequences of global warming as a result of human activity. Stronger evidence was starting to emerge that significant warming was a reality. The effects of changes in stratospheric ozone on global temperatures were not clearly understood. Nor were the possible influences of changing stratospheric temperatures on the Antarctic and Arctic depletion phenomena. The interaction and feedback between ozone depletion and global warming was emerging as another important aspect to be factored into the modelling.

As of 1994, then, although the stratospheric ozone problem had moved a little away from centre stage in the arena of public concern about scientific issues, there were still several important and ongoing areas for further scientific investigation. There is also a clear need for continuing attention to and fine tuning of public policy about inert chlorine compounds.

NOTES

1 Possible bromine involvement was first suggested by McElroy *et al.* in their chlorine based theory. (McElroy, M.B., Salawitch, R.J., Wofsey, S.C., & Logan, J.A., *Nature* **321**(1986), 759.) Bromine compounds are very much less abundant than chlorine compounds in the atmosphere, but their presence could open up reaction channels that depended less on light. Bromine involvement had been identified among the eleven questions addressed by the AAOE.

2 A definition of 'surprise', as the term is used here, might read something like 'an effect which is not anticipated'. The notion that 'surprises can still be anticipated' starts to sound like an interesting contradiction in terms! Of course it is not, because what is really being said is that we can anticipate that the state of knowledge in this area will continue to be significantly influenced by surprises. These surprises are unanticipated in the sense that we do not know what in particular they will be, nor when they will arise or be discovered. The conclusion of the sentence in the quotation is, on the other hand, a truism for which no excuse can be found.

Part II

Philosophical issues arising from the history

9   Prediction in science

The 1995 Nobel Prize in Chemistry was awarded to Sherwood Rowland and Mario Molina, and to Paul Crutzen. The basis of the award to Rowland and Molina was their work of 1973–6, where they first called attention to the importance of chlorine compounds in stratospheric chemistry, and investigated the possible effects of anthropogenic chlorine-containing compounds on the stratospheric ozone layer. Crutzen's earlier work (1968–73) involved the chemistry of trace substances crossing from the upper troposphere to the lower stratosphere, and investigation of the effects of water vapour and oxides of nitrogen on the ozone layer. For all three scientists there had, of course, been a continuing involvement in the investigation of stratospheric chemistry from that time onward. The particular focus of this chapter is on the early work of Molina and Rowland.

The award of a Nobel Prize, while arguably influenced by significant political factors, is a clear mark of recognition and great respect by a scientific peer group for the piece of scientific work involved. In this case, there is ample additional evidence that Molina and Rowland's work is very highly regarded in the community of atmospheric scientists.

An important aspect of Molina and Rowland's early work is that their initial scientific findings led them to publish material which incorporated predictions – predictions with both scientific and public policy implications. Several philosophers of science have written about the part that prediction plays in the practice of science and the gaining of scientific knowledge. Here is a case where some of those ideas might be tested.

A closer examination of Rowland and Molina's original work raises some interesting questions concerning the nature and status of 'scientific prediction'. In this chapter I will argue that:

- their original argument, while impressive, was seriously flawed. Logically, the flaws might have been detected at the time. But in practice it is doubtful that anyone was in a position to notice the problems.
- there is an important distinction between 'prediction' as deduction of the consequences of a theory, and 'prediction' as an attempt to foretell and describe the future behaviour of a system under scientific study.

- in scientific practice, there is normally an interaction between these two senses as different aspects of any particular prediction. This makes them difficult to distinguish.
- in the case of Rowland and Molina's celebrated work, prediction in both senses played a large part. But in both senses there was an element of failure in the predictions. The prediction that was made could not be seen as a test of the validity of the theory, because observation could not confirm the sort of ozone depletion that was entailed. Some of the other chemical implications of the theory could be directly observed. In terms of future behaviours of the system, and the practical import of the theory, they were correct in suggesting that restriction of the use of chlorinated fluorocarbons would be necessary to avoid significant damage to the ozone layer. But they were quite wrong about the detail of the type of damage that would occur.

In a series of papers on scientific prediction, Brush (1989; 1994) examines two important questions. The first, a philosophical question, is what meaning scientists and philosophers attach to the word 'prediction'. The second question is the historical question of how much the acceptance of any particular theory by the scientific community has actually relied on accurate *predictions* (as opposed to retrodictions) that could be evinced from the theory. In practice, does an entailment count for more in support of a theory if its observational embodiment was unknown at the time the theory was developed? And in logic, ought it to? These are complemented by a third question that has been addressed by many philosophers of science. It concerns the evidential value that is to be attached to prediction – possibly in each of several slightly different senses of the word.

The main distinction that Brush makes between different senses of the term 'prediction' is quite a different distinction to the one that I will emphasise. It is therefore important from the outset to be very clear about the meaning of our terms. Both Brush's distinction and mine are clear distinctions that can validly be made. But this is not to say in either case that they can always validly be separated in dealing with a particular case.

One issue in the meaning of the word prediction is the sense of the prefix 'pre-'. One interpretation is to take it as meaning 'ahead of time', so that 'prediction' becomes synonymous with 'prophecy' or 'forecasting'. On this reading, a scientific prediction from a theory would only count if it were evinced 'before the event'. The alternative is to take the prefix as meaning 'before' in the broader sense of 'a priori'.

Brush argues that a consequence of a theory can count as a prediction, even if it is not evinced until after the event, provided that it is something that is capable of being deduced from the theory without foreknowledge of the event. He cites Margenau, who claims this definition for use of the word as a scientific term, in contrast to its usage in everyday language. Brush demonstrates the regular use by scientists of the term 'prediction' in this broader sense. A prediction of a theory is a deducible consequence, not necessarily a prophecy. He argues that what matters to physicists is whether a particular result is deducible from a theory – a logical issue – rather than whether it actually was deduced before the fact – an historical issue.

Prediction plays a large role in Popper's account of the scientific method. A theory only counts as scientific if it makes 'bold predictions' – that is, if it has consequences that are somewhat surprising on the face of it, and that are capable of being clearly at variance with a possible result of an experiment. Popper saw 'prediction' in the narrower sense of forecast.

Popper was very suspicious of 'prediction' after the event as a test of a theory. There is a very real possibility that any foreknown result will subtly influence the detailed formulation of a theory, and thereby not stand as a truly independent test of the theory. Adjustment of a theory to fit foreknown observational results might even be made unconsciously. These same results might then be sincerely presented as deducible from the original theory. A 'prediction' made after the event can hardly be described as 'bold' or 'surprising' in the sense intended by Popper.

The comeback (Brush, 1994) is that an observation always requires some interpretation before it can be seen as confirming or contradicting an entailment of a theory. The way that a particular observation is interpreted is equally coloured by what theories were in place at the time the interpretation was made.

In the case of the work of Molina and Rowland, which forms the main historical reference point of this chapter, the distinction between prediction before the event and 'prediction' after the event is an unimportant one. There was simply too little known about the stratospheric chlorine/ozone system for there to be any question of entailments of their theory matching facts that were already known. There was a general, and rather patchy record of stratospheric ozone levels as measured at many ground stations around the world over a fifteen-year period. But no reliable measurement of the stratospheric concentration of any chlorine compound had ever been made when their first publication on chlorine-mediated depletion of stratospheric ozone appeared (Rowland, 1996, p. 1790)!

I therefore draw no conclusions about the respective roles of 'retrodiction' and 'forecasting' in science. We will set this issue aside, and focus on a different ambiguity of the word 'prediction'.

Brush also introduces a second distinction that can be made within the meaning of 'prediction' as a scientific term. This distinction is central to the case I am considering. But the two meanings are rather more difficult to distinguish and demarcate than the relatively simple issue of forecasting versus retrodiction.

There is an important difference between prediction in terms of the foretelling of essentially timeless experimental or observational results, and prediction as forecasting the future evolution of some system under scientific study. It is not always clear whether this is a distinction of degree or of kind. Brush's notion of an 'essentially timeless' prediction is exemplified in Prediction 1: 'If I release a large stone from the top of this 400 foot cliff, it will take just five seconds to arrive at the bottom.' But this sort of timelessness is largely restricted to the experimental and manipulative sciences, and becomes a little more problematic in branches of science where the basis of investigation is observation rather than experiment. Is there a difference in kind, for example, between Prediction 2: 'The comet of 1682 will return in 1758', and Prediction 3: 'The fine weather will last through most of tomorrow, but late in the day there will be increasing cloud, and showers'?

The distinction that I want to make is that in the first case (Prediction 2) the main purpose of the prediction was as a test of the hypothesis that at least some comets have closed orbits which lead to their regular return to the inner solar system. The advance warning to stargazers was distinctly secondary. In the second case, on the other hand, the prediction arises out of a very complicated interaction of physical laws, in a way that precludes its being a real test of any one of them in particular. Its main purpose is to assist the local population with the various plans they are making for tomorrow.

In late twentieth-century science, a new variation of this latter aspect of prediction has become very important. In several areas of science, prophecy is attempted by feeding everything that is currently believed about a certain system – its history, the detail of its present state, and the 'laws' governing its behaviour – into a very large computer model, and attempting to calculate future states of the system. The computer models that are routinely used now to provide four-day weather forecasts are a clear example.

Prediction of this sort differs mainly in its complexity and aims from the other sorts of prediction. The state of the local weather three days hence is an important problem in its own right – a problem that the community has asked scientists to solve. The success or failure of the prediction is not a direct test of any theory in particular, because the model depends on a very convoluted and somewhat arbitrary conjunction of theories. In addition, there are usually departures from the 'state of the art' treatments of individual aspects of the system, and approximations frequently replace 'exact' solutions. This is done to make the equations governing the system easier to solve, reducing the requirements in terms of computer size and time to realistic levels.

Because of these factors, predictions of this sort are not a critical test of a theory. A failure of the prediction might be due to a failure of an approximation, or an instability in the numerical part of the simulation, rather than a failure of the underlying physical laws from the theory that are incorporated into the model. Nevertheless they remain a test in a weaker sense. Poor performance of a weather prediction model will always initiate a strenuous search for improvement – where is it breaking down? Is there a factor that has been overlooked altogether? Is there an approximation that might be shaky and need replacement?

Testing the entailments of one or more of the incorporated theories is at most a very minor sideline for these model calculations.[1] The focus and central role of such scientific prediction as prophecy is as a practical application of the scientific knowledge in the area.

The ambiguity, then, lies in the distinction between attempting to test a theory by checking its predictions against the behaviour of the natural system, and in attempting to use the theory to predict the detail of the future natural behaviour of the system.

Prediction qua entailment is primarily focused back on the theory. It is pure science, a check of the performance of the system against how the theory says it ought to behave. It is thereby at least a critical, and possibly crucial test of the theory.

Prediction qua prophecy looks forward to the applications of the theory. It takes the theory, and other understandings of the system, to project a best guess scenario for the future behaviour of the system. It is applied science. It is doing this to inform us about the system itself, to help on a social level in our dealings with the system.

It is this difference in aim that makes the clearest practical way to distinguish these two meanings.

Molina and Rowland (1974) published a paper in which they warned that the continued widespread use of chlorinated fluorocarbons was likely to lead to a future depletion of the ozone layer amounting to about 13 per cent.

The significance of this announcement has been discussed in earlier chapters. Chlorinated fluorocarbons (CFCs) are synthetic compounds that were developed since the 1930s as refrigerants, and also found application in several other areas. They are characterised by non-toxicity and extreme unreactivity.

Ozone is a trace gas in the atmosphere. Even in the stratosphere (15 to

50 km altitude), where it is most concentrated, it still forms only a few parts per million of the atmosphere. However this very small amount of ozone performs two vital functions. It absorbs solar ultraviolet radiation in a wide wavelength range. This radiation would be lethal if it were to reach the surface of the earth unfiltered. The side effect of this absorption is a heating of the upper stratosphere. As a result, the stratosphere is vertically stable (warmer air overlies cooler), and puts a 'lid' on the turbulent weather systems of the lower atmosphere.

Molina and Rowland's paper clearly incorporates predictions. The particular predictions have strong aspects both of entailment and of prophecy. Observation of significant ozone depletion is presented as a possible strong test of current understandings of stratospheric chemistry. And the prediction of significant future ozone depletion is a warning to planning authorities to consider carefully any future widespread use of CFCs.

A summary of the arguments that Molina and Rowland used, and the evidence that they brought to bear has been given in Chapter 5. It was an indirect argument. CFCs were unreactive, as was known from laboratory studies. They were therefore not removed from the lower atmosphere by any of the processes that usually get rid of trace gases, and so they were accumulating. This was confirmed by measurements of Lovelock and others of actual background CFC levels in the atmosphere. When a compound accumulates in the troposphere, some of it finds its way up into the stratosphere. It was known from laboratory studies that ultraviolet light with wavelength between 190 and 215 nm can decompose CFC molecules, splitting off atomic chlorine. Any CFC molecules that found their way into the stratosphere would encounter this light, and be transformed from unreactive materials to very reactive chlorine atoms. The catalytic chain reaction in which atomic chlorine can destroy ozone in the presence of ultraviolet light was, again, well known from laboratory studies. It had not, at that stage, been observed as a natural process in the atmosphere, but the conditions were right for it to proceed.

Their argument was backed up with the results of some computer model calculations which suggested that the extent of ozone depletion was likely to be around 5 per cent at the time, and could be expected to reach an eventual level of about 13 per cent if the current CFC usage patterns continued.

This is a clear example of prediction in science. What is not clear cut is which sort of prediction is involved. The 'predicted' consequences of the theory were already available to be measured. The claim was that ozone levels should already be about 5 per cent below their natural values. The crucial measurements had arguably already been made, since stratospheric ozone data had been continuously monitored from a series of ground stations around the earth since 1957. But nobody had found cause to remark on any significant trend in the data. Did the fact that there was no convincing demonstration of a significant depletion contradict, disprove, or falsify the theory?

Unfortunately, it did not. The nature of the prediction was not nearly as clear-cut as it would seem on the surface. There were two main problems.

At the level of an entailment of the theory, ozone depletion is a qualitative prediction. The extent of that depletion is predicted in quite a different way, as the result of a computer model with known shortcomings and inadequacies.[2] Provided that the qualitative prediction is borne out (that is, that ozone does not actually increase), failure of the *quantitative* prediction has little direct impact on the theory. It would be attributed rather to failure of the computer model.

The other problem with the prediction was that it was 'ceteris paribus'. There were many other factors known to affect ozone levels. Some were global effects, others regional, and yet others were global effects that affected regions differently. Ozone levels vary with such things as the season, the level of sunspot activity, the state of the quasi-biennial oscillation, the amount and intensity of volcanic activity, and several other factors. Not all of these variations were well understood at the time. The variations involved with these factors were of magnitudes comparable with those predicted for chlorine chemistry by Molina and Rowland.

Ozone levels that were actually observed during the late 1970s and early 1980s were such as to neither confirm nor contradict the theory. Average ozone levels at the various ground stations appeared to have declined slightly, but the decline was much too small to have any statistical significance, particularly when other factors known to affect ozone levels were allowed for. It was not until the Ozone Trends Panel report of 1988 that a statistically significant pattern of ozone decline could be discerned. Data from ground stations between 30°N and 60°N were carefully analysed, and the effects of the eleven-year sunspot cycle and the quasi-biennial oscillation were factored out. The results showed a decrease of 1.4 ± 0.7 per cent[3] from 1965–75 to 1976–86 (NASA, 1988, p. 36) – a significant, but fairly marginal ozone depletion.

Probably of more interest to philosophers are the flaws in the argument on which the theory was based. An interesting, if not very significant example is in Rowland's *New Scientist* article (Rowland, 1975). The central point at issue is why anthropogenic CFCs, in particular, should be blamed for any changes in atmospheric chlorine chemistry. They represented only about one part per thousand of total chlorine emissions to the atmosphere. So the first point of the argument stresses that once released to the atmosphere, CFCs remain there for at least a matter of several decades. These compounds therefore tend to accumulate in the atmosphere. By contrast, about 98 per cent of chlorine emissions to the atmosphere are in the form of hydrogen chloride and sodium chloride. These two compounds have a high affinity for water, and consequently a lifetime of only a week or two in the atmosphere before they are returned to the surface in rainfall. The other significant natural form of chlorine emission is methyl chloride, which has an atmospheric lifetime of a year or two. The argument is that, although all chlorine compounds have the potential to be carried upward into the stratosphere, this is a very slow process, and so only very long-lived and persistent chlorine compounds will ever arrive there in significant quantity.[4]

Rowland presented the results of some direct measurements of stratospheric HCl as evidence that most of the hydrogen chloride in the stratosphere originated from CFCs and related compounds. If chlorine were entering the stratosphere as hydrogen chloride from the lower atmosphere, then the proportion of HCl in the stratosphere would decrease with increasing altitude. The opposite is observed. If the proportion of hydrogen chloride in the stratosphere decreases with decreasing altitude, a source of hydrogen chloride at or above the top of the stratosphere is indicated. There is ample evidence that hydrogen chloride is not raining down into the stratosphere from outer space. The only explanation is that chlorine is entering at the tropopause in some inert form, moving upward through the stratosphere, and reacting to form hydrogen chloride at the required high altitudes. This is illustrated in figure 9.1.

But this argument, convincing as it seems, has a logical problem. It is a one-dimensional argument. When the effects of latitude are considered, a very different picture might emerge. Nearly all of the material transfer from troposphere to stratosphere takes place in the equatorial region. The most important stratospheric circulation pattern is a circulation which carries material upward at the equator, moves to higher latitude in the upper stratosphere, descends in the winter temperate region or summer polar region, and returns to the equator along the lower stratosphere.

The next few paragraphs and diagram are an attempt to point out a logical flaw in Rowland's argument. This is a difficult task, because there is no error of fact. It is quite true that the vast majority of stratospheric HCl is generated high in the stratosphere as the eventual product of chemical decomposition of inert compounds carried up from below. There is now ample evidence of this. It is also quite true that the mixing ratio of hydrogen chloride increases with altitude in the stratosphere at all latitudes (except for possible complications at the winter pole). So instead of hydrogen chloride, we will consider hypothetical compound Z.

Altitude

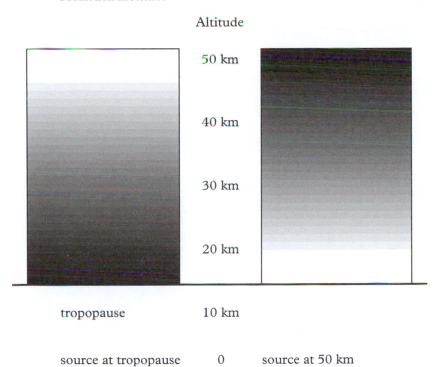

50 km

40 km

30 km

20 km

tropopause   10 km

source at tropopause   0   source at 50 km

Figure 9.1 Expected stratospheric distribution of HCl for low and high sources. (Darker shading indicates higher mixing ratio. One dimensional viewpoint.)

Compound Z enters the stratosphere from the troposphere at the equatorial tropopause, and is then slowly and uniformly removed as it follows the prevailing stratospheric circulation first upward and then poleward. There is little transport of compound Z across the tropopause at temperate latitudes.

A probe which measured mixing ratios of compound Z at different heights might then observe a decrease with decreasing altitude if it were operating in the temperate zone; only in the equatorial regions would the proportion decrease with increasing altitude as the one-dimensional argument would suggest.

Figure 9.2 illustrates a crucial difference that might emerge with the two-dimensional picture. Thus compound Z, which enters the stratosphere from below, might yet have an inverse mixing ratio profile at temperate latitudes.

Rowland was specifically talking about hydrogen chloride, though, and

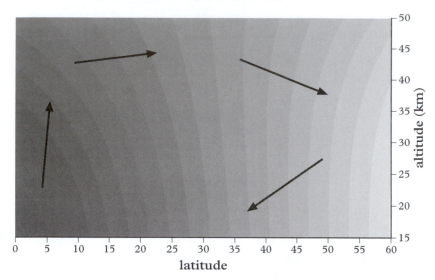

Figure 9.2 A possible two dimensional mixing model for source at bottom of equatorial stratosphere. (Bold arrows indicate the prevailing stratospheric circulation. Note that a rocket probe launched at about 40° latitude may encounter increasing mixing ratio with increasing altitude.)

the mixing ratio profile of hydrogen chloride is nothing like Figure 9.2. There is in fact no known compound that quite fits in with this picture. But that does not matter. The possibility of compound Z shows that observation of an inverse mixing ratio at temperate latitudes does not guarantee an elevated source. There is no suggestion that Rowland's conclusion was wrong – only that his argument was invalid.

The only actual measurements of stratospheric hydrogen chloride available to Rowland when he formulated and presented this argument were from two rocket flights, both in the temperate zone (Lazrus *et al.*, 1975; Farmer *et al.*, 1976). But given the pattern of the stratospheric circulation, an increase in HCl fraction with altitude in the temperate zone might possibly arise for a low equatorial source, as well as for a high source. The measurements of Farmer's group and Lazrus' group did not therefore provide the logical proof that Rowland's argument required.

It is important to note that my claim that Rowland's argument was flawed at this point does not represent a claim that he was wrong in fact. Anthropogenic CFCs do make the dominant contribution to stratospheric HCl. This has been demonstrated in many ways in more recent work.

I am not even claiming that the circulation pattern shown in figure 9.2 would necessarily produce an inverted profile at mid latitudes; only that it is a logical possibility that it may do so. The picture presented in figure 9.2 is an over-simplified one – the actual profile for any compound is crucially affected both by the boundary conditions at the tropopause, and the actual distribution of stratospheric sinks.

My claim is rather that the argument presented as evidence for a high stratospheric source of HCl does not quite work, and that Rowland in this paper presented no other evidence.

The problem was very much tied to the date of Rowland's paper. No evidence at all on this point had been presented in the first paper (Molina & Rowland, 1974) because it predated even these first direct stratospheric measurements of hydrogen chloride. Within a year after Rowland's paper, direct stratospheric measurements of CFCs themselves were available, which complemented the hydrogen chloride results (Schmeltekopf *et al.*, 1975; Heidt *et al.*, 1975).

By far the more serious flaw in Rowland's argument is his claim for completeness of the mechanism. A list of just six reactions involving chlorine is presented as incorporating, 'The important chemical reactions for chlorine in the stratosphere' (Rowland, 1996). And this is followed with a claim that, 'No quantitatively important stratospheric chlorine chemistry has been omitted.'

There are two strands of justification of this claim. The first is by the experiment of trying the inclusion of other known reactions into the model, using the best laboratory data for their rate constants. In this way it could be shown that a number of other reactions that had been suggested as possibly important were likely rather to have only an insignificant effect on the system. The other justification was to show how well the models based on the scheme presented matched up with the few direct measurements and observations relating to stratospheric chlorine chemistry that were available. If this scheme can match the behaviour of the actual system so well, the argument ran, there cannot be too much wrong with it. In fact, very little of the behaviour of the actual system had at the time been measured with sufficient accuracy to provide a critical test. When it was measured during the investigations of the next few years, inadequacies and discrepancies soon became apparent, and extensions of the reaction scheme were incorporated. By far the most important was the formation and photodegradation of chlorine nitrate as another important reservoir of stratospheric chlorine. But the real death-blow to this argument came with the discovery of the Antarctic springtime ozone anomaly. There was no way of accounting for it within the original Molina–Rowland chemical model. The ozone hole constituted a clear falsification of the contention that all of the important stratospheric chlorine chemistry was incorporated in Rowland's six reactions, by then extended to ten. It demanded the inclusion of yet more chemical reactions into models of the system. This was particularly the case once investigation of the phenomenon had shown that circulation patterns alone could not provide an explanation.

We have discussed 'scientific prediction' as providing a test of a theory by checking its observable consequences. Did Molina and Rowland's argument bring out consequences for the system that could be tested against observations? On the face of it, the central entailment of their theory can, to a limited extent, be tested by reference to measurements on the natural system.

But the prediction of ozone depletion is a rather vague one – its extent cannot be evinced directly from the theory, but only as the output of a model, with significant and known shortcomings. There is an epistemic commitment to an ozone depletion as a result of chlorine chemistry, and to this depletion increasing as a result of anthropogenic inputs of inert chlorine compounds. There is arguably a commitment to its extent being 'significant'. But the figure of 5 per cent thrown up by their model is somewhat arbitrary – either 3 per cent or 10 per cent as a measured value would have been regarded as a confirmation rather than a falsification!

There is an additional problem in an implicit 'other things being equal' clause. Many other factors were known to affect stratospheric ozone levels, and at least half a dozen of them in the same 2 per cent to 10 per cent range anticipated by Molina and Rowland. Any observed change in ozone would have been seen as the outcome of a convolution of all of these factors (which would be roughly additive).[5]

When others during the following years produced calculations based on the Molina–Rowland chemical scheme, there were many changes. Additional significant chlorine reactions were recognised. And more complicated and sophisticated computer treatments became available. Predicted levels of ozone depletion ranged from almost none to more than double Molina's figures. But by the early 1980s, smaller depletions were usually predicted – typically about 1.5 per cent rather than 5 per cent.[6] This smaller figure seemed to agree well with the limited observational evidence then available. Unfortunately at the same time the problem appeared to be only a minor one, unlikely to be of much significance. If the more recent figures were correct anthropogenic ozone depletion could no longer be seen as a matter of major concern. The National Research Council reported in these terms in 1984. Even the scientists centrally involved recognised that concern had waned at that time (e.g. S.Solomon, 1988, p. 131).

The conclusion must be either that ozone levels themselves did not provide a crucial test of the Molina–Rowland theory, or that the theory failed the test!

It is important to point out at this juncture that several secondary entailments of Molina and Rowland's argument did match observations very well: such matters as the quantities and vertical distribution of CFCs and HCl in the stratosphere, for example.

The second sense of scientific prediction concerns 'scientific prophecy'. In this sense, Molina and Rowland were saying that the continuing and increasing anthropogenic injection of inert chlorine compounds into the atmosphere could be expected to have serious future consequences for stratospheric ozone levels. This is 'prediction' at the level of public policy. The emphasis is not so much on testing the theory as on practical use of the theory. Right from the outset, Molina and Rowland saw that the consequence of their work was the need to lobby for a change in social policy: the need to limit any use of inert chlorine-containing compounds that would lead to their emission to the atmosphere (Molina, 1996b).

An analysis of Molina and Rowland's work from this point of view shows that they were right, but for many of the wrong reasons. The public policy prediction was that use of CFCs ought to be curbed, lest significant and lasting damage be done to the ozone layer. The perceived consequences were an increase in UV light reaching the earth's surface, and an increased incidence of cancers and cataracts, particularly in the sunnier areas.

But the detail of their prophecy was not borne out. For some time, there was no evidence of any significant ozone depletion. The prophecy began to look wrong, or at least drastically overstated. Later refinements of model predictions suggested much smaller ozone losses, adding to the idea that the problem had been overstated.

Perhaps nature has a strong sense of irony! A significant and increasing ozone depletion did begin just three years after their initial announcement. But it sneaked past the scrutiny of scientists. Its discovery occurred five years later, and was not announced for another three years. The Antarctic ozone hole was not the sort of depletion that Molina and Rowland had foreseen. The degree of depletion was much larger than anything that had been anticipated – up to 60 per cent, when atmospheric scientists had been struggling for years to try to untangle a chlorine-mediated depletion of 2 or 3 per cent from all of the other factors that affect ozone levels. The ozone hole was highly localised and seasonal. Only the Antarctic continent was affected, and only for a period of six to eight weeks each springtime. Subsequent investigation clearly tied this phenomenon to chlorine chemistry, and to anthropogenic chlorine inputs in particular.

The chemical scheme of Molina and Rowland did not fit the Antarctic phenomenon either. Their mechanism clearly indicated a fairly global ozone depletion, concentrated, if anywhere, in the tropical and warm temperate regions. Moreover, the Molina–Rowland scheme indicated that the largest effect would be on ozone levels around 40 km altitude; investigation of the Antarctic phenomenon soon showed that it affected ozone levels mainly between 15 and 25 km altitude.

In the years since the announcement of its discovery in 1985, the Antarctic ozone hole has grown year by year, and the associated depletion is now significantly affecting ozone levels throughout the Southern Hemisphere, as ozone poor air from the Antarctic stratosphere is carried Northward during late spring and summer. In the last few seasons there have been indications of a related but slightly different phenomenon causing large depletions in the Northern Hemisphere. The Molina/Rowland ozone depletion can also be observed as an almost completely separate phenomenon, showing up particularly around the 40 to 50 km level at low latitudes. As a whole, significant ozone depletion can be shown to have occurred, with trends ranging from roughly zero at the equator to about 5 per cent per decade at high latitudes in both hemispheres (WMO, 1994, pp. 1.13–1.16).

Thus, although right in general, the Molina–Rowland chemical scheme has shortcomings in detail, even as a prophecy of the future behaviour of the system. The current ozone depletion affects high latitudes particularly, and has no measurable effect in the equatorial zone; the Molina–Rowland prediction was of a fairly evenly distributed depletion, probably largest in the equatorial zone. The current ozone depletion affects mainly the lower stratosphere below 25 km; the Molina–Rowland scheme clearly pointed to an effect in the upper stratosphere at around 40 km altitude. Concerns about increased UV light incidence have shifted from California and Queensland to Patagonia and New Zealand.

Given these shortcomings of Molina and Rowland's work as prediction, how should it be seen? The award of the Nobel prize indicates that it is regarded, twenty years later, as having been extremely important and influential. The respect that is accorded their work within the community of atmospheric scientists would certainly seem to reinforce this impression.[7]

In the deduction sense of prediction, they were correct in emphasising the importance of chlorine compounds in the overall chemistry of stratospheric ozone. For many years only reactions of oxygen compounds had been considered. The influence of water and related hydrogen-containing compounds was incorporated into ozone reaction schemes in the mid 1960s, and of oxides of nitrogen in the early 1970s. Chlorine compounds are present in much smaller amounts, and their involvement would seem a priori less plausible.

They were also correct in their crucial deduction that the main source of stratospheric hydrogen chloride was the photochemical breakdown of inert chlorine compounds, rather than the direct upward transport of hydrogen chloride and sodium chloride from the troposphere. Stratospheric hydrogen chloride mixing ratios are currently believed to have roughly tripled from their natural background levels as a result of recent use of CFCs and similar compounds.

Finally their reaction scheme, though it was crucially incomplete, did serve as the basis for an overall understanding of stratospheric chlorine chemistry. The reaction scheme eventually used to provide an explanation for the Antarctic phenomenon includes all of their reactions as the main driving reactions in stratospheric chlorine chemistry. But there have been added a few other special reactions that are significant only in very special conditions that obtain in the Antarctic springtime – reactions that require the combination of visible light and the surfaces of ice crystals in stratospheric clouds.

The prophecy aspect of their work turns out to have been enormously important and influential, though to some extent this was serendipitous. The damage to the ozone layer that they had foreseen did not eventuate to nearly the extent that they had expected. A different type of ozone depletion, also chlorine mediated, did!

A coupling of the rapid increase in input of CFCs into the lower atmosphere, their virtual indestructibility, and the long lag times before their build-up in the stratosphere, means an inevitable continuing significant increase in stratospheric hydrogen chloride. If chlorine is significantly involved in ozone chemistry, it is very likely that something will change at some stage during this long and inexorable build-up, even if it is not the exact process that was predicted. In practical terms, the fact that Molina and Rowland made this prophecy had two major practical outcomes. Firstly, the work caught the public imagination, and increased public awareness of both the importance and the delicate nature of the earth's ozone shield. Before long there were significant public and political movements in several countries seeking to limit the use of CFCs. These filtered through to a very high level, so that the negotiations that led to the international agreements to restrict CFC usage were already well under way *before the Antarctic ozone hole discovery had been announced.* Clearly this meant that the international community was much better placed to take realistic action when the dramatic nature of the Antarctic phenomenon became known, and further investigation firmly linked it to chlorine chemistry.

Secondly, the work caught the attention of scientists. It opened up a series of measurements and investigations that needed to be made to more firmly identify and clarify the role of chlorine in stratospheric chemistry. These parallel mobilisations on the socio-political and scientific fronts interacted in important ways: the public interest in the issues, and the public policy implications of the issues, led both to a significant injection of research funding into atmospheric science (and atmospheric chemistry in particular), and an elevation of its status from a minor backwater of science to something of a glamour area. The result was that when the Antarctic ozone hole announcement was made, a very thorough scientific investigation was immediately triggered. Although the announcement was completely unexpected, and the phenomenon was a complete surprise, the problem of its mechanism was effectively solved within three years, and worked out in fine detail within five years.

The overall outcome was that action, both political and scientific, was taken immediately, which actually led to a turn around in chlorine trends within a decade of the ozone hole announcement, and is projected to lead to recovery of a situation where the hole will no longer appear within fifty years.

Flawed as the Molina–Rowland prophecy may have been, it was the primary factor in a fortuitous state of affairs. In one sense the Antarctic ozone hole was a phenomenon that came as a complete surprise. But in another sense its discovery actually came in circumstances where we were very well prepared to deal with its implications! For this, we have Molina and Rowland to thank – both for their scientific investigations, and for the fact that they saw the need and were willing to publicise their findings in the broader community and the political domain.

The analysis of this episode in recent science highlights some surprising aspects of the value that is placed on prediction in science. In terms of evidential value, the failure of a correctly evinced prediction should normally constitute a Popperian falsification of a theory. But the important question is whether it does so in a way that calls for 'fine tuning' of the theory by minor modification and extension, or in a way that calls for its radical overthrow. This is the sort of question addressed by Kuhn and Lakatos in their respective critiques of Popper's approach. There do not seem to be any practical or realistic suggestions from philosophers of science for its resolution.

Often in science, a seemingly clear prediction can be exceedingly difficult to check in practice. In this case, the atmosphere is a very complex system. There are many factors which can influence its behaviour in terms of circulation and detailed chemical composition. The prediction of a scientific theory is often *ceteris paribus*, and the trend can be difficult to discern among the many other factors that affect the system. Molina's evaluation in this case was (Molina, 1996a, p. 1780):

In the decade following the publication of our Nature paper, field observations corroborated many of the predictions based on model calculations and on laboratory measurements of reaction rates. However, the effects on ozone were unclear, because the natural ozone levels have relatively large fluctuations.

Rowland also emphasises the success of some of their other predictions, predictions that were clearly implicit, but not explicitly evinced in the original papers (Rowland, 1996, p. 1790):

Our original calculations about the behavior of CFCs in the stratosphere were actually predictions of the vertical distribution, because no measurements were then available for any chlorinated species in the stratosphere, and certainly not for CFCs. During 1975, two different research groups sent evacuated containers equipped with pressure-sensitive values [the intended word is 'valves'] up on high-altitude balloons, and recovered air samples from the stratosphere. The measured mixing ratios for CCl_3F (Fig. 6) were in excellent agreement with the vertical profiles calculated by us in the previous year. This fit between theory and experiment demonstrates both that CFCs reach the stratosphere and that they are decomposed there by solar ultraviolet radiation at the altitudes predicted earlier.

It is significant that these scientists talk a lot about 'prediction' in retrospectively evaluating their own theory. Clearly, the scientists see predictive success as an important issue. They seem to be thinking more of prediction qua entailment than prediction qua prophecy, but this is not entirely clear. It is also significant that they turn to the success of these 'subsidiary' predictions when facing the failure of their major prediction. This is not just making excuses. The issue seems to lie in the impact of a failed prediction: the awkward question of whether it calls for abandonment of the theory, or modification and adjustment of the theory. In this case, as, I suspect, in many others, it was the success of the subsidiary predictions that convinced scientists that there was a hard core of content in the theory that was 'right', and that work along the same lines directed to modification and adjustment was likely to be a more fruitful course than abandonment of the theory.

But is not this approach of 'adjusting' and 'modifying' a theory an ad hoc rationalisation, after the event? Is not this the very sort of science that modern philosophers have warned us against?[8] Should it not be seen as unscientific clinging to a discredited hypothesis, or attachment to a degenerating research programme? In this case, at least, there is a difference. There is ample independent evidence that the reactions that Molina and Rowland included in their mechanism are important reactions in stratospheric chlorine chemistry. The mechanism fails because they are not *the only* important reactions. The 'smoking gun' experiment, and various other results from the NOZE and AAOE suites of experiments, provided direct information about a number of other chemical species that amounted to independent evidence for the detailed mechanisms being proposed.

Rowland and Molina's theory is seen not as a flawed one, but as an incomplete one. The original theory is being extended, not 'patched up'. The claim that CFCs are broken down by ultraviolet light in the upper stratosphere, and make a significant contribution to the active chlorine compounds present in the stratosphere is unaffected, and strongly confirmed. The claim that active chlorine compounds make a significant contribution to stratospheric ozone chemistry, in spite of their relatively low concentrations, similarly stands up, with strong confirmation. The reaction scheme that Rowland and Molina had proposed to account for stratospheric chlorine/ozone chemistry had already been supplemented with a few extra reactions before the Antarctic ozone hole was discovered. The chemical theory that followed from the investigation of the Antarctic phenomenon still contained all of the reactions in Molina and Rowland's scheme, together with the new ones that had already been added. A further half-dozen reactions were also included in the scheme.

But these new additions were in no way arbitrary ones. It was not the case that 'if you want to understand what is happening in the Antarctic you need to arbitrarily include these extra reactions'. Each of the new reactions in the scheme depended to some extent on the specific Antarctic conditions. Some of the additional reactions involved the requirement of an ice crystal surface. It does not matter if you include these reactions in a treatment of other regions of the stratosphere. They will have no effect. Ice crystals are only present in the stratosphere in Antarctic winter and spring, and the Arctic winter. The anomalous polar stratospheric chemistry is only observed in just these places and seasons. The other new reactions involved the new species generated by the ice-surface reactions. Significantly, some of these also required visible light. The requirement for both ice crystals and visible light restricts the full-blown ozone depletion to the Antarctic spring (There is an absence of light during the winter season at either pole).

So the recent, and currently accepted chemical theories that deal with the Antarctic phenomenon are seen as resting strongly on the Molina–Rowland theory as a foundation, as extensions of that theory, and as strongly confirming its general approach. Although they extend and complicate the theory, they do not really undermine or weaken the original version in any way.[9]

On balance, then, it seems that the important thing was that *some* of the surprising predictions (qua entailments) of the new theory were successful. It does not seem to have mattered too much that others, including even the one that was the main focus of their original paper, were not. In this case there were enough successes to convince that the basis of the theory was largely correct. Modifications or extensions from that basis looked to be the more promising course.

Prediction (qua prophecy) in this case played a rather different role. It was important that the prediction in this sense was broadly right, but mattered little that it was not right in detail. It was the fact that the particular prophecies drew attention to a possible area of public concern, that provided impetus for both scientists and policy makers to tackle problems in this area. In the longer term it was shown that there was indeed a legitimate cause for public concern. Even though the problem that did emerge did not exactly match the prophecy, the calling of attention to the right general area was an important part of the eventual justification of the work, and the basis for its acclaim.

NOTES

1 Large computer models of this type are often used for hypothesis testing, but in a rather strange way. They are usually associated with sciences like meteorology, that are clearly observational rather than experimental. But although the natural system cannot be directly manipulated, the large computer model can be, and is therefore available for a sort of experimentation. This raises philosophical problems of its own, that will be visited in Chapter 13.

2 The most serious over-simplification was that the particular model used was 'one-dimensional'. That is, it took into account variations in the concentrations of chemical species with altitude, but did not allow for variation with latitude or longitude. Nor could it properly take into account the other consequences of horizontal circulation. The main circulation pattern in the stratosphere is a pair of circulation cells in which air rises at the equator, moves to high latitudes, and then descends. At least a two-dimensional model is needed to provide an adequate account of this.

3 The stated error is twice the standard deviation.

4 A simple discussion of the cycling of chlorine compounds through the atmosphere can be found in WMO *Scientific Assessment of Ozone Depletion*: 1994, p. xxix, and pp. 2.1–2.38.

5 A discussion of other factors affecting ozone, and how they can or cannot be factored out of a statistical analysis of measured ozone depletion can be found in NASA, 1988: pp. 33–41.

6 It is important to remember that, quite apart from any new insights into the chemistry, the period involved was one of a rapidly changing state of the art both in treatment of atmospheric circulation, and in computer technology. More sophisticated model calculations were rapidly becoming more feasible and more accessible.

7 I record two off-the-cuff remarks by leading atmospheric scientists in interviews: 'Their [Molina & Rowland's] work was really worthy of the Nobel prize.'
  'Even though they did not get it quite right, they certainly did make a bold
prediction, that was largely borne out.'

8 Popper's concern with this sort of approach, for example, was that if a theory
can be so readily modified whenever an observation does not match, the theory
may have no logical content. It is committed to nothing, and therefore telling us
nothing. One must be suspicious that it could be twisted to provide an explanation, whatever was observed.

9 This is an exact parallel with the way that more recent treatments of stratospheric ozone chemistry have built on Chapman's model as their foundation,
and the high regard in which Chapman's work is still held.

10   The crucial experiment

When an area of scientific understanding and investigation seems to take a major change in direction or make a sudden leap forward, there is often talk of a 'crucial experiment'. The idea is that the change can largely, or perhaps entirely be attributed to insights which came from the result of a single decisive experiment. It is clear that this is not always the case. Philosophers and scientists have disagreed widely as to whether it occurs frequently, rarely, or not at all.

There are at least two reasons why an experiment that was not really crucial might be constructed as a 'crucial experiment' after the event in telling the history. Firstly, it can add drama and colour to the story. Secondly, it gives an opportunity to clarify some of the confusion and ambiguity that would probably have been present at the time. The logical foundations of the present understanding of the subject can then be more clearly linked in with the history.

The 'crucial experiment' has been characterised as follows: it must give a result that is simultaneously in accord with a clear prediction of one scientific theory, and in contradiction of the clear predictions of all of its serious current rivals. This definition is given both by Lakatos (1974) and Franklin (1981). But Lakatos believes that 'no experiment is [i.e. can be] crucial at the time it is performed' (Lakatos, 1974, p. 320), while Franklin does believe in crucial experiments, and cites several examples which he sees as qualifying. Popper takes a slightly different view. He sees a crucial experiment only as one which has the potential to cause abandonment of a theory by falsification (insofar as that is possible). The experiment is crucial in that it provides the justification for one approach to be abandoned, and another to be taken up (Popper, 1959, p. 277). It makes little difference whether the new theory was already in place, or whether the formation of a new hypothesis has to be stimulated by the falsifying experiment.

In this chapter we will re-examine the idea of a crucial experiment, and look at a crucial experiment in the investigation of the Antarctic ozone hole.

I will argue that the primary characteristic of interest is the effectiveness of the particular experimental result in determining a clear direction for further scientific effort. If this is the case, then there are at least three possible types of crucial experiment which must be considered, of which the Lakatos/Franklin characterisation is just one.

A second possibility can arise when an experiment leads to a completely surprising and unforeseen observation, and science changes course as a result. A striking example is the simple action by Leeuwenhoek of turning a microscope to the examination of semen (Leeuwenhoek, 1677). The observation of swarms of spermatozoa, completely unexpected, very rapidly[1] led to a radical change in the direction of research effort and theory development in the field of human and animal generation.

I will also argue for a third type of situation where a scientific investigation can provide convincing evidence for one theory from among a number of rivals, even at a rudimentary stage of theory articulation before clear and decisive predictions can be evinced. This is closely related to Francis Bacon's notion of a crucial experiment as the 'fingerpost at the crossroads' – an experiment which provides a clear indication of the fruitful direction to follow. There is a possible example of this in the investigation of the Antarctic ozone hole. The possibility is also recognised that there may yet be other ways in which an experiment can yield crucial evidence which leads to a major change in direction in an area of science.

In principle, then, an experiment can be seen as having been crucial if, taken in its historical context, it provided scientific evidence sufficiently strong to be a legitimate cause of the pursuit of one theory of a significant phenomenon, and the abandonment of all of its current serious rivals. This criterion is, of course descriptive, in contrast to the normative criteria presented earlier. It focuses more on whether the experiment did in fact influence the course of scientific endeavour, than on whether it provided evidence which ought to have done so. But by taking up this descriptive view, we can see that the normative models may have been too narrowly construed.

By interpreting 'legitimate cause' in a very narrow way, we can make this definition match identically with the normative criteria of Lakatos, Franklin, or Popper. But it is possible to consider the notion of 'legitimate cause' much more broadly. On the narrow interpretation, the only legitimate causes of abandonment of a theory are cases where the theory makes a prediction that is not borne out by the results of observation or experiment. This is part of the general falsificationist line, and while Lakatos argues strongly that even a number of such cases are never *sufficient* legitimate cause for the abandonment of a line of theory, he also clearly implies that one or a number of such cases are a *necessary* part of the legitimate cause for theory abandonment.

Consider the situation where there are a number of rival theories of a particular small area of science. Each of the theories has a similar degree of empirical success in accounting for known phenomena, observations, and experimental results. That is, they all get it roughly right, with just one or two small anomalies that might require further work or special pleading. There are not sufficient empirical grounds for preferring any one of these theories over its rivals. But then a new experiment is done which produces a significant and surprising result. One of the theories can be extended to explain this result in a fairly obvious and straightforward way (though the result was never 'predicted'). The rival theories cannot even start to explain the result. Perhaps, for example, the observation was of an electrical phenomenon, and only one of the theories made any mention of electricity in its chain of explanation. Any electrical phenomenon would then have been completely irrelevant to each of the other theories and quite inexplicable within their contexts. In no sense has any bold prediction been vindicated, nor has any rival theory been falsified. But it is quite clear that the breadth of one theory can readily be extended to take in new electrical phenomena, while the others would require a very elaborate and somewhat ad hoc superstructure to do so. Electricity is clearly going to play some role in explanations in this area of science from now on, and only one of our current theories can handle that! This sort of situation could be seen as a legitimate cause for theory adoption and abandonment.

There is a possible example of this type of crucial experiment in the story of the Antarctic ozone hole, but when we examine it closely, we will find that it is problematic.

The 'smoking gun' as a crucial experiment

The discovery of the Antarctic ozone hole, and the investigation of its causes has been discussed in earlier chapters. We will review the main points.

In 1985 a paper was published reporting a marked decrease in ozone levels in the stratosphere each Antarctic spring since 1976 (Farman *et al.*, 1985). The report came as an enormous surprise to scientists for several reasons. Firstly, the effect was very large – 30 per cent and more. Secondly, it was very localised. It was restricted to a particular geographic region, and a period of six–eight weeks annually. Thirdly, no such effect had been reported from the weather satellites, which were supposed to be monitoring worldwide ozone on a regular basis, and were naively thought to be more sophisticated. Fourthly, a great deal of scientific research and computer modelling had been devoted to theories of stratospheric ozone depletion, and an effect of this sort had never been predicted, and was not readily explicable. Finally, there had been an extensive search for clear evidence of ozone depletion of any sort, and no result of anywhere near this magnitude had previously been observed. Stratospheric ozone depletion, indirectly resulting from widespread use of chlorinated fluorocarbons, had earlier been predicted. The possibility had caught the public imagination. The issue was a politically important one at the time, and worldwide conferences were working on the issue of restricting use of these compounds because of their possible involvement. But up until this point there had been no convincing evidence of any significant ozone depletion.

The report of anomalously low ozone levels was rapidly confirmed. Satellite measurements were re-examined and found to show similar very low results for Antarctic spring ozone (Stolarski et al., 1986). Careful measurements were made of Antarctic stratospheric ozone in subsequent spring seasons, and convincingly showed that the 'hole' continued to deepen. The scientific community was thus faced with clear and convincing evidence of an important phenomenon that could not be explained within the current framework of understanding – an anomaly that required new insights.

Three main rival hypotheses (each with several variants) emerged. Firstly, it was suggested that the ozone depletion was indeed being caused by the presence of chlorine-containing compounds. Atmospheric mixing ratios of several of these compounds had increased greatly over the years as a consequence of human activity. The second theory was that a major climatic shift had occurred in about 1976, so that in the springtime, lower atmosphere air, which contains little ozone, was upwelling into the Antarctic stratosphere in a major plume. The third theory was that the period of observed ozone decrease between 1976 and 1984 corresponded to a period of increasing solar activity, and that solar interactions with the upper atmosphere in polar regions led to the production of compounds which could destroy stratospheric ozone after being transported downward.

There are two important points to be made about these three hypotheses. The first is that each of the hypotheses arises from a different traditional branch of science, and tends to move the main part of the problem into the particular sphere of its own discipline. On the face of it, the problem does relate to several areas of science, and calls for an interdisciplinary approach. But the first proposal suggests that atmospheric chemists will provide the answers. A little help from meteorologists might be needed to explain what is special about Antarctic circulation, that might lead to concentration of pollutants, or similar effects. The second proposal suggests that meteorologists can probably handle the issue without reference to anyone else. The third would imply that upper atmosphere physicists should find the answers, with some reference to well understood chemistry! But this does not imply any failure by scientists from the three disciplines to communicate properly. The very real problem of inter-disciplinary communication in modern science does not seem to be nearly as insurmountable as Kuhn's account (1962, pp. 144–59) of 'incommensurability' between disciplines would suggest. In fact the debate throughout seems to have been characterised by significant, if not always amicable, inter-disciplinary communication and collaboration.[2]

The second point is that all three hypotheses were speculative in the extreme, and each had great weaknesses. Each was in effect a suggestion for a direction of further research; no one of them was anywhere near providing a rigorous scientific explanation of the phenomenon.

In particular, the chemical hypothesis (which was ultimately confirmed by the experiment) was starting from a very weak position. The only known mechanism by which chlorine atoms could remove large amounts of ozone from the stratosphere involved strong sunlight, and vertical sun conditions as a necessary ingredient; the Antarctic springtime with weak horizontal sunshine was almost the last place it was to be expected. Moreover the chemists had been very much involved with the prediction of a generalised global ozone depletion due to chlorine compounds, but the predictions of the scale of the depletion had decreased as the computer models were improved to take better account both of new chemical understandings and of circulation effects. None of these models had ever predicted an Antarctic anomaly of any sort, let alone one of such major proportions. On the other hand, meteorologists had no specific evidence of the particular circulatory changes that might be associated with the proposed spring upwelling, and only inconclusive evidence of a climatic watershed in 1976. Finally, the tying in of the ozone hole with the sunspot cycle could only be achieved phenomenologically if fifteen years of data prior to 1972 are ignored – there was no ozone hole in 1959, for example, when there was a strong solar maximum. There is also the problem of whether nitrogen oxides could be generated in sufficient quantity in the extremely rarefied outer regions of the atmosphere, for such a mechanism to work. The argument that they could be was strongly presented, but far from compelling.

The eventual resolution of the issue between the rival theories arose out of interdisciplinary collaboration and agreement. The AAOE (discussed in Chapter 7) was a fairly large scale international effort. Two aircraft carried a number of instruments to make stratospheric observations of various sorts. One of them actually flew at stratospheric altitudes, and was able to take direct samples from and make direct measurements in the lower stratosphere. The other flew through the upper troposphere, and was restricted to slightly less direct observations. The airborne observations were matched by the intensive collection of ground-based data at a series of Antarctic stations (NOZE-2), and near simultaneous satellite observations.

In the event, the results of this experiment (or series of observations)[3] did effectively distinguish among the three explanations, and clearly pointed to a chemical explanation as the primary cause of the phenomenon.

The most dramatic result from the many chemical species whose concentrations were measured, was the association, both temporal and spatial, between ozone disappearance and elevated ClO radical levels. In the winter darkness, ozone levels were high, and ClO radicals very low. As soon as sunlight fell on the clouds that had formed in the local stratosphere during the winter, ClO radical levels rose 100 fold or more, and ozone levels simultaneously started to fall (see figure 7.1). The observation has since been referred to as a 'smoking gun' result. Among the other data that were collected, it was found that nitrogen oxide levels were particularly low – in exact contradiction of what the solar cycle theory would have required (NASA, 1988, p. 97). Direct evidence of major upwelling of tropospheric air was not found. Some results were interpreted as indirect evidence of some upwelling on a small and insufficient scale – both too local and too brief to support the purely circulation-based theories (Kerr, 1987, p. 157).

It is a matter of historical record that this particular data collection project very rapidly and effectively shifted the bulk of research effort, and the general view of most scientists in the field, firmly behind a chemical explanation of the Antarctic ozone hole. The specifics of Antarctic circulation patterns remained an important part of the story, but the notion of a plume of ozone-poor tropospheric air displacing ozone rich stratospheric air was abandoned as a primary explanation. The 'odd nitrogen' or solar cycle theory (based on solar interactions in the thermosphere) was similarly put aside.

There is a clear reason why the experiment might have been decisive for socio-political rather than genuine scientific reasons. The issue was seen as a socially important one, and the sponsoring agencies had provided funding in an effort to obtain a clear and decisive answer to what was causing the phenomenon. The scientists were under pressure to arrive at a definite answer. On the other hand, one might have expected some sort of rearguard action from those who found that the problem had been moved out of their field of expertise, and would expect to lose their share of any research funding involved. But in this particular case the value of the results of the experiment as decisive evidence seems to have been overwhelming.

For the next part of the discussion we will temporarily set the detail of history aside, and simply use a myth to address some philosophical issues. Suppose that there had been no further development, experimental or theoretical, after the rival theories were first articulated, and that the 'smoking gun' result from the AAOE had been obtained in isolation. Could such a result have been decisive in choosing between three rival embryonic theories? I am contending that it could have done so, and that it could have done so quite definitely. The essence of the result is that wherever ozone is disappearing, ClO levels are anomalously high. This does not provide any evidence, one way or the other, against the circulation theories (which have nothing to do with chemistry) nor the solar cycle theory (which does invoke chemical reactions, but none that involve chlorine compounds). But the third theory suggests that chlorine chemistry is causing the ozone depletion, while not being explicit about how. Elevated ClO levels may not be a necessary consequence of all of the chlorine theories, but they are certainly a likely consequence. One of the three murder suspects has dropped his calling card at the scene of the crime!

This is a situation where it would be quite reasonable to abandon the other theories and pursue the chlorine theory alone, even if there were no other evidence to falsify them. Suppose, for example, that there had been no other falsifying evidence against the circulation theory. There would still have been a difficulty with maintaining the theory, because the new phenomenon, ClO enhancement, could not have been accommodated in any comfortable way. Upwelling tropospheric air does not contain ClO. Even if 'unusual and exotic chemistry' accompanied an Antarctic upwelling of tropospheric air into the local stratosphere, it would not be possible to devise a scheme in which ClO enhancement occurred earlier than ozone depletion. The circulation theories saw stratospheric ozone being pushed aside rather than chemically degraded. Normal stratospheric air was seen as being replaced by upper tropospheric air that naturally contained little ozone. Upper tropospheric air does not contain high ClO, and even if it did, the arrival of ClO would occur at the same time as the loss of ozone rather than preceding it. The ClO enhancement and ozone depletion would have to be treated as two quite unrelated phenomena, and the elaborate spatial anti-correlation of the 'smoking gun' result would have to be a huge coincidence.

The 'smoking gun' result indicated a strong three-way association between elevated ClO, depleted ozone, and sunlight on clouds. The circulation theory simply has nothing to say about ClO. Tropospheric air is poor in ozone, but it also does not contain ClO at significant levels. The odd nitrogen theory also has nothing to say about chlorine compounds. Even in the absence of other evidence, or of further refinement of the theories, the result would be crucial.

This is just the sort of situation that might be seen as constituting an alternative 'legitimate cause' for the abandonment of two of the rival theories, and the adoption of the third.

Once the build-up of ClO radicals associated with ozone depletion has been observed, the outline of a chemical explanation is much more clearly indicated. All chlorine containing species are present in very much lower amounts than ozone itself. A chain mechanism, whereby a single free chlorine atom can destroy many ozone molecules, is therefore clearly required. The mechanism the chemists had been exploring for twelve years or so involved the following three reactions:

$$Cl + O_3 \rightarrow ClO + O_2$$

$$O_3 + \text{ultraviolet light} \rightarrow O_2 + O$$

$$ClO + O \rightarrow Cl + O_2$$

In this way, a single chlorine atom can continue to break up many ozone molecules, provided that there is plenty of ultraviolet light around for the second step, so that O atoms can be produced, and free Cl atoms regenerated in the third step.

But at Antarctic sunrise, insufficient ultraviolet light is available. There is nothing to prevent the first step from going ahead, however, provided some source of free Cl atoms is available. A build-up of ClO would then be expected as ozone is destroyed. For any significant ozone destruction, though, some alternative to the second and third steps above is required to regenerate free Cl atoms. What any chemical explanation required, then, was a new local source of free Cl atoms, and an alternative loop to the second and third reactions above to regenerate them and keep the chain going. Neither of the missing steps could require ultraviolet light, but visible light must be involved, since sunrise was important in the scheme of things. There was a further clue in the association of ozone depletion with polar stratospheric clouds. The lag of ozone depletion behind ClO build-up, and the large extent of that build-up suggested a rather inefficient chain – that is, a fairly slow reaction or series of reactions to regenerate atomic chlorine from ClO.

The discussion must now turn from this idealised version to take more account of events as they are presented in the record of the scientific literature, and the other published accounts.

What role did falsification really play in the abandonment of the rival theories? The solar cycle theory is perhaps the more easily dealt with. There was already fairly clear and convincing evidence from the NOZE-1 experiments and from ground data that levels of active nitrogen oxides were unusually low in the winter polar vortex. This was widely, but not universally, regarded as decisive evidence against the solar cycle theory, which attributed the phenomenon to increased nitrogen oxides moving down from above. Detailed measurements of the vertical ozone distribution, obtained in NOZE-1, NOZE-2, and the AAOE, clearly showed the anomalous depletion as occurring in the 15–22 km altitude band. Again, if the solar cycle theory were true, then the active nitrogen compounds moving down from above ought to have triggered a depletion in the upper rather than the lower stratosphere. At the time of the AAOE, most of the scientists involved saw the solar cycle theory as no longer viable. This is about as clear-cut as a case of direct falsification in a scientific investigation ever gets.

The AAOE plugged some remaining loopholes. It was fairly clear that nitrogen compounds had been removed from the situation mainly by reaction with water ice to produce solid or liquid nitric acid. A reservoir of active nitrogen may have remained in the immediate location. It still might have had the potential to regenerate active nitrogen oxides in appropriate conditions. The uptake of nitric acid into water was a phenomenon that might have been reversed by other chemical reactions. But the AAOE clearly showed that nitric acid was decisively lost from the stratospheric system as it settled downward with the larger ice particles. There was a genuine, significant, and irreversible loss of potentially active nitrogen compounds from the local lower stratosphere.

Nevertheless, in spite of this strong falsification, the theory had not been completely killed off. A paper published in a prestigious refereed journal a few years after the AAOE, was in essence an attempt to revive the solar cycle theory (Stephenson & Scourfield, 1991).[4]

The circulation theory was, on the other hand, still considered a viable theory at the time of the AAOE. It was also effectively falsified in the AAOE, by results from experiments other than the ClO/ozone correlation. Circulation data collected did not match the expected pattern associated with tropospheric upwelling, as predicted by computer models incorporating the circulation theory. But this could not be interpreted as particularly strong evidence against upwelling as such: the data were too sparse, and the models too uncertain.

The more serious evidence against the circulation theory came from the use of nitrous oxide as a chemical marker. Nitrous oxide is a relatively very unreactive oxide of nitrogen, and it also has a rather lower affinity for water than the other nitrogen oxides. On the current understandings of stratospheric chemistry, the nitrous oxide level in an air parcel could be used as an indicator of the highest altitude achieved by that air parcel in its recent past. The results of nitrous oxide measurements from the AAOE clearly indicated that the very air that contained the extremely low ozone levels, as measured at about 15 km altitude, had recently descended from about 30 km altitude (Loewenstein *et al.*, 1989). This was another enormous surprise in the AAOE, and on the face of it a very solid piece of evidence against the circulation theory.

But to what extent was it a falsification? According to the circulation theory, the ozone-poor air should have ascended from below the level where the measurements were taken; the nitrous oxide levels indicated that it had descended from above. But evidence from a chemical marker might not be completely reliable. Nitrous oxide is not completely inert. It is not significantly less reactive than, say, any of the CFCs, molecular nitrogen, nor even molecular oxygen. It was clear that there was a lot of unusual and poorly understood chemistry going on in the polar vortex. It was not inconceivable that nitrous oxide might be involved in some of the reactions. But in this case there was confirmatory evidence from other chemical markers that, like nitrous oxide, are destroyed in the lower stratosphere. Levels of both methane and CFC-12 were also very low, again indicating a descending air mass. There was strong concordance in the indications from several quite different chemical markers. An argument against the strong descent in the stratospheric polar vortex could not be sustained.

The situation with the chlorine-based chemical theories was much messier. Several quite different suggestions had been made about possible mechanisms. So at one level this was a family of theories, competing with the circulation and solar cycle theories. But at another level they could be seen as several distinct and rival theories, competing with one another. Taking the chemical theories as a family, and considering the chemical hypothesis in a broad sense, elevated ClO levels must be seen as a likely, rather than a necessary accompaniment of ozone depletion. But the two strongest individual hypotheses about mechanism had each identified elevated ClO as a necessary consequence of the proposal (S. Solomon *et al.*, 1987; McElroy *et al.*, 1986), and Susan Solomon's group had even calculated the ClO mixing ratio that would be required to make their mechanism work.

In the idealised version it was shown that the evidence from the 'smoking gun' experiment would have been sufficient to determine the issue between the rival theories, even in the absence of other experimental results and further theoretical development. The more complete picture that emerges from a closer consideration of events prior to and surrounding the AAOE allows the issues to be seen in terms of falsification and confirmation. In either event, a crucial experiment is involved. There was a rapid transition from a situation where there were several competing accounts of the phenomenon to one where a single account was accepted by a wide consensus of the scientists from all disciplinary backgrounds who had been involved. Further research effort shifted from deciding between accounts to filling out the detail of this account.

The two rival theories dropped rapidly out of contention. The solar cycle theory had been directly falsified. Nitrogen oxides were low rather than high, and the phenomenon was occurring exclusively in the lower stratosphere. There was compelling direct evidence against the circulation theory. To have any hope of surviving, it would need to have been revised to incorporate descending rather than upwelling air within the vortex. But it was a central notion of the circulation theories that the ozone depletion was actually a redistribution that had brought naturally ozone-poor air into the Antarctic stratosphere. There was no ozone-poor air at higher altitudes. On the face of it there was an impossible inconsistency. Any revived circulation theory could have borne no genuine resemblance to the original theories. The chlorine theory was clearly indicated as the fruitful direction to follow. The specific ClO mixing ratio prediction of Susan Solomon's group was quantitatively wrong, but qualitatively correct. Most of the rival chemical theories also strongly indicated an increase in ClO mixing ratio. It was apparent that the chemical approach was the only one that might be readily extended and articulated to provide an explanation of the new phenomena, after further investigation. According to one commentator, the scientists who had argued strongly for the circulation theory – those who had most to lose – made brief and abortive attempts to salvage something of their approach, and then admitted the evidence for the chemical theory as overwhelming (Roan, 1989, pp. 219–20).

Franklin suggests some additional criteria that characterise a crucial experiment. He refers to *importance*, in terms of the way the experiment relates to central concepts of rival theories, and *decisiveness*, in terms of clearly and rapidly pointing to one rival rather than another. In effect, his paper attempts a taxonomy of 'good' experiments. Franklin first distinguishes between 'sociologically good' and 'methodologically good' experiments – those that are actually highly regarded by the peer group, versus those which are intrinsically worthy of high regard. He then makes a further distinction between 'technically good' and 'conceptually important' experiments. He finally subdivides the latter category into several classes including 'crucial' experiments and 'strongly corroborative' experiments. As a part of this last classification, he characterises the 'crucial' experiment as not only strongly supporting a particular theory, but also as effectively eliminating any current alternatives. He takes the narrow view of support and elimination as consisting only in matching or contradicting a clear prediction. But even if we take a much broader view of what might constitute support for or legitimate grounds for elimination of a theory, there seems to be much of value in the remainder of his characterisation of the crucial experiment.

In the case of the AAOE, the issue was important to basic scientific understanding of the oxygen/ozone system in the earth's stratosphere, as well as in its current political and social interest. It does qualify as conceptually important. In view of the rapid convergence of opinion in the scientific community, the experiment must also be seen as decisive. There could be little argument with the contention that the experiment measures up as 'sociologically good' in Franklin's terms. But the case for 'methodologically good' might not seem so clear.

It is debatable whether the results of a single crucial experiment really did coincide with a logical entailment of one theory, and contradict some logical entailment of each rival. To obtain the necessary falsifications and confirmations, we have to look piecemeal at a wide suite of different types of measurement that were taken on the flights. It seems strange, in terms of previous discussions of crucial experiments, to describe a large and diverse exercise like the AAOE in the singular as 'an experiment'.

There are at least two quite different points of view that could be taken about the AAOE as a crucial experiment.

The more conventional approach would be to look at the situation in terms of confirmation and falsification. From this viewpoint, the AAOE as a whole is the crucial experiment. The AAOE was a set of experiments deliberately designed to distinguish between rival theories. With a few exceptions, each of the sets of measurements was intended and designed to provide evidence which would count strongly against or in favour of one of the rival theories. The hope was that after the event, one theory would emerge strongly confirmed while all of its rivals would be falsified in some sense. The extra sets of measurements were aimed at data collection to provide extra information in case no theory emerged unscathed, and some new theorising was required. The AAOE as a whole was deliberately designed as a 'crucial experiment', and it succeeded perfectly.

My own preference is to see the 'Smoking Gun' (ClO/ozone result) as the particular crucial experiment. It provides a clear example of a Baconian 'fingerpost at the crossroads'.[5] The important point here is that the experiment was one which was capable of discriminating between emerging theories at a relatively early stage of their respective developments. Franklin seems to have envisaged the crucial experiment as arising only in a situation where rival theories are already sufficiently developed to have made predictions by which they would stand or fall.

Predictions of phenomena and effects, other than ozone depletion as such, had been associated with each of the three families of theories. But because they were at an early stage of development, it is not at all clear that there was any real commitment to predictions that related directly to possible observations. That is, these predictions were not presented as effects by which the theory fell or stood, since there was still the possibility that further development and 'fine tuning' of the theory might have reversed some of them.

Elevated levels of oxides of nitrogen was a prediction of the solar cycle theory that was generally recognised as central to the theory. This was particularly the case because the mechanism envisaged by Callis and Natarajan involved increased NOx as part of the causal chain leading to ozone depletion in their theory. This theory was widely regarded as already rejected by falsification following the NOZE-1 indications of low NOx, and therefore not still a viable theory at the time of the AAOE. The AAOE suite of experiments did confirm low NOx in the polar stratosphere. But it is interesting to note that a variant of the solar cycle theory, where high energy protons took over some of the supposed role of the nitrogen oxides (Stephenson & Scourfield, 1991), was published even after the AAOE results!

But both chlorine and circulation theories were regarded as still viable at the time of the AAOE (S. Solomon, 1988, p. 145). Evidence collected before that time (including the NOZE-1 results, which showed elevated chlorine oxides and depleted nitrogen oxides) had not been regarded as falsifying either theory.

It is doubtful that the particular nature of the crucial result of the experiment was widely foreseen by those advancing chemical theories. In general terms, the experimental design involved measuring and monitoring concentrations of many chemical species on the grounds that if chemical processes were important, then some irregularities in these concentrations might be expected. The specific questions and aims on which the AAOE experiment design and selection was based were framed very directly in a confirmation/falsification model. ClO was one of the main species targeted. In the AAOE mission statement, high ClO was described as having a 'central role' in the chemical theories, and as being 'required' by those theories. Even so, experimental observation of high ClO levels was seen as a result which lent support to the chlorine theories. It is not clear that it was generally seen as one by which they might stand or fall.[6]

The very low NOx levels or the evidence of descent from the chemical tracers provided solid falsifications of the solar cycle and circulation theories respectively. But when a favoured theory is knocked down in this way, its supporters typically look at how it might be reconstructed to get around the difficulty. The 'smoking gun' result said, loud and clear, 'Don't even bother to try. Chlorine is the villain!'

There is another important difference from previous accounts of crucial experiments. It is not easy for an outsider to find elegance in the experimental design. Some atmospheric scientists assure me that it is certainly there. I have been reminded that beauty is in the eye of the beholder! There was a strong element of hypothesis testing in most of the experiments included in the suite. But much of the project was akin to a 'line search' – intensive data collection in the hope of finding a vital clue somewhere. The experimental design and execution was the work of a very large team of experts. The idea of taking the opportunity to visit and take as many measurements as possible directly in a very remote and difficult location such as the Antarctic stratosphere is quite an obvious one. There was no central 'bright idea' that could be attributed to any individual, but a lot of careful and collaborative design work. The design questions largely involved such things as planning flight paths, packing as many scientific instruments as possible onto the planes, choosing which quantities to measure, and ensuring the accuracy of the measurements that were made.[7] There was a balance between different experimental aims. Some were designed with the hope of specific vindication or rejection of each rival theory. Other experiments sought rather to collect a large volume of varied data to provide the basis for further analysis should none of the current theories prove particularly satisfactory. This aspect may be characteristic of the difference between some present day science and the science of the nineteenth and early twentieth centuries. It may be that the anecdotal consideration of the thinking and clever ideas of individual scientists, favoured by some historians of science, is an approach which will not be so well adapted to understanding the science of the late twentieth century as it has been to that of the previous few centuries. The sense of elegance and ingenuity of the ideas of individual scientists, implicit in much of the discussion of 'good experiments', fades away in considering an exercise of this scale and style. In this particular case there is also the issue of the difference between experiment qua manipulation of conditions in an apparatus contained in a small laboratory or private room, and experiment qua non-manipulative measurements on the stratosphere as a large external laboratory.

The methodological goodness of this suite of experiments arises in a manner quite different to that foreseen by Franklin. There is little to be seen of scientific elegance or ingenuity on the surface of what was done, though there may or may not have been a good deal of it in the fine detail of the planning and design. It is uncertain that the predictions of rival theories were sufficiently strong that their contradiction would necessarily lead to theory abandonment. But the planning was methodical and meticulous. A series of specific questions was picked out which might distinguish between the current rival theories, and individual experiments designed to address these questions. The exercise as a whole retained a clear focus. As a result, the experiment succeeded in distinguishing rapidly and decisively between rival theories, at an almost embryonic stage of their development.

The mythology of crucial experiments: a caveat

Identifying a significant change in scientific direction with a crucial experiment often occurs in scientific storytelling. Typically it is used as a pedagogic device, both to add interest to the story, and to provide a clear indication of why the presently accepted corpus of theory was preferred to its rivals (Gilbert & Mulkay, 1984). In addressing the latter aim, the nature of the experimental intention, design, and result, is often oversimplified to the point of gross historical distortion. The evidential issues are usually analysed with the benefit of hindsight, and a lack of appreciation of and sympathy for the contemporary point of view.

Gilbert and Mulkay (1984) refer to the frequent citing of 'key experiments' by working scientists. The scientists refer to these results to justify their present positions on contentious issues in their fields. But these authors argue that the stories the scientists tell are at best unreliable as history. As sociologists, Gilbert and Mulkay stress a widely recognised and important distinction. The experiments that may be cited to provide evidence to justify a position in hindsight, may not be those that actually were crucial or influential in an historical sense. Their claim is that the scientists often rewrite (or retell) the history to blur this distinction. This particular claim is also central to Lakatos' view of the history of science (Lakatos, 1974, p. 322).

Gilbert and Mulkay's analysis highlights an important caveat against retrospective claims that a particular experiment has been crucial. But we can be fairly certain that their particular concern does not arise in this case. The experiment was seen as crucial at the time it was conducted, by a wide group of scientists, and this is much more clearly documented than in most other examples that could be quoted. Indeed, the whole AAOE project was intended to be crucial. There was no guarantee beforehand that it would provide such a clear result as it did. It might easily have failed in this intention. But in the event it was successful beyond expectations.

The chlorine monoxide observations in the AAOE were successful in rallying the consensus of scientific belief behind one of a number of rival theories. This achievement was soundly based in the scientific evidence provided by the results of the experiment. One theory was strongly supported, and its rivals became untenable. Yet it could not really be said that the ClO/ozone result was in accordance with a prediction of one theory, and contradicted the predictions of the others. To be fair, though, it could be said that the AAOE suite of experiments, taken as a whole, did provide this confirmation and falsification.

The model that seems most appropriate to describe cases like this is to take the broader view of what might constitute legitimate grounds for theory rejection and adoption. It is then possible to recognise a number (at least three) of quite different classes of crucial experiment. Apart from the narrow model analysed by Popper, Lakatos, Franklin, and others, the sort of result that arises in cases like Leeuwenhoek's examination of semen is clearly a distinct, if somewhat rare type of crucial experiment. The 'smoking gun' experiment from the AAOE provides an example of a third type of crucial experiment, different in many ways from each of the others.

There are legitimate grounds for theory adoption and rejection other than the matter of matching or contradiction of theory predictions in an experiment.

History does not usually provide straightforward examples

When an historical example is used to make a philosophical point, it is easy to oversimplify the history, even to the point of distortion. Real cases seem to carry lots of extra twists and side-tracks. The result is a structure full of extra complication, and not nearly so clear in providing an illustration of the underlying philosophical principles. Moreover, the twists and side-tracks usually do not show up on superficial examination of the history (Fleck, 1946, p. 114).

There are therefore some grounds for presenting the history in a simplified way that illustrates the point more clearly, and avoids a lot of convoluted and largely irrelevant detail. But the caveat is always that the history must not be distorted in its effect. An assertion of the form 'had this complication not arisen, the scientists would have reached the same conclusions' involves a counter-factual, with attendant logical and philosophical difficulties. Yet it must be this hidden assertion that provides what justification there is for dismissing some material as irrelevant, leaving out the twists, and telling the story in its simplified form.

The construction of the history that has been presented here sees the 'smoking gun' result of the AAOE – the anti-correlation between chlorine monoxide and ozone levels – as the crucial observational result that decided the issue between rival theories. In doing so it did not need to falsify and confirm in the strong sense required by Franklin. It was able to be decisive without the need to meet this criterion.[8]

But quite a different construction seemed appropriate and natural to at least one of the leading scientists involved in the AAOE planning and execution. The AAOE suite of experiments as a whole can be seen as the 'crucial experiment'. The circulation theories are falsified in the strong sense, but by observations other than the 'smoking gun' result. The theory that is seen as strongly confirmed by the crucial experiment is not a vague group of chemically based theories, but one specific proposal put forward by Susan Solomon and others including Sherwood Rowland (S. Solomon *et al.*, 1986).

In this section, I will examine some of the complications that have been left out of the discussion in the argument of the first part of this chapter. The main aim is to convince that the simplification, of which I have clearly been guilty, does not amount to distortion. There is a secondary aim of comparing the merits of the rival constructions.

There are three main areas to be examined. Firstly, I have claimed that the rival circulation theories were not 'falsified' by the ClO/O_3 correlation. But there are results from prior to the AAOE that provide significant evidence against the circulation theories. More importantly, the nitrous oxide and whole air sample results from other experiments in the AAOE suite provide definite falsifications. Secondly, I have claimed that the 'smoking gun' result did not match a clear prediction of the chlorine based theories. But elevated ClO levels were a clear entailment of several of the proposed mechanisms that had been put up in the development of what was really a family of theories rather than a single theory. One of these papers had even calculated the ClO mixing ratio that would have been required to sustain the detailed mechanism that was being proposed. And thirdly, I have presented the AAOE as if it had followed straight on from the discovery of the ozone hole, and nothing important had happened on the experimental front in the intervening two years. In reality there was a considerable amount of experimentation and analysis – most notably the NOZE-1 series of experiments – that provided extra insight into the phenomenon.

I have tried to claim earlier that the observation of greatly increased ClO levels did not match a firm prediction of the chlorine theory. But several chemical mechanisms that might have accounted for chlorine-mediated depletion of Antarctic ozone had been proposed in the papers developing the chlorine theories. Increased ClO was an easily evinced consequence of most, but not all of these. It could possibly be argued, then, that there were in fact several different chlorine theories. In that case elevated ClO could be seen as a prediction of some of these theories, strongly confirmed by the 'smoking gun' experiment.

In one of the papers proposing a chlorine theory (S. Solomon et al., 1986, p. 756), elevated ClO is quite explicitly mentioned. The argument is not directly that chemical equations included in the proposed mechanism lead to an increase in ClO levels. Rather it is that the observed rapid decrease in ozone levels in early Antarctic springtime is difficult to achieve with a model based on a chlorine mediated radical chain mechanism. The model can only work if ClO levels rise dramatically. A very similar point is made in another paper (McElroy et al., 1986), though in the context of a much narrower exploration of mechanism. But there is no indication in either case that elevated ClO arises as a direct consequence of the chlorine theory. It is, logically, an entailment. But not in the direct sense of 'If mechanism M then (high ClO)'; the entailment only works in the indirect sense of 'If mechanism M then not (sufficient ozone depletion) unless (high ClO)'. There is no specific commitment in either paper to a necessity that elevated ClO should be both observable and observed, and that the chlorine theories should stand or fall on whether it was.

Elevated chlorine monoxide could be seen as a prediction of the chlorine theory. But the discourse had been within a particular family of mechanisms, and there was no commitment to any mechanism in particular at that stage.

The language of the two papers is particularly tentative and conciliatory:

We suggest here that the loss of O_3 in Antarctica may be attributed to . . . [one variant chlorine-based mechanism]. (McElroy et al., 1986)

A heterogeneous reaction between HCl and $ClONO_2$ is explored as a possible mechanism to explain the ozone observations. This process produces changes in ozone that are consistent with the observations. . . . Similar ozone changes are obtained with another possible heterogeneous reaction . . . (S. Solomon et al., 1986)

Had they been confronted with 'disappointingly' low ClO levels, the protagonists of the chlorine theory could still have tried to resurrect it with a broader approach to possible mechanisms.[9]

The consideration of the AAOE 'smoking gun' experiment as a crucially decisive result rests on the proposition that the experimental result was a new one; and that it was not merely a final confirmation of what was already generally believed to be the case.

A 'conspiracy theory' could, for example, be built around the idea that the scientists already knew about the ClO result, denitrification of the polar air, and the importance of polar stratospheric clouds. Relevant work that might have provided these answers had been done in NOZE-1. Or it was possible that information could be extracted from satellite data, or from data from any of a number of other projects. The AAOE could be seen as a publicity exercise that diverted a lot of funds to atmospheric sciences, enabled the collection of a mountain of extra data that really only interested the specialists, and allowed the findings on Antarctic ozone depletion to be presented to the public in a particularly dramatic way. If anything approaching this were the case, then it would be quite improper to see the AAOE as a crucial experiment, except perhaps in the very broadest sociological terms.

The official version of the state of knowledge about the Antarctic phenomenon prior to the AAOE can readily be gleaned from the relevant literature. Some of the specialist literature appears to anticipate many of the results of the AAOE, and to present arguments in a very forthright way, as though there were already no room for doubt or controversy. But the same could equally be said of the circulation theory papers, where quite different arguments were presented just as forthrightly.

A closer reading shows that even among the specialist atmospheric scientists, the issues were far from settled. The definitive position is presented in the planning paper for the AAOE (Tuck et al., 1989, p. 11181).

The NOZE-1 expedition to McMurdo in 1986 led to a great advance, in that it provided the first evidence that chlorine chemistry in the Antarctic during September and October was highly perturbed. It confirmed previous observations that the abundance of NO_2 was very low and also showed that HNO_3 was depleted. The column abundance of N_2O was observed to be much lower than in mid-latitudes. Ozone profiles were also measured, showing the depletion to be in the 12– to 20–km region, with frequent layered structure. Nevertheless, understanding was still limited by lack of data; apart from ozone, there was almost no profile information and almost no information about the dependence of the phenomenon on latitude and longitude, . . .

A crucial element in the proposed halogen-based ideas was the role of heterogeneous reactions on polar stratospheric clouds (PSCs), which were known to be present from the observations of the Stratospheric Aerosol Measurement (SAM)

II Satellite, but very little was known about size distributions or composition. [Embedded references in the original omitted]

Susan Solomon was leader of the NOZE-1 expedition. Her recent oral recollections are generally in line with this evaluation (S. Solomon, private interview, 1996):

So I think NOZE-1 was very successful. I think we got some of the first indicators that chlorine was what was causing the ozone hole. Now the advantage of flying an airplane is certainly many fold – you can get the measurement at a single point, whereas with remote sensing you are always going to be faced with the challenge of what you measure as some sort of integral between you and your light source. So, from that point of view, it is always more difficult to interpret. But if what you want to know is 'Is ClO a factor of a hundred times normal?', you can probably tell that. I think we showed that. I think that AAOE was a beautiful experiment. It was what was needed. I think you have to take the two together, though, to put it in a proper context.

In the AAOE planning paper, particular variants of the chlorine theory and dynamical theory were identified as remaining viable immediately prior to the mission. Eleven specific questions were presented for investigation, with the aim primarily of distinguishing between the theories, and secondarily of general data-collection to help refine the theories, or to prepare the ground to help devise a different approach should none of the current theories remain viable. Some of these questions were directed specifically at chlorine theories, while others looked at the dynamics. But four or five of them addressed areas of common interest to both sets of theories (e.g. 'What is the morphology of the ozone depletion?'), or of more indirect interest, relevant to both theories, but critical to neither (e.g. 'What is the water vapour mixing ratio?'). The very first question of the eleven reads, 'Is there sufficient ClO to sustain a fast enough non-O-atom chain or chains?' This particular formulation of one of the central questions addressed in the suite of experiments clearly shows that there was no great confidence in the ClO data from NOZE-1. It also sets up the ClO measurement in the 'bold prediction'/falsification model, and suggests that the chlorine theory may stand or fall on the ClO result.

There is one other indication that the AAOE in general, and the 'smoking gun' experiment in particular, were not a routine confirmation nor a dramatic demonstration of results that were already known. It is easily found by looking at the status of the circulation theories immediately prior to the AAOE. The tone of the papers formulating and advocating the circulation theories is quite as forthright and confident as the chemical papers. Several of the questions for investigation relate directly to the circulation theories (e.g. 'Is there a coherent pattern to the vertical velocities?'). The NOZE-1 results had had a significant influence. It was generally recognised prior to the AAOE that there was a 'chemically perturbed zone' within the winter and springtime polar vortex. Ozone loss, low NOx levels, and the presence of polar stratospheric clouds were well accepted. But low ozone, low NOx, and high water content, could all be characteristic of tropospheric air that had moved upward. It was also generally recognised that the stratospheric chemistry was somewhat changed in this region. This might possibly have been simply because of the different mix of trace substances present. Some of the NOZE-1 results on other trace species, most notably ClO and N_2O, were not generally trusted nor accepted (Kerr, 1987).

I have argued that it is possible for an experiment to be crucial in deciding between rival theories without actually providing any direct falsification or confirmation. This argument is unaffected by the complications in the history of the case that was used *as an illustration of the possibility*. My further argument that the 'smoking gun' experiment from the AAOE *is an example* of this type of crucial experiment does depend on the fine detail of the history. The story is sufficiently complex that I must concede that it might be 'simplified' and constructed in a different way for presentation as an example of a conventional confirmation/ falsification experiment. I have here tried to demonstrate that my own is the more natural and convincing portrayal. Certain experiments in the AAOE suite other than the 'smoking gun' experiment provided strong evidence against the circulation theory – evidence sufficiently strong to be classed as falsification. But it seems rather to have been the evidence of the 'smoking gun' experiment itself, much more than the negative indications from these other experiments, that was rapidly decisive in convincing the protagonists of the circulation theory to abandon rather than to seek modification of their approach. High chlorine monoxide had already been identified prior to the AAOE at least as a likely consequence of the chlorine theories, and even seen as a factor that would be necessary for the chlorine theories to work. But with the relatively incomplete stage of study of possible chlorine-based mechanisms then prevailing, there may still have been room to reformulate the chlorine theories had elevated ClO not been observed. Finally, it is clear that the AAOE in general, and the 'smoking gun' experiment in particular was a genuine investigation seeking new results. Elevated ClO had been anticipated in Phillip Solomon's results from NOZE-1, but the direct and convincing observation of elevated ClO, coupled with the observation of the remarkable detailed correlation with ozone depletion, was genuinely a novel and crucial result.

So I present the 'smoking gun' experiment as the type of crucial experiment that indicates a clear direction at the crossroads. The alternative characterisation is to consider not just the 'smoking gun', but the entire AAOE suite of measurements as a crucial experiment that simultaneously confirms and falsifies predictions of rival theories.

Why was the 'smoking gun' result so compelling?

It is fairly easy for the lay person to come 'cold' to the story of the Antarctic ozone investigation, and to recognise, in the result presented in figure 7.2, overwhelming evidence for the chlorine theory. Why should this be the case? What is it about the structure of the graph that makes it so convincing? What are the underlying arguments, and epistemological principles that lead to this estimation? Are they sound arguments and principles? Some of the issues involved have been raised before, most notably by Le Grand (1990). The scientific case he explores is the issue of what was to be made of the series of parallel magnetic reversals that could be observed near mid-ocean ridges. There are a number of curious parallels between this case and the 'smoking gun' experiment. But there is a centrally important and characteristic feature common between the pictures that Le Grand analyses, and the graph of the 'smoking gun' experiment. It is the combination of complexity and an element of randomness in the data with a strong symmetry or pattern.

Both of the graphs in figure 10.1 illustrate a perfect correlation. But because the curves in the left panel have a fairly simple shape, they carry no great conviction that the results they portray are related. The problem is that curves of a generally indistinguishable similar shape have been presented to us so many times before; they can easily arise in descriptions of many unrelated phenomena. In formal terms, the curves have a low information content.[10] The curves in the right panel are also simple, at first glance. They simply jump wildly up and down, seemingly at random. They give the impression that there is no message to convey, just noise. But a closer examination shows that the fluctuations in one curve, wild as they may be, are exactly matched by opposing fluctuations in the other. Random patterns do have a generally similar appearance, but they do not reproduce their fluctuations in this type of exact manner. There is overwhelming evidence that the two results plotted are connected. This is not merely a subjective conclusion. We can analyse the two sets of curves using the tools of statistics to obtain measures of the significance of the correlations, or using the alternative tools of information theory to calculate the information content of the evidence for correlation. In either case we will conclude that the evidence for a connection between the two results plotted in the right hand panel is many times stronger than that in the left.

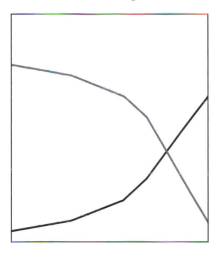 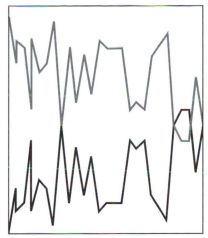

Figure 10.1 Correlations in simple and complex data.

So in this case, the instinctive judgement of seeing a strong connection when we see a pattern in complexity is found to be a sound one.

In the case of the magnetic profile of the ocean floor,

The clinching argument for most marine geologists and geophysicists was the single profile collected for Lamont by the research ship Eltanin on its nineteenth traverse across the East Pacific Rise. Other profiles made on the same voyage were set aside in favour of *Eltanin-19*. One could literally fold the profile along the ridge and match up anomalies from the opposite sides. It became the template against which other profiles were matched, evaluated, and resolved. To see this visual 'proof' was to become a believer in the symmetry thesis. (Le Grand, 1990, p. 255)

The *Eltanin-19* profile shows a sequence of about fifteen peaks, separated by troughs, leading up to the central ocean ridge. The same sequence is then reproduced in mirror image on the other side of the ridge, with very close matches in the height, separation, and detailed shapes of the peaks.

The 'smoking gun' result of the AAOE shows a broad correlation between falling ozone levels and rising ClO levels during a traverse from the mid-latitude stratosphere through a transition region into the polar vortex. But it also shows a remarkable matching of the fine structure. About six very sharp ClO peaks in the transition region match exactly with corresponding troughs in the ozone concentration.

There were results from ten flights plotted in Anderson's paper on the simultaneous ozone and ClO determinations in the AAOE. The first three, which occurred prior to the development of the spring phenomenon, show no significant ozone depletion, in spite of anomalously high

ClO within the polar vortex. The fourth and fifth show the beginnings of ozone depletion, and some complex structure in the transition region. Of the remaining five, which show fully developed ozone depletion within the vortex, the seventh is the one that is always presented as the 'smoking gun' result. There are four others that should show broadly similar structure, but the curves lack the complex peaks and troughs in the transition region that make the result look so impressive, and the correlation in the broad structure is not quite so perfect. This need not be regarded with suspicion, as a case of selectively emphasising results that support a particular point of view. The explanation must lie simply in the set of weather conditions that prevailed on 16 September. On that flight, the transition region on the edge of the polar vortex obviously contained a lot of fairly diverse and discrete air parcels that were not well mixed. On other days the transition region was generally narrower, and associated rather with a fairly smooth interpolation between the polar and mid-latitude air. But the parallel with the emphasis that was placed on *Eltanin-19* in the story presented by Le Grand is remarkable.

Remarkable, too, is the parallel of the reaction of the scientists in that case:

Vine himself commented when he saw this profile, 'It was all over but the shouting'. The reaction of marine geophysicists and palæontologists to this single image were similar . . . A. Cox '. . . a truly extraordinary experience . . . there was just no question any more that the seafloor-spreading idea was right'; W. Pitman: 'It hit me like a hammer'; or, even more tellingly from J. Worzel, a staunch opponent of Drift: 'It's too perfect'. (Le Grand, 1990, pp. 256–7)

In both of the cases, we find scientists from the opposite camp completely convinced by the evidence of this type of strong correlation. In the case of the ozone investigation, it is the conviction that the 'smoking gun' graph points so strongly to chlorine-mediated depletion that leads to abandonment of the circulation theory approach. Had it not been for that, the negative evidence of the nitrous oxide profile, and the rather ambiguous evidence of actual circulation patterns, may not have been enough to prevent attempts to modify and save the circulation theories. They would ultimately have been given up, but not without a struggle.

There are other aspects of the 'smoking gun' experiment that need some discussion. The mechanism that was accepted to account for that result produces a correlation involving four main components: ozone, ClO, visible light, and ice crystals (hence polar stratospheric clouds). Denitrification, too, must be taken for granted. The presence of ice crystals and very weak visible light is sufficient to lead to greatly elevated ClO levels. There is a delay and possibly the need for stronger visible light before a chain reaction gets well established; this will lead to a further doubling of ClO, and removal of ozone.

The 'smoking gun' result clearly links ClO and ozone. The role of visible light in the two stages mentioned can be seen in a comparison between results early in the flight programme and later in the flight programme (see figures 7.2 and 7.3). The differences must be connected either with an increase in the solar zenith angle as the season progresses (and hence increased light intensity), or with a slow build-up timescale for some parts of the process, or both.

But there is nothing to tie in the clouds to the rest of the story. Was it the case, for example, and could it be demonstrated that the pattern of sharp local peaks and troughs in ClO in the transition region, corresponded to patches of cloud and clear along the course of the flight? If not, what were the alternative explanations for why ClO levels were fluctuating so much in different parcels of local air?

Measurements of aerosol particle concentrations and size distribution were taken on the same flights as the ozone/ClO measurements. A different team of investigators were associated with these measurements. The apparatus was slung on the right wing of the ER-2 plane rather than the left (Tuck *et al.*, 1989, pp. 11182–3). Results of the monitoring of ice particles on 16 September, the day of the 'smoking gun' result, are reproduced in figure 10.2. The left hand panel shows small ice particles (0.05–0.25 μm radius), the right hand panel shows a larger fraction (0.53–5.5 μm radius). The horizontal axis shows elapsed time on the flight. Direct comparison with the 'smoking gun' results from the same flight is difficult. The horizontal axis of figure 7.1 is latitude. The ClO/ozone readings were taken only on the Southward portion of the flight. There is no visually striking reproduction of the shape of the ClO or ozone curve in the ice data. The strong peaks occurred only when the plane descended to lower altitude. The strongest, and only visible correlation, is between ice particle numbers and altitude. Greatly increased ice particle concentrations are associated with lower altitudes: take-off and landing at the ends of the graph, and a planned descent from 20 km to 13 km at the turn-around point of the flight, the middle of the graph, followed by a climb back to the higher altitude. The authors of the ice paper comment on the correlation between ice and ozone (Ferry *et al.*, 1989, p. 16471): 'Ozone is the lowest when the particle concentration peaks'. This does not seem particularly profound when the peak referred to is directly associated with the deliberate mid-flight descent. Of course the upper troposphere contains lower ozone levels than even the polar stratosphere! More telling is what follows:

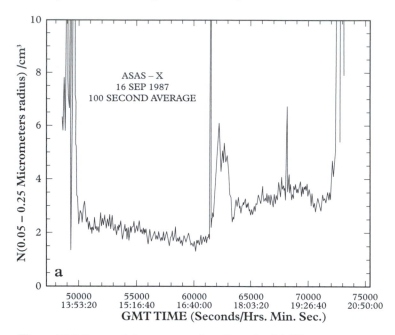

Figure 10.2 Ice particle concentrations from the AAOE.
Reproduced from Ferry *et al. J. Geophys. Res.* **94** (1989), 16470, Fig. 10.
© American Geophysical Union.

The Southward flight (on which ozone & ClO readings were taken) is
represented on the left hand part of this graph – between 50000 and
61000 seconds UT. A descent and climb at the Southern extremity of
the flight path is associated with the ice crystal peak between 61500 and
63500 seconds, and the flight back to Punta Arenas occupies the right
hand part of the graph.

However, there is also an ozone depletion beginning at 58,500 s UT that is not
associated with an aerosol increase nor an altitude change. On the return leg,
ozone increases beginning at 63,900 s UT without any change in aerosol
concentration, and without an apparent change in altitude. (Ferry *et al.*, 1989, p.
16471)

The ozone changes referred to here are the very broad changes associated
with entering and leaving the chemically perturbed region in the polar
vortex. There is no real difference in ice particle densities. None of the
broad structure of the 'smoking gun' result is reproduced in the ice data,
let alone the fine detail of the transition region.

There are reasons why the ClO/ozone might not be reflected in the ice
data. Small ice particles can evaporate in a matter of minutes in response

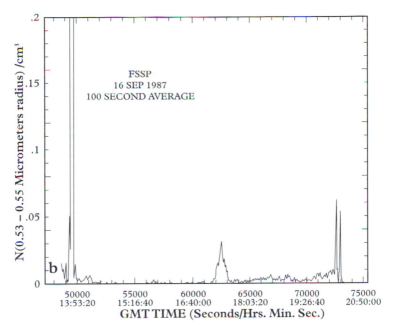

Figure 10.2 (*cont.*)

to changing atmospheric conditions; chlorine monoxide and ozone require hours and days respectively to respond to changed conditions. Ice crystals are certainly needed for the initial production of high ClO levels, and might or might not be needed to sustain the chain reaction. But they did not vary in association with the varying ClO and ozone levels found in the 'smoking gun' experiment.

If chlorine monoxide is the villain left holding the 'smoking gun', then particulate ice is the nervous accomplice who has rapidly fled the scene of the crime!

NOTES

1 It actually took a decade or two, but some allowance must be made for the more leisurely pace of both science and communication in the seventeenth century.

2 e.g. The tone of the acknowledgement in 'Stratospheric Ozone 1988' (HMSO, London,1988), p. 55 makes very clear that good communication between scientists from different disciplines had made an important contribution to the then state of understanding.

3 I do not wish to draw a distinction between observation and experiment.

Some philosophers like to maintain a strict distinction between observations, as measurements of what is happening naturally, and experiments, where a natural system is deliberately disturbed, or a particular arrangement of entities and their interactions artificially brought about for the purposes of observation. Scientists working in areas of earth sciences, as well as astronomy, and similar areas (indeed, even in archaeology) are seldom really in a position to do experiments at all, if this distinction is to be maintained. Yet the decisions about what to measure, where and when to measure it, and what methods to use, are essentially the same problems of experimental design faced by other scientists. The issue is well discussed by J.E. Tiles, *Brit. J. Phil. Sci.* **44**(1993), 463–75.

4 There could be a Lakatosian criticism of this work for 'clinging to a degererating (degenerated?) research program'. The fact that this letter was published shows an impressive open-mindedness and generosity on the part of the editors and/or referees of *Nature*. (At least, that is the way I prefer to read it; at least one of the scientists centrally involved feels rather that the referees made a bad mistake!) This is perhaps a strong piece of evidence against the accusation of a conspiracy among the atmospheric scientists on the Antarctic ozone phenomenon.

5 See e.g. Ian Hacking, *Representing and Intervening* (Cambridge University Press, 1983), pp. 249–51. Hacking particularly makes the point that the fingerpost is a strong indicator of the fruitful direction to follow, rather than a logically compelling stricture.

6 There was a prior publication by Phillip Solomon's group in the NOZE-1 experiments, which claimed the *observation* of elevated ClO levels from a ground station [De Zaffra, R.L., Jaramillo, M., Parrish, A., Solomon, P.M., Connor, B., and Barrett, J., *Nature* **328**(1987), 408–11]. It is suggested in Kerr's report [*Science* **238**(1987), 156.] that the work was not highly regarded nor widely accepted. It is difficult to see why it would not be, if elevated ClO was a clear prediction of one of the main rival theories. The main objection to the work seemed to be that it was simultaneously showing levels of nitrous oxide which were anomalously low (i.e. many times lower than expected). Susan Solomon and others took these high ClO results seriously, but only saw them as 'a strong indication that halocarbon chemistry plays a significant role in the ozone hole phenomenon' [Solomon, S., *Rev. Geophys.* **26**(1988), 144.], or 'suggestive that photochemistry was at least partially responsible for the ozone decline' [Jones *et al.*, *J. Geophys. Res.*, **94**(1989), 11529.]

7 Including such issues as how to measure very low levels of nitrogen oxides in the atmosphere, from a jet aircraft whose own exhaust contains quite high levels of nitrogen oxides, for example.

8 A scientifically trained reader of this section was horrified at my suggestion that scientists would take a "mere" correlation as decisive evidence of causality. An awareness of philosophical enquiries into causality makes this seem less surprising. Over 200 years ago, David Hume argued that the notion of causality was itself an artificial construction and an illusion, and the only thing that was real was the observable factor, that is, the correlation. This position formed a large part of the basis of the empiricist school of philosophy, and it has never been refuted. I would not want to take such an extreme position. But

a century later John Stuart Mill made a milder claim which I would consider correct and uncontroversial: in normal circumstances the only available evidence of causality comes from correlation.

A scientist cannot say that correlation is not a good enough basis for a scientific theory – ultimately it is the only basis that can be found.

The really important points about correlation and causality are:

(1) that correlation only provides good evidence of causality when it is strong and persistent; and

(2) that while a good correlation clearly indicates the fact of causality, it cannot of itself indicate the direction of causality nor the length of the causal chain.

9 It is debatable whether there was room for an escape of this sort. The consideration of mechanism, as presented in the paper, is not exhaustive. But one of the leading scientists involved assured me that other possibilities were considered informally, and even tested in preliminary laboratory work, before they were dismissed. For example, heterogeneous reactions at ice crystal surfaces had been considered in terms of precursor production for a gas phase radical chain mechanism. But there had not been consideration of the possibility of surface reactions directly involving either ozone or the chain carriers themselves in the argument of S. Solomon *et al.* They were probably not relevant, but might have provided an escape from the need for greatly elevated gas phase ClO. Apparently these possibilities were considered and dismissed, but not reported on.

10 There is a formal and productive branch of mathematical science called Information Theory, where notions like 'information content' are given precise definition and quantification. See, e.g., Brillouin, L. 1962, *Science and Information Theory*, 2nd Ed. Academic Press, New York.

11 Positive and negative evidence in theory selection

Many scientific textbooks include a small section headed 'The Scientific Method', or something similar. It contains a brief description of the way that the authors believe scientists investigate, evaluate evidence, and incorporate new knowledge into the body of science. It is usually very idealised, and often prescriptive and over-simplified. Consider the following two extracts from such sources:

An important point to remember about theories is that they can seldom be proven to be correct. Usually, the best we can do is fail to find an experiment that disproves a theory. (Brady, 1990, p. 5)

Theories are, however, only tentative. A theory continues to be useful only as long as we fail to find any experimental facts that cannot be accounted for by the theory. But only one fact that the theory cannot explain will cause the theory to be modified or replaced by a new theory. (Gillespie *et al.*, 1986, p. 91)

The essential feature of Popper's philosophy of science that has been so influential among scientists and philosophers alike is his breaking of the symmetry between confirmation of a theory, and falsification of a theory. The idea is that it is possible to use experimentation to disprove a theory, but not to establish it. The notion that falsification is possible, while confirmation is not, is an over-simplification. It is substantially undermined by the Quine-Duhem problem, and its inadequacy is reflected in Popper's adoption of his own type of scepticism (the philosophical view that it is not possible to be certain about knowledge claims), and his later, deeper analysis of the problems of rational theory adoption and rejection. Nevertheless, this simplified view of Popper's philosophy has been taken up by many working scientists. Even among philosophers of science it is Popper's legacy that falsification is sometimes seen as more respectable than confirmation.

One of Popper's main targets in his analysis was the inductivist view of science – that scientific theories or laws arise as inductive generalisations of a series of observations, and are confirmed by further examples which fit the generalisation. It is hardly surprising, then, that he works with the notion that a law or theory in science may be represented in the form 'All As are B'.

In an analysis of the practicalities of theory adoption and rejection, I will contend:

- Firstly, that many scientific laws or theories cannot be reduced to the form 'All As are B'.
- Secondly, that much of the asymmetry between confirmation and falsification depends on this form, and cannot be extended to some scientific theories, particularly in their developmental stages.

The contention that there is asymmetry between confirmation and falsification has previously been challenged from a neo-inductivist perspective by Grünbaum (1976) and others. There has also been a challenge using Bayesian analysis, where an attempt is made to put a statistical measure on both corroboration and falsification. Here I will take an approach quite different to either of these. My point is rather that many scientific theories have a form which simply cannot be cast as an inductive generalisation.

We will continue to consider the case of the investigation of the Antarctic ozone hole, and the 'smoking gun' result that I have argued was decisive in its influence on theory adoption and rejection.

At the time of the experiment, there were several rival hypotheses, each in effect seeking to attribute a large and anomalous local ozone depletion to quite different causes. A carefully designed suite of observations and experiments was carried out. Observational evidence relating to the new phenomenon was collected. The hope was that the results would distinguish between these rival hypotheses, and also help in developing the detail of whichever one or more contenders remained viable.

The main rival hypotheses may be summarised as follows. Firstly, it was suggested that the ozone depletion was being caused by increased levels of chlorine-containing compounds in the local stratosphere. This increase had in turn arisen as a result of increasing human use of inert chlorine compounds, and release and build-up of these compounds in the surface atmosphere.

The actual mechanism whereby a global increase in stratospheric chlorine compounds would lead to a dramatic effect only in the Antarctic, and only at one time of the year, was far from certain, though rapid progress had been made in developing some of the ideas. There were, in effect, several quite different proposals about the detail of mechanism in what was essentially a family of closely related theories (S. Solomon et al., 1986; McElroy et al., 1986; Molina & Molina, 1986; Crutzen & Arnold, 1986).

The weakness of this approach at the time was its tentative and speculative nature. Stolarski and Schoeberl (1986) argued priority for a circulation-based approach on the grounds that it should be examined 'before any unusual and speculative chemistry is introduced into the problem'. The then known chemistry could *not* provide an explanation. Ultraviolet light was an essential part of the known chlorine cycle. In the Antarctic at this time of the year the sun stays very low in the northern sky, and the ultraviolet levels are consequently very low. Models based on known chemistry had never predicted an Antarctic anomaly.

A second family of theories attributed cause in quite a different way. A major climatic shift was supposed to have occurred about 1976, so that in the springtime, lower atmosphere air, which contains little ozone, was pushing aside the ozone-rich stratospheric air in the Antarctic (Tung *et al.*, 1986; Mahlman & Fels, 1986).

In winter the Antarctic vortex forms, isolating polar air in both the lower atmosphere and the stratosphere. With springtime sunrise, the vortex starts to break up. The proposal was that in this break-up, lower atmosphere air may be forced up in a plume into the stratosphere, pushing stratospheric air aside. This was supposed to be a new pattern that started around 1976. In this case the weakness was lack of direct evidence – either for large scale vertical movement of the air mass, or for a climatic change in 1976.

Another theory attributed the anomalous ozone depletion to solar interactions with the upper atmosphere. It was noted that the period of onset of the observed ozone decrease between 1976 and 1983 largely corresponded with a period of increase in solar activity to a particularly strong maximum. Charged particles emitted by solar storms are deflected to polar regions by the earth's magnetic field. Here, they could interact with the upper atmosphere to initiate reactions leading to the production of oxides of nitrogen in large amounts. These in turn could destroy stratospheric ozone after being transported downward (Callis & Natarajan, 1986).

But the atmosphere at 200 km altitude is very rarefied. The authors' argument that enough nitrogen oxides could be produced is not entirely convincing. Moreover there is not the same sort of correlation between solar activity and ozone levels in the period from 1957 to 1972.

The problem was seen as an important one, socially and politically as well as scientifically. There were clearly different social policy implications depending on which theory proved correct. A massive effort was made to sort the problem out. Several programmes of data collection were undertaken. Fairly early in these investigations it became apparent that nitrogen oxide levels, far from being enhanced, had actually fallen to extremely low values in the region of the Antarctic ozone depletion. The third theory was a clear candidate for conventional rejection via falsification. But both chlorine and circulation theories remained viable, and at least one further attempt was made to resurrect the solar theory.

The AAOE in 1987 was carefully and deliberately designed to sort out the uncertainty. The individual experiments were planned with a view to collecting data that might falsify or confirm any of the then viable theories. Despite the generally falsificationist views expressed by modern scientists, there is little evidence of asymmetry between confirmation and falsification in the planning for this exercise.

The results of one of these experiments, the 'smoking gun' experiment, was hugely influential. Other experiments in the suite also provided important results, which included strong confirmatory or falsificatory evidence for some of the theories. But it was largely this single experiment which very rapidly led to the adoption of the chlorine theories (and arguably to one of the variant proposals from among the chlorine theories), and the abandonment of the rival circulation theories. An analysis of the case reassures us that the adoption and abandonment were based on reasonable evidential grounds, rather than political motivations. The conventional Popperian story would be that crucial data must falsify the theory that was rejected (insofar as scientists were unwilling to abandon the auxiliary hypotheses involved in data interpretation), leaving the triumphant theory as 'last man standing'.

The difficulty is that Popper's story simply does not fit this case particularly well. The result that was most influential in achieving the rejection of the circulation theories, was a result that bore absolutely no relation to those theories.

The observations in the 'smoking gun' experiment involved chlorine monoxide. The circulation theory had nothing to say about chlorine monoxide, directly or indirectly. Chlorine monoxide is a reactive, free-radical species that was being observed in quantities many times its natural level at any height in the normal atmosphere. It is neither naturally present at high levels in the lower atmosphere, nor generated in solar interactions with the outer atmosphere. Its presence is not inconsistent with the circulation theories as such (nor for that matter with the solar cycle theory), but an explanation of it is called for, quite independent of, and unrelated to these theories themselves. Chlorine monoxide did enter directly into most of the chlorine theories, but at that stage there was not a consistent commitment among these theories to a detailed mechanism that would entail increased concentrations. Even so, the result looks more like a confirmation than a falsification. That is, a *direct* confirmation; not a Popperian confirmation by failure to falsify.

The crucial result involved a close association between ozone disappearance and elevated chlorine monoxide radical levels. In the winter darkness, ozone levels were high, and chlorine monoxide radicals very low. With the return of sunlight to the clouds that had formed in the local stratosphere during the winter, chlorine monoxide radical levels rose 100 fold or more, and ozone levels started to fall dramatically. It was this result that had a large influence in determining the issue between the theories for the specialist scientists involved in the AAOE, and that was alone effective in deciding the issue for the broader scientific community.

But, in the light of Popper's analysis, how can anything that looks so much like a *direct* confirmation, and so little like a falsification, be so powerfully effective in redirecting the course of a branch of scientific enquiry?

This is even more interesting in view of the fact that there was a falsification of the circulation theories in the results from other experiments in the AAOE suite.

At first sight, it does not seem likely that the circulation theories could have been falsified. Because they were very general theories about an upwelling of air in the Antarctic region at that time of the year, they were not prescriptive about the fine local details of circulation patterns.

Monitoring the whole of the airflow over the Antarctic region during a spring season was not a logistically feasible exercise. This was particularly the case because it takes only a very small vertical air velocity to move a large volume of air vertically in a matter of days. There was no guarantee that the vertical movements were steady or consistent, either from time to time or from place to place within the Antarctic region. Any attempt to use measured airflows to falsify a circulation theory would have depended on checking a rather sparse set of observations against the predictions of a computer circulation model based around the detail of the theory. The theory had not developed to the point where such a model could be reliably generated. In any case, a mismatch betweeen the model results and the observational data set would always, at least in the first instance, be attributed to a failing of the detailed implementation of the model rather than a failing of the underlying theory on which it was based.

The falsification of the circulation theories that was produced in the AAOE was of quite a different type. Atmospheric circulation mixes the gases in the troposphere very effectively, and quite effectively in the stratosphere as well. Only gases that readily undergo chemical reactions, or that have a high affinity for water, show significant local variations in mixing ratio in the troposphere. In the stratosphere, there is a third group of gases that can show local variations: those that decompose in ultraviolet light.

There is a group of gases that are totally unreactive in the troposphere, but are susceptible when they rise into the stratosphere. Either they are decomposed when they reach heights where an appropriate wavelength of ultraviolet light is not filtered out, or they react with some of the reactive species that participate in stratospheric chemistry, but are usually absent from the troposphere. Nitrous oxide, N_2O, is one such gas. It is uniformly present in the troposphere at a level of about 300 parts per billion. It takes almost no part in any chemical process there, having an average atmospheric residence time of at least several decades.[1] But when it rises into the stratosphere it starts to encounter ultraviolet light that can break up its molecules. In the absence of unusual air circulation, the mixing ratio of nitrous oxide falls rapidly with increasing altitude in the stratosphere. The fall-off starts around 15 km, and by the time an altitude of 30 km is reached, there is almost no nitrous oxide present. This very rapid change of nitrous oxide mixing ratio with altitude allows nitrous oxide to be used as a marker gas to determine the greatest altitude recently achieved by a stratospheric air parcel. When extremely low levels of nitrous oxide were consistently observed in air samples taken from Antarctic stratosphere in the AAOE, it was a clear indication that the air being sampled at around 12 km had recently descended from a height of at least 30 km.

But there was a possible flaw. The samples were taken from what was being called the 'chemically anomalous region'. Nitrous oxide is very unreactive, unlike the other oxides of nitrogen that were involved in the anomalous chemistry. But when no-one was quite sure just exactly what was going on, there was an outside chance that nitrous oxide was being removed from the local air by some unusual chemical process.

The closing of this possible loophole came from yet another of the experiments in the AAOE. There are gases other than nitrous oxide that show a similar pattern of rapid fall-off with increasing altitude in the stratosphere. Two of these had been measured, and were also showing extremely low levels, characteristic of air from 30 km or above (Heidt *et al.*, 1989). One of these gases, perhaps ironically, was dichlorodifluoromethane – one of the most important CFCs. The other was methane.

So there was a falsification of the circulation theories in the results from the AAOE. But somehow it was the chlorine monoxide result that was more influential and decisive in the abandonment of this approach.[2] Nevertheless, this particular case is a complicated one, and a Popperian story can be made to fit by downplaying the chlorine monoxide experiment and emphasising the marker gas experiments. The fit does not seem to be a natural one.

A rather different account must be devised to deal with the case of the formation of a consensus behind the continental drift theory. The parallel between continental drift and this case has already been introduced in the previous chapter. Here again, the continental drift theory started out as just one of a number of rival theories seeking to explain certain phenomena of the earth's topography. It did not even seem to be the strongest among the rivals. A magnetic survey of the Atlantic Ocean was totally and rapidly decisive in achieving a consensus behind this theory.

But the data that were collected seemed to have nothing at all to do with any of the theories that were rejected. What was observed was that magnetisation directions in the rocks of the ocean floor changed in quite an irregular fashion every twenty or thirty kilometres, but that the changes were symmetrically disposed about the mid-ocean ridge.

Now this was a spectacular and visually compelling piece of evidence, but evidence of what? It did not, on the face of it, falsify any prediction of any of the current theories. Nor did it even match an entailment of the continental drift theory.

But it became a solid confirmation of continental drift as soon as attempts were made to explain it. It was quite inexplicable using any theory of topographic and geological features other than continental drift. It could be explained using continental drift only with the super-structure of some additional suppositions. It had to be supposed that Africa and South America were moving apart in a fairly steady and gentle fashion, and that this motion was accommodated by a flow of lava from below into an ever-widening crack along the mid-Atlantic ridge. If this were the case, then a scale of distance from the mid-Atlantic ridge would also be a scale of time since the lava of the local sea floor had solidified. And when molten rock solidifies, the current magnetisation due to the earth's magnetic field becomes fixed into the rock. The result would then be a record of reversals of the earth's magnetic field as a time series, moving backward in time as we moved away from the ridge. And this record could be traced, and would look exactly the same, on either side of the current ridge. The case is discussed in detail by Le Grand (1988, especially pp. 176–81, 202–26).

What is happening in a case like this is neither falsification nor confirmation of a theory in the conventional sense. Some other logical structure is involved. We will seek to establish what this structure is, and to show that it is operating in the adoption of theory in the ozone hole case, in a very similar way to the way it operates in the continental drift case.

The first point is that the theory of continental drift cannot fairly be encompassed in one, or even several statements of the form 'All As are B'. 'All ocean floors spread' and similar propositions do not really meet the case. Continental drift is not really about an inductive generalisation over four oceans or seven continents, or even twenty-one major plates! It is not realistic to see continental drift as the last remaining pillar of theory, after all of its serious rivals have been knocked down like ninepins by a series of falsifications. Symmetric disposition of magnetic reversals about mid-ocean ridges looks more like some sort of confirmation of continental drift than a falsification of rival theories (which do not even seem to address the possibility). But it is by no means an entailment of the theory, nor the fulfillment of some sort of 'bold prediction'.

The first task in providing a new framework is to restore some of the symmetry between confirmation and falsification. We start with a new notion: that any theory can be matched with another theory that is its direct opposite in some sense. We will refer to the antithesis of a theory. Insofar as a theory can be encapsulated in a simple proposition, its antithesis is encapsulated in the negation of that proposition. If a theory has the form 'All As are B' (as Popper suggested that all well-formulated scientific theories ought), then it can be falsified by the discovery of a single A that is not B, while any number of new As that are found to be B will not overcome the Humean[3] objection that the next new A might not fit in. The negation of the statement is that 'There exists at least one A that is not B'. That is a statement that can be confirmed, but never empirically falsified unless the entire population of As is finite and can be examined. Why should not this statement be used as the model of a possible type of scientific theory – the theory that would be the antithesis of the original theory? The apparent objection is that it is, at least on the surface of it, a statement about an individual rather than a class, and so may not fulfil some sort of universality requirement for a scientific law statement.

But does that really mean that it cannot be a scientific theory? Suppose we take some liberties with the history of science, and become naïve particle physicists. We know about positrons, and have been very impressed by a particle which is equal and opposite to the electron in every way, and mutually annihilates in collision with an electron with a large release of energy. So we come up with a postulate that there ought to exist a particle that stands in similar relation to a proton.

Probably, in the long term we have in mind a postulate of a general nature, like 'every elementary particle has an equal and opposite anti-particle', but for the time being, our 'theory' is restricted to 'there exists (or can be generated) a particle equal and opposite to the proton, which will produce a certain precise series of observable effects, including a spectacular firework show when it bumps into a proton'.

There are theories very much like this within the body of mainstream science. It is hard to find a good reason why a scientific theory should not have this form. But such a theory would fail Popper's demarcation criterion. It is clearly verifiable – in an experiment one day the right sort of tracks were found, and we could say 'Yes, we were right. There are anti-protons after all.' But it could not be falsified. Years of experimentation that failed to produce anti-protons might simply mean that we had not hit on the recipe for producing them! Is this sort of particle physics a pseudo-science?

Popper recognises and discusses exactly this point (Popper, 1959, pp. 68–70). His solution is to regard existential statements of this sort as metaphysical, and not truly empirical.

If a scientific theory does not have the form 'All As are B', then its antithesis may also be an acceptable scientific theory. If this antithesis is falsifiable, then a falsification of the antithesis also constitutes a confirmation of the original theory.

To summarise: Falsification of a theory necessarily constitutes direct confirmation of its antithesis. If it is possible for the antithesis of any scientific theory to also be a legitimate scientific theory, then at least one of the pair must be directly confirmable.

What I believe is happening in cases like the *Eltanin-19* profile and continental drift, or the 'smoking gun' experiment of the AAOE, is an effective direct confirmation by falsification of the antithesis.

With the type of confirmation used in an empiricist model, and effectively shown to be valueless by Hume, Popper, and others, the argument goes much as follows:
- We have observed O, as we have many times before in these circumstances.
- Our theory T entails that we should observe O in these circumstances.
- Therefore T is right, because it would be a huge co-incidence if we were to keep on observing O, and T was not right.

With this type of confirmation there is quite a different argument:
- We have observed O, which is a very surprising result that demands an explanation.
- It is not possible to frame an explanation of O unless T is right.
- Therefore T is right.

The crucial and unusual part of this argument is its second sentence, and this is where the antithesis and the falsification comes in. The antithesis is the theory not-T. Like any theory it can have entailments (when taken in conjunction with appropriate auxiliary hypotheses). If one of those entailments is not-O, then an observation of O falsifies theory not-T.

There is good evidence that in the actual unfolding of the ozone hole story, the antithesis of the chlorine theory was a genuine 'theory' involved in the debate, not simply a construct in hindsight. The antithesis could be expressed:

chemical reactions of chlorine-containing substances are not a significant causative factor in the anomalous ozone depletion in the Antarctic spring.

The early protagonists of the circulation theory were saying quite explicitly that chlorine chemistry did not need to be invoked to explain the

Antarctic ozone depletion. The whole effect could, they believed, be explained in terms of air circulation alone. This represented both an appeal to Ockham's Razor,[4] and a commitment to the antithesis of the chlorine theory.

Consider, for example, the following statements taken from Stolarski and Schoeberl (1986):

> These observations suggest that the variations within the spring season in south polar total ozone are governed by dynamical redistribution rather than chemical processes.
>
> We find that there is very strong circumstantial evidence that during any one year the September decrease in total ozone at high latitudes is due to a dynamical redistribution of ozone rather than a chemical loss.
>
> Our results suggest that no new chemistry or chemical processes are required to explain the intra-seasonal decline in total ozone at South Pole.
>
> The recent observations of a significant decrease in Antarctic total ozone during the spring months should be examined in light of both photochemical and climatological constraints before any unusual and speculative chemistry is introduced into the problem.

Their eventual abandonment of their position was as much a result of the dramatic refutation of the antithesis of the chlorine theory, as of the bearing on their own theory of the evidence collected.

The form of the argument can be applied to the ozone hole investigation in the following way:

- Theory: Chlorine chemistry is causally involved in ozone depletion in the Antarctic stratosphere.
- Antithesis: Chlorine chemistry is not causally involved in ozone depletion in the Antarctic stratosphere.
- Hypotheses auxiliary to the antithesis in interpreting the observation:

  (i) It is not possible that ozone depletion itself could cause a chlorine monoxide enhancement that temporally precedes it.

  (ii) It is not possible that any factor that could simultaneously deplete ozone and enhance chlorine monoxide would not involve reactions of chlorine-containing compounds.

  (iii) The instrumental readings of the observations reliably and accurately indicate mixing ratios of chemical substances via the analysis procedures adopted.

- Falsifiable entailment of the antithesis:

  Greatly enhanced chlorine monoxide levels (or indeed, large anomalies in the mixing ratios of any chlorine-containing substance) ought not to be observed in close correlation with Antarctic ozone depletion.

The falsifiable consequence of the antithesis can then be seen as constituting genuine confirmation of the theory. The confirmation is direct; it is quite different to the notion of 'confirmation only by failure to falsify'.

The symmetry is restored – direct confirmation works in a way quite unforeseen by Popper, and it works in exactly the same way, and to exactly the same extent, that direct falsification does!

For any theory, there is an antithesis. Falsification of the theory is logically equivalent to direct confirmation of the antithesis, and vice versa.

If the theory has the form of a generalisation, then its antithesis will have the form of a particularisation. But some theories may themselves be particularisations, and have generalisations for antitheses, while many theories are neither generalisations nor particularisations. Usually, generalisations are falsifiable but not capable of direct confirmation, while the sort of particularisations that arise as their antitheses are confirmable, but not directly falsifiable. Popper has considered such particularisations, qua existential statements, recognises that they form a part of the scientific corpus, but regards them as beyond the pale in his discussion of empirical science. I will not examine here his arguments for so doing. But if a theory has a form which is neither generalisation nor particularisation, then it may be capable of either confirmation or falsification in the direct sense, as may its antithesis. This possibility does not seem to have received specific attention.

Confirmation by falsification of the antithesis has a very characteristic property. The confirming result need not be manifest as a direct consequence of the theory. It is not a 'prediction' in the sense that 'if this theory holds, then X ought to be observed'. Rather, it has the form 'It is just not possible that X could be observed unless this theory holds'. It is not difficult to devise a possible scheme for chlorine-mediated ozone depletion that would not entail an increase in observed chlorine monoxide levels. But it is impossible that such a strikingly enhanced chlorine monoxide concentration would be observed in correlation with ozone depletion unless chemical reactions involving chlorine compounds were a significant part of the ozone removal process.

In real science, direct confirmation of theory can play a genuine role, just as falsification can. This is particularly the case in the early stages of investigation of a problem arising from a new phenomenon.

Popper seems to have seen very clearly the logical status of the possibilities of confirmation or refutation for different types of statements. But he does not seem to have seen that 'All As are B' is much too restrictive a model for the types of statement that might be involved in a scientific theory. Even respectable and genuinely empirically based theories are much too diverse to be captured in this way.

A dialogue of objections[5]

Your characterisation of the situation sounds convincing, but it is surely only one of several possible characterisations. In particular, the thesis of the chlorine theory, or any of the other theories, can easily be incorporated into the form, 'All As are X', and a conventional Popperian analysis would work out just as well.

My claim in the previous section is that a scientific theory like the chlorine theory – 'anomalous Antarctic ozone depletion is caused by reactions of chlorine-containing molecules' – has a form which cannot be reduced to 'All As are X'. But you are now saying that it can be cast in this form. How do you get from 'C is the efficient cause of E' to 'All As are X'?

That is fairly straightforward: 'E is caused by C' must mean either 'E is <u>always</u> caused by C', or 'E is <u>sometimes</u> caused by C'. A Popperian analysis then comes very simply. In the first case, a simple re-wording achieves the desired form of generalisation 'All observations of effect E are occasioned by cause C'. In the second case, the statement is an existential statement, and cannot be regarded as a mature scientific theory. Until further investigation is undertaken which leads to 'E is <u>always</u> caused by C when conditions P, Q, and R apply', there is not a complete scientific theory on the table for evaluation.

This question gets to the very centre of the point I am making. I think that this type of model restricts the notion of a scientific theory in an inappropriate way. It misses much of the meaning and flavour of what a scientist is saying when proposing a theory which attributes efficient cause in this type of complicated system. The attribution of cause is neither an 'always' nor a 'sometimes', but a 'normally'. Scientific attribution of cause, once one gets away from the very simplest systems, is *ceteris paribus* – other things being equal.

It is certainly true that in this case the rival theories were not 'mature'. But they were not the sort of theories that were ever intended to mature in quite the sense intended by Popper. No-one expected the final form of the theory to include an 'always'.

Jonathan Shanklin brought out this very point when I talked to him in 1996 about the Antarctic investigation, his role in it, and his view of its conclusions. The claim that the Antarctic ozone hole was caused by anthropogenic chlorine compounds was not, he maintained, a claim that this was the only possible cause of such a phenomenon. It was quite conceivable that anomalous ozone depletion might also be caused in some other way, like an unusually large volcanic eruption in the region, or a close encounter with a passing planetoid. But the theory was never intended to cover eventualities like these. Rather, the claim was that this is what had caused the depletion over the last eighteen spring seasons, and was likely to cause a springtime depletion for many years to come.

If this is the type of claim that is being made in a statement of a scientific theory, then it can readily be seen that a Popperian search for a counter-example is entirely inappropriate and irrelevant – a counter-example simply does not falsify! If, on one occasion, a huge volcanic eruption led to a major loss of ozone in the Antarctic region, it really would have very little to do with the substance of the actual chlorine theory. But it would constitute a perfect falsification of the artificially constructed Popperian model theory, "On all occasions of major ozone depletion, chlorine chemistry is the efficient cause".

As a result, any attempt to cast such a theory in a Popperian mode in this way would lead to a statement with a lengthy (infinitely lengthy?) string of seemingly *ad hoc* caveats, which would become increasingly bizarre as the list extended:

Anomalous Antarctic ozone depletion is always caused by reactions of chlorine-containing molecules, unless an unusual factor is present, such as a huge volcanic eruption, a close encounter with a passing planetoid, a visit by ozone-eating aliens to the region, . . .
and so on.

Now there is a consensus among scientists that the anomalous depletion is accounted for by the type of mechanism envisaged in the chlorine theories. Most of the fine detail of mechanism has been filled in. The status of the accepted theory matches the Popperian model to only a very limited extent. Certainly its acceptance is provisional. But ongoing work is aimed at refining understanding of the details of mechanism. There is no interest in searching for counter-instances to the contention that 'anomalous Antarctic ozone depletion is *always* caused by reactions of chlorine-containing molecules'. A counter-instance would not be seen as falsifying if it were associated with any other unusual circumstance whatever.

You state quite clearly and forthrightly that the Eltanin-19 type profile of magnetism in the Atlantic was not an entailment of the continental drift theory. But about the main example you are using you are much more ambivalent, perhaps even inconsistent. Was a large increase in ClO in association with ozone loss an entailment of the chlorine theory?

A large increase in ClO mixing ratios was clearly and explicitly mentioned in two of the articles where possible chlorine-based mechanisms were discussed, as well as in the planning documents for the AAOE. The context was that a mechanism of the type being discussed could only reproduce the observed phenomena if the ClO mixing ratio reached a certain level. This is quite a different thing to the mechanism accounting for an increased level of ClO. Increased ClO is an entailment of the sort of mechanism proposed by Solomon's or McElroy's groups, but only in the same sense that a hole in the victim's mosquito net is an entailment of the theory that malaria is caused by a mosquito-borne virus.

Looking more broadly and generally at the chlorine theories, it is clear that increased ClO mixing ratios were a direct consequence of most of the variant mechanisms that were under serious consideration. Mechanisms that would not have involved ClO increases – most notably the mechanism originally proposed by Farman *et al.* – had been shown to be flawed, or to be incapable of fitting the rapid onset of the phenomenon. But chlorine-mediated ozone depletion that did not involve increased ClO mixing ratios remained a theoretical and logical possibility, if not a practical one.

Is it fair to say that the crucial result of the AAOE did not match a clear prediction of the chlorine theory? After all, a prediction does not have to be something very precise like

(1) ClO levels rise by 157 per cent.

There are several progressively weaker forms of predictive statement, like

(2) ClO levels 'rise substantially'.

(3) ClO levels 'change significantly'.

(4) 'Some Cl species' to 'change significantly'.

Surely, even in a preliminary form, the chlorine theory must make an assertion at least of (4)!

Surprisingly, this is not the case. The reason is quite complicated. There are two quite separate strings to it:

(1) If a theory is sufficiently ill-formulated to admit either of two diametrically opposite consequences, then it has no genuine consequence of that type.

(2) Systems of coupled chemical reactions in general, and chain reaction systems in particular, have strange properties. It is quite possible, and not at all uncommon, for reaction conditions to change in such a way as to increase rate of formation of a particular product without any discernible effect on the concentration of the chain carrier species directly involved in the reaction step that leads to the product.

I should also re-iterate that in one sense, both Solomon's and McElroy's articles had made a prediction at level 2 of your question – that ClO levels would have to rise substantially in association with ozone loss.

Would you explain your first point? We are talking here about a theory that is saying that chlorine chemistry is involved in a phenomenon. But we are (at this stage) not sure of the detailed mechanism. Suppose that with one possible mechanism a crucial concentration will show an increase; with another, a decrease. In either event the crucial concentration will show a <u>change</u>. It seems to me that such a theory is saying:

Either C1 or C2
If C1 then P
If C2 then P,

and the consequence is surely P.

This argument is sound in itself, but overlooks one possibility. If a theory allows for two different mechanisms, it would also normally allow for both to operate in concert. If mechanism **M1** leads to a decrease in the crucial concentration, and mechanism **M2** leads to an increase, then it is likely that a combination exists that will leave the concentration unchanged. Certainly for additive mixing it can be simply shown that such a combination exists, and the corresponding weightings of the two mechanisms can be readily calculated. The consequences of two mechanisms operating in concert are not necessarily simply additive. But some combination will exist, in most cases, such that the increase occasioned by the one mechanism will be exactly balanced by the decrease occasioned by the other.

Perhaps so, but is not this idea of the theory admitting of different mechanisms, and separate mechanisms operating in concert a rather artificial one? And would not the particular weighting that leads to no change in the crucial concentration be an enormous coincidence?

To deal with the second question first: yes, it would be a coincidence. But we are talking here of an alleged predictive entailment of a theory, and such a statement should be a matter of necessity. Coincidence is no excuse. Moreover, the coincidence would not be as great as it might seem, because we are not talking about a single fixed value as being the 'normal concentration' of the crucial substance. Trace constituents of the atmosphere can vary enormously in concentration from day to day and from place to place – the range would typically span a factor of 2, and for some minor constituents it would be much greater. The crucial changes in ClO concentration measured in the AAOE were much greater – a factor of 100 or so.

To see the importance of the idea of a theory allowing for different mechanisms, and the possibility of different mechanisms operating in concert, we will examine the nature of the chlorine theory immediately prior to the AAOE.

The chlorine theory was never a single theory, but rather a family of theories. Roughly paraphrased, they agreed on the following points:

• the Antarctic phenomenon is caused by a build-up of chlorine compounds in the stratosphere. This explains its recent onset.
• the Antarctic phenomenon is predicted by none of the computer models incorporating normal understandings of stratospheric chlorine chemistry and circulation.

- there must therefore be some additional reaction or reactions involving chlorine-containing species that have been overlooked in the computer modelling. These must take on a special significance in the special conditions pertaining to the Antarctic springtime stratosphere.

They then proceeded to differ in their suggestions for the particular chlorine reaction or reactions that might be most influential, and that should be considered for further investigation.

In general, there was no real commitment to a particular reaction or reactions as the crucial part of the mechanism. (If for no other reason, there was the very real risk of snatching defeat from the jaws of victory!). The tentative tone in which particular detailed mechanisms were proposed in the several articles contrasts remarkably with the very forthright tone of the rest of the debate between the protagonists of the rival theories. Other similar theories were seen as allies rather than rivals, because (i) they directed attention to the same general area, and (ii) they were usually not mutually exclusive. If mechanism a and mechanism b were both realistic possibilities, then there is nothing wrong with a reaction scheme incorporating both a and b.

Turning to your claim about the properties of coupled chemical reactions, can you provide an illustration that makes this point fairly, clearly and simply?

Of the proposed schemes, Farman's mechanism is one that has only very minor consequences for concentrations of ClO and other chlorine-containing species. But the illustration can be made most clearly with a fanciful artificial example.[6] The mechanism of a radical chain reaction usually involves at least four steps. In the first, or initiation step, reactive free radicals are formed from a less reactive species. The second and third steps are propagation steps. Firstly, a free radical A reacts to produce a product and a different free radical B. Then B reacts to form a product, which may be the same or a different one, and regenerate A. Finally, there must be a termination step in which reactive free radicals are removed from the system by formation of some more stable product.

Suppose then, that in the normal stratosphere, the following mechanism accounts for ozone removal (NB this mechanism does not actually account for stratospheric ozone depletion – it is artificial, inaccurate, and over-simplified):

$ClONO_2 + light \rightarrow ClO + NO_2$	Reaction [1]	Initiation step
$ClO + NO \rightarrow Cl + NO_2$	Reaction [2]	$\Big\{$ Propagation
$Cl + O_3 \rightarrow ClO + O_2$	Reaction [3]	steps
$ClO + NO_2 \rightarrow ClONO_2$	Reaction [4]	Termination step

Now suppose that in the Antarctic, in the presence of ice clouds, reaction [2] shuts down because all of the oxides of nitrogen are taken up into the ice, and NO concentrations have fallen drastically. However, it just happens that a different reaction can take its place. This reaction cannot occur in the gas phase, since it is catalysed by the surface of ice crystals.

$ClO + O_3 \rightarrow$ (ice catalyzed) $Cl + 2 O_2$ Reaction [5]   1st propagation step.

It also just happens, to make the analysis simple, that the rate of this reaction [5] in the ambient polar conditions is equal to the rate of reaction [2] in the normal stratosphere, and that the rate of each of the other reactions remains the same. In that case, the reaction system is completely unchanged as far as every chlorine-containing species is concerned, and so there will be no changes in the concentration of any of these species. But now, there are two molecules of ozone being removed from the system for each cycle of the two propagation steps, instead of only one. It is clear that:

• Ozone depletion has increased significantly – doubled, in fact.
• Ozone depletion is being directly caused by chlorine chemistry.
• No chlorine-containing species has changed its concentration.

It is found more generally with radical chain mechanisms that steady state concentrations of the chain carriers are often very insensitive to changes in concentrations or reaction rates. In particular, for the simple four-step reaction mechanism, concentrations of the chain carriers – ClO and Cl in this case – depend only on the substance concentrations and rate constants involved in initiation and termination. The two propagation steps have little or no influence. If the two propagation steps increase their rates in proportion, neither chain carrier is much affected, even though both are involved. Even if changes in the propagation steps are out of proportion, the sum of concentrations of the two chain carriers remains the same. For schemes relating to stratospheric ozone, ClO is always much more abundant than Cl. So the sum of chain carrier concentrations is effectively the ClO concentration for any simple scheme where there are the only two chain carriers. The only circumstances in which a significant change to ClO levels will occur is if there is a major change in an initiation or termination reaction. Linking of other carriers into the chain will also cause changes, but relatively smaller ones.

Farman's chlorine theory model is a case of the type where only propagation steps are affected, though NOx chain carriers are linked into the scheme. Changes in ClO levels predicted by this model are small, and of uncertain sign. McElroy's crucial reaction involves linking some bromine-containing radicals into the reaction scheme. But in this case, extra initiation and termination steps are also considered, and so a significant ClO increase is indicated.

I think that I can see the point. But I am not a chemist, and not used to working with these reaction mechanisms. Is there any sort of analogy to something more familiar that might make it easier to understand?

I also have difficulty with this sort of thing. Let us try to build up an analogy that works.

Clarissa (chlorine) is a criminal well-known to the police (scientists). They suspect her involvement in some of the financial transactions associated with a new drug-smuggling operation (ozone depletion). They try to collect evidence against her by monitoring the daily balances (concentrations) in her various bank accounts (chlorine compounds). But what can they reasonably expect to find? There are a number of theories. Most expect to find the balances in at least a few of the accounts increasing, because she is presumably in the action expecting to make a significant profit. But a few point out that the balances might also be decreasing, because she is probably buying into a share of the new operation. Now the equivalent of my first objection is that in this situation, it is equally a possibility that she is both enjoying a profit and building up an investment, and that it would not be a silly move to simply balance the investment against the profit by putting just the profit – no more and no less – back into the business. In this case, the account balances would show no change. The equivalent of my second point is that Clarissa's bank accounts are almost certainly not the final resting-place of any profits that might be being made, but simply a conduit. Because the police can only collect the daily balances of the accounts, but not monitor individual transactions, the enormously increased flow of money through the accounts cannot be directly observed. And an increased throughput will probably have little or no effect on the daily balances (it is supposed that her account activity is at the level of numerous transactions per day).

Looking at the overall picture, there can be no prediction of a necessary increase, nor of a necessary decrease, nor even of a significant change in the daily balances of any of Clarissa's accounts. Nevertheless, if a series of major changes were to occur in one or more accounts, and if the dates were found to correlate with the shipment dates known to the police from other aspects of their investigation, it might constitute significant circumstantial evidence of Clarissa's involvement.

With regard to the circulation theory, it seems to me as though you are describing a simple and straightforward case of Popperian falsification. If the theory says that the air ought to be moving upwards, and the AAOE finds air moving downwards, there ought to be an open and shut case.

The essence of the circulation theory is a claim that (1) there was an important change in Antarctic circulation patterns around 1976, and (2) the current circulation pattern is such that ozone-poor tropospheric air is carried aloft into the Antarctic stratosphere in early spring, displacing the ozone-bearing stratospheric air away from the pole to lower latitudes.

What evidence was collected in the AAOE that relates directly to the circulation theory? The planes were fitted with instruments which measured wind speed and direction, including vertical components. But the analysis of these is not as simple as measuring whether the vertical wind direction is upward or downward at various places. Winds are variable from time to time, and local wind directions are affected by many things, including surface topography. All of the data were collected on a dozen flights. All were collected on paths more or less along the meridian of Punta Arenas. They are hardly enough to give a global picture of what is occurring in the Antarctic.

There was also a major bias built into the flight data on atmospheric circulation. The ER-2 aeroplane had very stringent take-off and landing requirements. The twelve days out of forty on which data were collected therefore corresponded to the only twelve days with particularly fine and still conditions at Punta Arenas. It would not be unreasonable to presume that this might correlate with special, and probably atypical, weather conditions further South!

The collected data could nevertheless be compared with predictions from computer models of Antarctic circulation into which the proposed upwelling had been incorporated. If the result of this comparison is a poor match – as it was – it can be taken as disappointing, or even discouraging. But the problem could be with other details of the computer model, and it may well be that a bit of 'tuning up' of these other details could provide a good fit. It would not be seen as sufficient grounds for rejection of the theory incorporating upwelling in the polar regions.

Surprisingly, the strongest indication that the upwelling was not taking place was chemical evidence from trace gases (Loewenstein *et al.*, 1989). Extremely low nitrous oxide levels indicated that polar stratospheric air measured at 15 to 20 km altitude had recently descended from above 30 km altitude. And any suggestion that the nitrous oxide was being affected by the local anomalous chemistry, and that perhaps it could not be trusted as a height marker in the usual way, was ruled out by similar results for two other trace gases.

It is quite clear that the trace gas analyses from the AAOE provided firm evidence of descent of the air in the polar vortex. It could therefore be seen as a direct falsification of that theory. But in spite of this direct falsification, the general abandonment of the theory seems to have arisen mainly out of the positive evidence for the chlorine theory.

Sharon Roan (1989, p. 219) refers to a working conference after the AAOE, where the main protagonists of the circulation theory

... tried to salvage what they could of their arguments. But, one by one, the theories were dismissed. The evidence for chlorine was overwhelming. And even the chemists were stunned by Anderson's data.

As you have said, Popper's notion of a scientific theory is restricted to an empirical generalisation. But the sort of theories you are talking about involve the attribution of cause. This is a very different idea of what a theory is. And yet you are trying to use what is still basically a Popperian framework for the discussion. Would it not be more appropriate to be talking about 'theory selection' rather than 'falsification and confirmation', and to be using an approach more like that of Mill, who was thinking of scientific theories as attribution of cause?

Mill's framework does seem to fit the case I have outlined very well. His position is that if phenomena A and B are strongly correlated, then there is some sort of causal connection between them: either one is the cause of the other, or both are different effects of a common cause (Mill, Ch. 8, 5th canon). The rival theories in the case of the Antarctic ozone hole were indeed different attributions of cause, and the crucial observation was a correlation which linked in one of the theories, but not the others.

But my purpose was to highlight the narrowness of the Popperian view of scientific theory adoption and rejection, and why a broader view is needed. This is best done from within a quasi-Popperian viewpoint. Otherwise the point is not effectively made. Popper was, after all, familiar with Mill's writing, and that did not deter him from developing his own approach.

There are also problems with applying Mill's system to the Antarctic ozone case. Strong correlations can also be found between Antarctic ozone levels and such surface phenomena as surface sea temperature, and areas of Antarctic sea-ice.[7] On a cursory examination, though not on deeper analysis, such correlations appear to point to a circulation theory rather than a chemical theory of the Antarctic phenomenon.[8] One underlying problem for Mill's system is that the causal connection that he sees implied in a strong correlation need not be a proximate one; there may be a very long and complicated chain of causality involved.

There is a real problem with your antithesis proposition. The example out of which it has come to you is both highly technical, and not particularly clear-cut in some of its aspects. Perhaps it would be easier to see how your logical scheme works, and why Popper's is inadequate, if you could come up with some everyday, non-technical example.

Well that should be possible, though it is not particularly easy on the spur of the moment ... [long pause] ... Perhaps I could come up with a detective story example.

There was once a man who died after two or three days of agonising suffering. The reason was not obvious, and all medical treatment had failed. At the inquest it was discovered that he had been poisoned by a very rare alkaloid – there was no previous case of poisoning by this substance in the local records. The circumstances were regarded as suspicious, and the detectives were called in.

After some brilliant preliminary work, the detectives came up with two theories of where the poisoning might have taken place – the questions of how, and by whom, were left until a later stage. The first theory was that the poison had been administered at his home. The second was that it had been administered a few nights earlier, when he had dined with his sister and brother-in-law, who lived a considerable distance away.

The investigation was at an impasse until a surprising new piece of evidence emerged. It turned out that his sister's pet cat had died a similar agonising death at about the same time. Following exhumation, traces of the same alkaloid were found in the cat's remains. The detectives promptly abandoned the first theory, and worked on the second! To forestall a number of other twists and objections, it should be pointed out that the detectives ascertained there had been no other contact between members of the two households for some months previously.

How is this case to be seen in Popperian terms? The new evidence has in no way falsified the theory that the poison had been administered at the victim's home. Nor in any sense does a bold prediction that the family cat will die arise out of the theory that the poison had been administered at the sister's house.

But in terms of the model I am proposing, everything falls into place. The theory that the poison had been administered at the sister's house has an antithesis: 'the poison had been administered somewhere other than at the sister's house'. With the help of auxiliary hypotheses that 'two cases of poisoning at the same time by a substance previously unknown in the district are not unconnected', and that 'the cat was not deliberately poisoned to mislead', we can take the death of the cat as strong positive evidence for the theory, or as a falsification of its antithesis. Same container of poison, same time, precludes different place. Notice that the evidence calls for refinement of the theory. There are still unsolved questions of mechanism to be worked out. Why did the cat die? Was the poisoner experimenting on the cat? Did the cat manage to eat some scraps of the food in which the poison was administered?

All right, I can see what you are getting at there. And in most ways it does seem to be a very good analogy for your characterisation of the ozone hole story. But it also seems to bring out the weight of one of my previous objections. If you are going to frame your auxiliary hypotheses in such a way that you can say

'Same container of poison, same time, precludes different place', then you will have to admit, on the same grounds, that the new evidence constitutes a falsification, indeed, a Popperian falsification of the first theory.

Yes, that is a slightly unfortunate feature of the example I chose. In this case, the two theories are clearly mutually exclusive. That was not the case with the various theories of ozone depletion – there was no *logical* reason why upwelling from the troposphere and perturbed chlorine chemistry should not both contribute to ozone depletion. The practical objection to this possibility was only the Ockham's razor argument. In the absence of explicit evidence, why propose the conjunction of two mechanisms to account for a phenomenon when either mechanism had the potential to account for it on its own?

Nevertheless, I must concede that in this case the new evidence does, in a convoluted way, constitute a Popperian falsification of the rejected theory. But it only does so as a side effect. Its primary effect is direct confirmation of the favoured theory. Moreover, the Popperian story encourages us to focus on the theory to be falsified, and to collect evidence relating to its predictions and possible shortcomings. If that had been done in this case, then a strenuous attempt to falsify the theory that the poisoning was done at the man's own house would never have uncovered the crucial evidence. The death of a family pet many miles away is hardly a police matter, and would simply never have come to their notice had they not been actively considering the alternative theory involving that household. The crucial evidence would in any case be placed in the 'sister's house' section of the case file.

I consider that this particular effect is one of the great weaknesses of the Popperian model of scientific investigation. In the ozone hole investigation, and probably in many other cases, the approach of conducting research primarily by trying to find falsifications of the best available theories would lead to overlooking vital evidence that would point in another direction: evidence that would only be uncovered if the appropriate alternatives were being strenuously and directly investigated.

Your story of the Antarctic ozone investigation brought to my mind not Popper's model of how scientific theories are proposed and then rejected by falsification, but rather some recent articles on 'Arched Hypotheses' (Thomason, 1994). How do you think your idea of 'Falsification of the Antithesis' is related to the notion of 'Arched Hypotheses'?

There is certainly a close family resemblance that may even amount to some sort of logical equivalence. But there are also differences in the flavour of the two approaches. Falsification of the Antithesis, for example, seems to relate to absolute approaches to confirmation and falsification, whereas Arched Hypotheses sits more comfortably with a probabilistic or

Bayesian Approach – the idea is that, in terms of scientific explanations, the conjunction of two improbables is not necessarily improbable. Because of that, I think there will be individual case studies where one rather than the other seems to fit the picture.

One story where the Arched Hypotheses has been applied concerns a simplified view of an aspect of Galileo's advocacy of the Copernican system. The balance of evidence was against the Copernican theory, and also against the reliability of the newly-invented telescope for celestial observations. But celestial observations with the telescope matched certain detailed predictions of the Copernican theory.

Does this story sit comfortably with the Falsification of the Antithesis approach? Consider the situation from the standpoint of the Copernican theory – a new theory facing a considerable struggle because the older established theory seems in many ways to be performing better. There is no prediction that telescopic observations will provide a particular series of planetary sizes or brightnesses, even though these sizes and brightnesses are the consequence of the Copernican theory for an ideal terrestrial observer. The notorious unreliability of celestial telescopic observations precludes that. But when the telescope produces precisely those observations that correspond to what the theory predicts for an ideal terrestrial observer, there is a strong confirmation of the Copernican theory. The contention that the Copernican theory *does not apply* has been falsified, because this antithesis predicts that no observer, reliable or otherwise, should produce precisely the ideal Copernican set of results. That is, although the telescopic observations obtained were not a prediction, or even a likely consequence of the Copernican theory, it is most implausible that they could be obtained if the Copernican theory did not apply. The antithesis of the Copernican theory is effectively falsified by the observations, even though those observations might not be particularly reliable.

To re-iterate the point, if the Copernican theory is true, then it is by no means certain, or even likely, that the telescope will reveal the observed phenomena. But if the Copernican theory is false, it is quite inconceivable that that particular set of phenomena would be revealed by the telescope.

So the Falsification of the Antithesis approach does fit this sort of case, but admittedly not as naturally as the Arched Hypotheses approach.

What about turning the consideration inside out. Does the Arched Hypotheses approach provide a description – perhaps even a superior description – of your story of the ozone hole investigation?

Well in this case we have to find two unlikely hypotheses. In the case of sixteenth-century astronomy, one of these was internal to the 'theory' and the other was more or less external to it – more to do with interpretation of the observations. An exact parallel with this case would have us formulate our argument in terms of the chlorine theory being somehow *a priori* less plausible than the circulation theory, and the link between ozone depletion and chlorine monoxide enhancement also being somehow unlikely. But this simply will not work. Although chlorine monoxide enhancement is not a necessary consequence of the chlorine theory, it is clearly a likely one. And although the chlorine theory was having its difficulties as a suggested explanation for the ozone depletion phenomenon, it was faring no worse in this regard than either of its main rivals. In the case of the ozone hole investigation there does not seem to be an unlikely aspect external to the theory itself.

To achieve a description in terms of Arched Hypotheses, it would seem that both of the unlikely hypotheses would have to come from somewhere inside the chlorine theory. This, perhaps, we can do. It could be seen as unlikely that anthropogenic chlorine compounds could be causing a major ozone depletion in the Antarctic stratosphere. After all, years of extensive investigation had shown that they produce only a minor effect, barely measurable, in the rest of the stratosphere. The Antarctic is the region most remote from the sources of anthropogenic chlorine. It is also the region least exposed to intense ultraviolet light, which was theoretically seen as a necessary co-requisite with chlorine compounds for effective ozone depletion. So if we take this as our first unlikely hypothesis, then a second could be to do with the unknown detailed mechanism. It could be an unlikely hypothesis that a special chemical mechanism involving reactions that had never been included in the previous extensive and highly successful modelling of stratospheric chlorine/ozone chemistry was somehow becoming prominent in special conditions that obtained in the Antarctic springtime.

But if we try to obtain an Arched Hypotheses model on this sort of basis, we have something very different from the other case. Before we do a single experiment or make a single observation, we need to put these two unlikely hypotheses together to have even the chance of an explanation. Quite clearly a chlorine theory must consist in an overall hypothesis that embraces both of these as a 'package deal'.

Overall, I think I would have to concede that there would be a way of stringing together a story of the Antarctic ozone investigation that could fit in with the Arched Hypotheses model, but that in this case it seems a less natural model than my approach of Falsification of the Antithesis.

Can you see any better or more natural way of telling this story in the framework of Arched Hypotheses?

No, I cannot. But I do not think you need to worry about the two unlikely hypotheses fitting together as a package deal. Surely the whole idea of the Arch is that both arms must stand or fall together.

There is some truth in that. But in this case the arms stand so closely and necessarily together that it is difficult to consider one without the other – they seem more like the top and bottom halves of a pillar. The top half of the pillar – exotic chemical mechanisms – does not even arise unless the bottom half of the pillar – anthropogenic chlorine compounds exercising a surprising large influence in the affairs of the Antarctic stratosphere – is in place. To be effective, the arms of an Arch must stand apart!

But let us get this into some sort of structure. Can you demonstrate more simply the nature of your "falsification of the antithesis" argument. How might it give the same logical result or a different one to 'Arched Hypotheses' – or to Popper, for that matter?

I will deal with Popper first. For that purpose I need to re-iterate the logical structure of my argument. It is a very simple one, and I can claim no great originality for the logic.

If a proposition admits falsification but not confirmation, then its complement will admit confirmation but not falsification. Popper's original claim is, in essence, that any 'scientific theory' is represented by a proposition that will admit falsification but not confirmation. My argument is simply that he is taking much too narrow a view of what is meant by a scientific theory. My anti-proton story is intended to show how the complement of a scientific theory may itself be what would usually be considered a scientific theory – this case Popper considers, and explicitly denies. I go further to say that many scientific theories are in fact best represented as propositions that may admit either falsification or confirmation, and that there is no asymmetry. Popper (1954, ¶ 15, p. 70) explicitly agrees that there is no asymmetry *among propositions,* but takes a very restrictive view of what sort of propositions may represent a scientific theory. My disagreement with him is about representation, not about logic.

Popper's position is that an experimental or observational result cannot entail the proposition that represents a theory, but that it can be mutually incompatible with the proposition. That is the same thing as entailing its complement. My contention is that the antithesis of a scientific theory may also be a scientific theory, and that these two theories are represented by complementary propositions. If a result is mutually incompatible with a theory, then it entails its antithesis, and vice versa. In this way a theory may be subject to direct confirmation instead of, or as well as falsification.

In the case of 'Arched Hypotheses' we have to come to grips with Bayesian statistics; it is an argument about the value of evidence in probabilistic terms. The situation described by the model involves a theory which consists in the conjunction of two unlikely independent hypotheses.

It is shown that a piece of evidence can be strongly confirmatory of the conjunction (in Bayesian terms), without being a confirmation of either unlikely hypothesis standing alone.

The only real difference is that in the Bayesian Approach a finite but very small subjective probability is allowed for every possibility that is not completely excluded by logical requirements. I have taken the more simple-minded approach of assuming that falsification by evidence may be treated as absolute.

NOTES

1 The atmospheric lifetime of N_2O is apparently very difficult to determine (Warneck, 1988, pp. 442–52). Values from the late 1970s and early 1980s range from four to 100 years, with Warneck eventually suggesting a figure around thirty years, and considerable reservation. The more recent 1994 WMO Report suggests a value around 120 years (WMO, 1994, p. 13.6).

2 At one stage, I was trying to argue that there had not been an effective falsification of the circulation theories, or at least that the falsification had not been particularly influential. One of the leading scientists involved argued strongly that there had been a proper falsification, and that that was the important factor. In summing up his case he wrote that 'the trace gas results did effectively falsify the circulation theories, *and the chlorine monoxide result was the clincher*'. (My emphasis – a Freudian slip?)

3 David Hume, eighteenth-century Scottish philosopher, stressed the problem of induction. The fact that a generalised proposition has never produced counter-examples, gives us no rational warrant to assume that it will not do so in future.

4 Ockham's Razor is the name given to an ontological principle attributed to William of Occam, a fourteenth-century philosopher. The principle is that an ontology should strive for an economy of entities. A system incorporating fewer types of entity is to be preferred over one that unnecessarily introduces more types of entity. In modern usage, it is frequently (and perhaps loosely) extended to the closely related epistemological principle that if two explanations are equally in accord with the available evidence, the simpler is to be preferred.

5 This dialogue takes place between the author and an anonymous critic. The critic is actually a composite of questions raised by Konrad Talmont-Kaminsky, Neil Thomason, John Christie, and Brian Ellis, with some of my own doubts and misgivings.

6 I am indebted to John Christie for producing this scheme, and for much of the analysis of chemical kinetics in this section more generally.

7 Austin, J., Jones, R.L., Palmer, T.N., & Tuck, A.F. 'Circulation Changes and Chemistry: Implications for the Destruction of Ozone in Antarctica'. Unpublished paper, 1987. The Abstract reads, in part:

Interannual changes in Southern Hemisphere sea surface temperature show a high degree of anti-correlation with October mean total ozone from Halley Bay over the period 1960–85. Similarly, the area of sea ice surrounding Antarctica in late winter/spring is highly correlated with the area of the 'ozone hole' in October, 1979–85. Also there is evidence of an equatorial shift of the circumpolar tropospheric westerlies over the period 1976–85. These changes in tropospheric circulation form a coherent pattern, and are qualitatively reproduced by a general circulation model under an imposed SST [i.e. sea surface temperature] perturbation.

Adrian Tuck (private communication) refers to this paper in these terms:

Despite the fact that both referees liked it, *Nature* rejected it on grounds of length. By the time I got it back from *Nature*, I had seen the first results from Punta Arenas, and it wouldn't have looked right to modify it from there. We were right about downwelling and chemistry! The SST, sea ice, angular momentum, and TOMS correlations have never been published.

It seems somehow inappropriate that the evidence contained in this paper has never been put before the scientific jury!

8 The surface phenomena are, in the paper, linked with the conditions for production and persistence of polar stratospheric clouds, and thus to a chemical rather than a circulation model for polar ozone depletion.

12 Branches and sub-branches of science: problems at disciplinary boundaries

Science has expanded enormously over the last century and a half. This applies both to the volume of its subject-matter, and the number of practitioners who would regard themselves as scientists. Science has expanded less by broadening the areas of experience that it addresses, than by uncovering and exploring ever finer detail, and proliferating new phenomena within the general scope of its traditional subject matter.[1] As an almost inevitable result, the working scientist has defined an area of research expertise in ever narrower terms. The chemist of today still has a basic training in the whole of chemistry, and a disciplinary orientation in one of perhaps three to six major subdivisions of the subject (organic chemistry, physical chemistry, etc.). But a claim to familiarity with the frontiers of human knowledge, and/or research expertise, would only extend to one specialised area (or possibly two or three) of perhaps thirty to 100 that would encompass the subject of chemistry.

Right from the outset, unravelling the science of stratospheric ozone was a problem that overlapped several boundaries between traditional disciplines. The Chapman model described ozone formation and removal in terms of the type of mechanism and approach that arises in the chemical sub-discipline of gas kinetics. The correlation of column ozone values with surface weather conditions clearly required a direct tie-in with air circulation and meteorology. And the fact that ozone levels were influenced to some extent by solar activity indicated some role also for solar physics and/or upper atmosphere physics. In this case, the interaction between scientists from different backgrounds was a particularly interesting one. There had previously been little or no interaction between chemistry and meteorology. Until recently, very few chemists would have had any training at all in meteorology. Even many of the atmospheric chemists had little or no meteorology background. Again, until recently, most meteorologists had little or no training in chemistry. Typically they were trained in physics, geophysics, or applied mathematics, and may have studied chemistry to first year university level, if at all.[2]

In 1962, Kuhn put forward his well-known 'incommensurability thesis', which related to communication problems between different groups of scientists. He was actually addressing alternative and rival theoretical formulations of a single problem, which might more usually mean a failure of communication by different camps within a single discipline area. But his arguments applied equally to problems at discipline boundaries. There would inevitably be differences that had crept into the connotations and finer shades of meaning denoted by the technical terms as used by the different groups. In his later revision of this work, Kuhn complained that his own meaning had been widely misinterpreted:

A number of them [philosophers], however, have reported that I believe the following: the proponents of incommensurable theories cannot communicate with each other at all; as a result, in a debate over theory-choice there can be no recourse to good reasons; instead theory must be chosen for reasons that are ultimately personal and subjective . . . The point I have been trying to make is a simple one, long familiar in philosophy of science. Debates over theory-choice cannot be cast in a form that fully resembles logical or mathematical proof . . . Nothing about that relatively familiar thesis implies either that there are no good reasons for being persuaded or that those reasons are not ultimately decisive for the group. (Kuhn, 1970, pp. 198–9)

Even if one does have reservations about Kuhn's incommensurability thesis, or its application to this type of situation, it would be no great surprise to find that problems of interdisciplinary communication had influenced the course of development of this particular area of science.

The first issue that I will briefly consider is the tendency of scientists, when faced with a particular problem, to seek a solution within the framework of their own expertise. This can extend even to seeking to redefine the problem so that it more readily falls within that framework.

The division of opinion among atmospheric scientists about the probable cause of the Antarctic ozone hole in the period between the announcement of its discovery and the AAOE, was largely along disciplinary lines. Most of the atmospheric chemists supported chlorine-based theories, while circulation-based theories were supported largely by meteorologists and circulation dynamicists.[3]

Why do scientists seem to favour their own discipline or sub-discipline in seeking a solution for a complex scientific problem? Working from within the framework of one's own area of expertise is the obvious starting point for attack on any problem for which it might yield results. If the scientist becomes convinced that this will not work, it is obviously necessary either to shelve that particular problem and tackle another, or to seek a collaborator with the expertise appropriate to the more promising approach. Those chemists who are not removed from the problem by this sort of natural selection will therefore become the initial advocates of

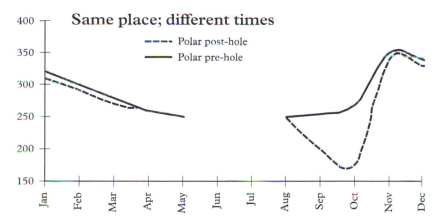

Figure 12.1 The comparison which shows springtime ozone depletion.

chemical approaches to the theory of a phenomenon, while the meteorologists who remain will support meteorological approaches. A chemist
who becomes convinced that a meteorological theory of the phenomenon
is more likely to be correct will either turn to working with a meteorological group, probably as a junior partner, or turn to a different problem. In
either event, independent[4] publications will not be produced supporting
the theories from the other discipline!

In attempting to explain the Antarctic phenomenon, the atmospheric
chemists always referred to an 'ozone depletion', while the dynamicists
often spoke instead of an 'ozone redistribution', pointing to a ring of
stratospheric air in cool temperate latitudes surrounding the Antarctic,
where ozone abundances increased at the same time as the polar decrease
was taking place. A very explicit report reads:

Further analysis of satellite measurements show[s] that during any one year the
September decline in total ozone near the South Pole is compensated by an
increase at mid-latitudes. The total ozone amount from 44°S to the pole remains
almost unchanged from August through November, even though both the polar
and mid-latitude values reach extremes during this period. These observations
suggest that the variations within the spring season in south polar total ozone are
governed by dynamical redistribution rather than chemical processes. (Stolarski
& Schoeberl, 1986)

This difference of view could not easily be resolved. There was a problem
with the respective frames of reference. The chemists focused on the
polar region, and compared the then current seasonal ozone profile with
the pre-ozone-hole profile. Stolarski and Schoeberl, as advocates of a
theory based on air circulation, took quite a different focus. They compared the polar and cool temperate zone profiles for ozone, using post-
ozone-hole data.

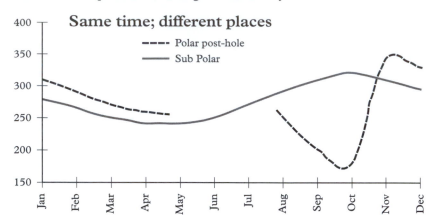

Figure 12.2 The comparison showing springtime ozone redistribution.

When allowance is made for the fact that the cool temperate zone covers a much larger area than the polar zone, it becomes clear that the ozone changes very little over the total southern region during August to November. The change, according to this frame of reference, ought to be seen as a redistribution of ozone from the pole to lower latitudes during September and October.

The only way any real judgement can be made between these two different, but very plausible stories, is to look at the broader picture. The full picture does not resolve the issue, but does seem to lend more support to the chemists than the dynamicists. If we were to take the dynamicists' approach to the post-ozone-hole data, and apply it to the pre-ozone-hole data, we would find that over the region in total, what used to be an ozone build-up from August to a late October maximum had become a steady ozone level through the period. That is not actually a depletion, but it is the next best thing! The chemists' view was of an actual depletion local to the South polar regions, and fairly minor changes in the situation elsewhere. Nevertheless, the issue ultimately is incapable of resolution, because of the different frames of reference.

Another issue for consideration is the matter of possible 'blind spots' arising because of demarcation issues between the disciplines near the boundary line. There are certain questions that cannot even arise, and consequently theoretical approaches that cannot be considered, until there is effective communication and dialogue between the two groups across the disciplinary divide.

Some of these blind spots are fairly trivial as far as the science at the frontier is concerned, but important in the consensual acceptance of the science. Rowland (1994) became acutely aware of this:

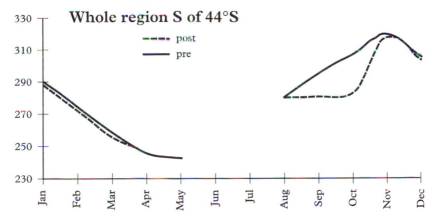

Figure 12.3 The broader picture. Schematic ozone profiles in the Southern Hemisphere. The 'hole' shows up as a 'redistribution', but there is still a significant loss relative to earlier years.

The chemistry community especially was sceptical of the assumed ready transfer of molecules much heavier than air into the stratosphere. The meteorological community, in contrast, was already quite familiar with the overriding importance of the motions of large air masses in transporting molecules around both the troposphere and the stratosphere, and also knew that the molecular weight of individual gases was of no importance in such mixing . . . Surprisingly, 19 years later, with literally tens of thousands of measurements of CFCs and other halo-carbons in the stratosphere, opinion pieces and letters to the editor from seem-ingly qualified chemists and physicists (and the occasional climatologist) still appear in which transport of CFCs to the stratosphere is denied or questioned on the basis of their excessive molecular weight.

Another example of a blind spot has been discussed in Chapter 9 of this book. Rowland himself misjudged one of his arguments because he failed to fully appreciate some of the limitations of the one-dimensional circula-tion and chemistry model that he and Molina used in their attempt to quantify ozone depletion. In doing so, he over-estimated the force of his argument about hydrogen chloride distribution.

It would be a mistake to think that, back in the 1970s, there was a com-munity of stratospheric chemists, who could have set Rowland right on this or any other point. As the history outlined in Chapter 2 of this thesis suggests, there were very few chemists working on stratospheric prob-lems; there were very few stratospheric problems in chemistry perceived as interesting. The discrepancies in the Chapman scheme (see Chapter 2 in this book) for stratospheric ozone chemistry had been allowed to remain for decades; it was not until the late 1960s and early 1970s that any real progress was made in clearing them up. Molina and Rowland themselves were very new to the area:

When Mario Molina joined my research group as a postdoctoral research associate later in 1973, he elected the chlorofluorocarbon problem from several offered to him, and we began the scientific search for the ultimate fate of such molecules. At the time, neither of us had any significant experience in treating chemical problems of the atmosphere, and each of us was now operating well away from our previous areas of expertise. (Rowland, 1996, p. 1787)

There was a small community of atmospheric chemists whose most noteworthy achievement had been sorting out the very complicated chemistry of photochemical smog in the 1960s. Gas kineticists occasionally turned their attention to stratospheric problems, as did a few climatologists with some chemical background.

Rowland reports that, on discovering that stratospheric decomposition was the likely fate of CFCs, and that the decomposition products would initiate a catalytic chain decomposition of ozone:

... both of us went to Berkeley just after Christmas 1973 to talk with University of California chemistry professor Harold S. Johnston ... we wanted to make contact with the atmospheric science community because we had carried out all of our work to this point in isolation. (Rowland, 1994)

In the ozone investigation generally, the most prominent blind spot appears to have been an unpreparedness to consider in detail a possible role for chemistry at solid or liquid surfaces in the generally gaseous stratospheric medium.

At the time of the SST debate, the initial concern related to water from the aircraft exhaust. As the debate continued, the emphasis shifted to oxides of nitrogen. In the modelling, water was given a dual role. On the one hand it was seen as providing a source for hydroxyl and hydroperoxy radicals that could become involved in catalytic cycles which destroyed ozone. On the other hand it was recognised that direct injection of water could lead to cloud formation (a 'vapour trail') which could affect the local radiation balance and circulation. The possibility that was little considered was that the ice particles might alter the chemistry by providing solid surfaces which afford alternative (heterogeneous) reaction pathways. Proposed mechanisms were always sets of gas phase (homogeneous) reactions,[5] coupled with models for irradiation and circulation.

Similarly, and perhaps more excusably, Molina and Rowland were thinking mainly in terms of gas phase chemistry when they put forward their suggestion about the role of chlorine compounds in stratospheric ozone chemistry.

Our initial 1974 article had specifically stated that all of our calculations to that time had not included any heterogeneous reactions because none that we had examined seemed likely. (Rowland, 1994)

The last part of this passage is important. Molina and Rowland did seriously and rigorously consider possible heterogeneous reactions, and find them likely to be unimportant. It is not easy to find evidence that the possibility of surface reactions on aircraft vapour trails were so seriously considered in the modelling associated with the SST debate.

Several computer model studies in the period immediately following Molina and Rowland's paper sought to estimate the likely extent of ozone depletion via the Molina–Rowland mechanism. Most did not include any heterogeneous chemistry.

When Farman, Gardiner, and Shanklin (1985) were analysing the anomalous ozone results, the tentative mechanism they put forward was based on chlorine chemistry. The thinking was entirely in terms of gas phase chemistry. In the discussion, there is even a suggestion that the *homogeneous* reaction between chlorine nitrate and hydrogen chloride to produce molecular chlorine might be important. The currently accepted mechanism for the phenomenon includes the same *heterogeneous* reaction on ice crystal surfaces as one of the crucial reactions.

After the announcement of the discovery of the Antarctic ozone hole, the chemists were faced with the problem of what was special about the Antarctic that could cause such an effect. It was only then that they turned to talking seriously with meteorologists about Antarctic weather and circulation, and became aware of the possible importance of polar stratospheric clouds. Heterogeneous reactions at ice crystal surfaces were clearly indicated. The first clear suggestion of a role for such reactions appears in S. Solomon *et al.*, in 1986. The first significant investigation of the reactions is reported by Molina *et al.* in 1987. Interestingly, Molina had begun to investigate heterogeneous reactions before the published announcement of the Antarctic ozone anomaly. He had been intending to investigate the sort of effect that volcanic aerosols of sulfuric acid in the stratosphere might have in perturbing the Molina–Rowland ozone destruction mechanism (Rowland, 1994).

At one level then, we are looking at a 'blind spot' between chemistry and meteorology. The meteorologists tended to underestimate the importance of chemical reactions in the system generally, while the chemists did not know about clouds in the Antarctic stratosphere (and hence ice crystal surfaces). Reactions on ice crystal surfaces were therefore completely overlooked in modelling stratospheric processes until the Antarctic ozone hole dramatically called attention to the possibility.

But at another level, we are also looking at a 'blind spot' involving the boundaries of one of the sub-disciplines of chemistry.

At first sight, the failure to include heterogeneous reactions might seem a strange sort of oversight for the chemists. After all, heterogeneous reactions are surely a part of chemistry! It was not, of course, a universal failure. How can this oversight be accounted for? The simplest answer involves the chemistry/meteorology divide. Any chemist not familiar with polar meteorology would be thinking of the stratosphere as a cloud-free region, with no particle surfaces to provide reaction sites. Most of the chemists, initially, were simply unaware of polar stratospheric clouds.

But there is another very significant aspect, involving the relationships between sub-disciplines of chemistry.[6] Atmospheric chemistry is a discipline that has arisen largely out of gas kinetics. Many of the leading atmospheric chemists were trained, and worked for some time, in the field of gas kinetics. Atmospheric chemists constantly rely on the studies of gas kineticists to obtain the reaction rates that they need for their models of atmospheric reaction systems.

Gas kinetics is concerned with obtaining the mechanisms of reactions that occur in the gas phase – that is, in breaking up the reactions into a number of elementary steps. It is further concerned with devising experiments that enable the rates of each of the elementary steps to be deduced.

In terms of theoretical understandings of chemical reactions, gas phase reactions are the simplest. They hinge around collisions between two or three isolated molecules. There is no environment to be considered, that might add extra complications.

The presence of a surface that might get involved in a reaction system is therefore the bane of the gas kineticist's life. But laboratory studies of a gas reaction cannot be undertaken without using some sort of containing reaction vessel, which inevitably will have surfaces! The typical gas kinetics study of the 1960s or 1970s involved carrying out the reaction in a pyrex reaction vessel which had been pre-treated by decomposing organic compounds in it to 'season' the surface – that is, to give it a hard, waxy, and unreactive surface coating. The reaction rates measured in such a vessel would be compared with rates measured in the same vessel filled with similarly treated small pyrex beads. In this way the surface area was changed by a large factor, but everything else remained the same. Any change in reaction rate that was observed would be attributed to the greater surface area, and therefore to surface reactions. It was always hoped that rates would not change! If they did not change too much, a simple correction for surface area could be made, that would supposedly eliminate the surface effects, and give the rate of the 'pure' gas phase reaction.

There was therefore an ethos within the field of regarding surface reactions largely as a 'nuisance', and hoping to find that they exerted little or no influence on the behaviour of the reaction system under study.

In consequence, when gas kineticists turned their attention to the atmosphere, they would tend to start with a sigh of relief – at last a reaction could be studied without a containing vessel, and the accompanying surfaces where reactions might occur. In the lower atmosphere there were some problems with dust, particulate pollution, and clouds, but by and large the reaction systems that were studied involved gas phase reactions with only minor surface perturbations. The stratosphere is above the clouds; only two types of surface problem might remain – volcanic aerosols, of which most atmospheric chemists were aware, and polar stratospheric clouds, of which many of them were not!

The other point that should be recognised is that it would not just have been a case of allowing for heterogeneous reactions by adding extra equations to the scheme, and including them in a model for the overall system. Heterogeneous reactions are much more difficult to quantify than homogeneous gas phase reactions. They do not reliably follow such simple rate equations, and factors like the size and shape distribution of the aerosol particles themselves can make large differences. A whole new layer of complexity is added to attempts at modelling by the inclusion of heterogeneous processes.

With the increasingly fine focus of recent science, scientists have tended to define their areas of expertise ever more narrowly. Sub-disciplines of the various branches of science have proliferated. With this subdivision has come increased scope for interdisciplinary communication problems. The problems raised by the investigation of stratospheric ozone overlap the boundaries of at least three major disciplines, and several sub-disciplines within each of them.

In this particular case, each of the specialist disciplines has a distinctive and technically complex approach to the particular problems it deals with. And there had been little history of previous interaction or debate between them. These factors ensured that interdisciplinary communication was difficult. The three characteristic features of such a situation can be very clearly seen in this case. Each group tried to devise a theoretical approach that would allow the problem to be dealt with within the framework of its own discipline, with only minimal input from the others. Each group saw and formulated the problems in subtly different and incompatible ways. And there were some aspects of the stratospheric ozone system, and of the theory necessary to provide a satisfactory account of it, that remained hidden until a late stage of the investigation. There were problems that could not be noticed and dealt with, until a good measure of interdisciplinary dialogue and communication was eventually achieved.

NOTES

1 It is not expected that the reader will find this claim either original or controversial. Relevant discussion can be found, among other places, in

a) de Solla Price, D.J., 'Little Science, Big Science', Columbia University Press, New York, 1963, pp. 4–10.

b) Atkinson, M., *Stud. Hist. Phil. Sci.* 25(1994), 147–58, but especially around pp. 149–50.

2 There are exceptions. Adrian Tuck, for example, was the chief planner of the AAOE. In his early career he had obtained a higher degree in chemistry before getting a position with the UK Meteorological Office, and being trained as a meteorologist.

3 I have not undertaken the sociological census, except in the most superficial way. This reading of the situation seems to be uncontroversially accepted among the atmospheric scientists involved.

4 As will be evident from the scientific articles referenced in this thesis, collaborations of two to six authors are the norm in this area of science. Single author papers are relatively rare. Some of the collaborations are interdisciplinary, but many are among groups of chemists or circulation dynamicists.

5 A homogeneous reaction is one that takes place between molecules in a single phase – in this case the gas phase. A heterogeneous reaction takes place at the interface between two phases – the surface of a solid or liquid particle. A gas phase reaction involves a simple collision between two or three molecules, in which the molecular structure gets re-arranged. The heterogeneous reaction, on the other hand, involves molecules sticking on the particle surfaces, and reacting there. A heterogeneous reaction between particular substances always proceeds with different rate behaviour to the homogeneous reaction, and sometimes gives different products.

6 The material that follows is largely based on discussions with Dr John Christie, who trained as a gas kineticist.

13   Scientific evidence and powerful computers: new problems for philosophers of science?

Rapid developments in the technology of electronic computers in the latter half of the twentieth century have led to dramatic changes in the ways that consequences of a scientific theory can be calculated and presented.

There does not seem to be a difference in kind between the way that the detailed motions of the planets might have been calculated in the nineteenth century, and the way that five-day weather forecasts are calculated today. In both cases, for example, approximation methods need to be introduced at some stages in the calculation to keep the computational task within reasonable bounds. Atmospheric circulation is clearly a three-dimensional problem, but one-dimensional and two-dimensional models are and were commonly used to reduce the size of the computational task to reasonable bounds. In an exactly analogous way theoretical chemists of earlier times reduced problems to over-simplified one-dimensional or two-dimensional models to make them possible to solve. It was only in this way that quantum mechanics could be applied to chemical systems prior to the computer age. But although there are no differences in kind between manual and machine computational models, there do seem to be important differences of scale.

Firstly, a modern computer model can be sufficiently complex for there to be a danger (or an opportunity, depending on your point of view) that it can become an end in itself.

The large computer models developed and used in the last few decades have somehow taken on a life of their own. What, for example, is to be made of a published paper entitled 'The 40 to 50 day oscillation in a perpetual January simulation with a global circulation model' (Pitcher & Geisler, 1987)? What it means is that a very large computer model of world climate has been allowed to run for a few simulation years as though there were no succession of seasons. The purpose was to check out some of the properties of the model – how it responds to various fluctuations. But to what end? Clearly it is not intended to produce a direct comparison between the behaviour of the model and the real system. We cannot observe the real world in 'perpetual January'. Is it perhaps to help diagnose some possibly aberrant behaviour of the model? That may be a valid use for such a simulation. But in that case it would be hard to find justification for the referees to allow its publication in one of the more prestigious scientific journals, in effect claiming it as a significant advance in human knowledge! A reading of the abstract shows a purpose slightly different to either of these possibilities. There is apparently a natural cycle of variable length between forty and fifty days that shows up in some climatic measurements. The model was run to see if this cycle was reproduced. Cycles of generally similar characteristics were generated by the model with a period of twenty-eight to thirty-one days. I suppose the results were regarded as a partial success – the model threw up the right sort of behaviour, but with the wrong frequency pattern. It would be possible to interpret the results as showing that the fifty to sixty-day cycle could probably be explained without any underlying dependence on seasonal factors. The 'perpetual January' of the model did not seem to matter. If the model produced nearly the right sort of cycles with the succession of seasons turned off, then presumably the succession of seasons was unlikely to be a factor with a major real world causative influence on these particular cycles.

Even so, there is a deep strangeness in this type of science. Science is supposed to be about investigations of natural systems and phenomena. But here the investigation is of a model. There is no guarantee that the model correctly and accurately represents the natural system. And it is being run in a mode that cannot possibly represent the natural system. The methodology seems to be quite inappropriate. And yet the results of the investigation are deemed, by the authors and journal referees at least, to be a contribution to scientific knowledge. And perhaps it is! There seems to be an issue here for philosophical investigation and analysis.

An overview of the scientific enterprise brings out another problem with this type of large computer simulation. The scientist's task consists largely in trying to account for the complex phenomena seen in the real world, in terms of basic natural laws or principles. The linkage is to be via a chain at least of pattern or correlation, and preferably of causality.[1]

A very large computer model is devised for a physical system. It is based on a set of equations and algorithms representing the best current understandings of the natural laws that govern the system. Its output is a set of calculated values of various quantities that can be measured by observation of the natural system. If the calculated and observed results consistently match, then this produces some reassurance that the behaviour of the system is governed by the natural laws of science incorporated into the model. The reassurance is very limited, though. It has the same evidential status as instantiation of a generalisation. There may well be other quite different sets of laws that would produce the same result.

One situation where an inaccurate or incomplete model can produce a good empirical fit with observations is where two or more factors, whose effects tend to cancel each other out, are overlooked.

A slightly different situation arose in the ozone hole story. In that case, computer models around 1984 were producing a very good fit with observed data. But about a dozen reactions that can be important in stratospheric ozone chemistry were missing from the models. At the time, most of them were unknown reactions. Those that were known were not believed to be important. In normal circumstances, none of these reactions are important. They become important only when two unusual conditions co-incide. The Antarctic winter must be cold enough for polar stratospheric clouds to persist until after springtime sunrise. And the level of stratospheric hydrogen chloride must be at least double the natural level.

Until these special conditions arose, and scientists became aware of them, there was no possible indication that the models were in any way incomplete, and no driving force to investigate the incorporation of extra reactions into the model.

The fact that a model works well is no guarantee that it accurately represents the natural system. The fact that a model works well, and has always worked well, is no guarantee that it will always work well, especially if there is some subtle change in the system.

Another problematic area is perhaps best brought out by consideration of an idealised and abstract situation. Suppose that we were able to produce a 'perfect' but very complicated model for the behaviour of a physical system. Input conditions could be entered, the computer program could be run, and a series of outputs would eventually be produced that exactly matched a set of observations on the system.

The difficulty is that this use of the model provides no satisfying explanation of *how* the behaviour of the system arises out of the laws that were incorporated into the modelling. The complexity of the model, like the complexity of the system, is largely beyond the comprehension (qua ability to contain) of the human mind.

Logically, the problem might be considered solved. There has been a clear demonstration. The physical laws have been incorporated as input into the computer model, and the correct behaviour of the system has emerged as an output. But the problem persistently appears to remain. Its focus is the search for an intermediate level of explanation; for a pattern in the complexity. The computer has not revealed the intermediate steps in the chain of causality.

We can imagine a situation where the problem of the anomalous Antarctic ozone depletion might have been solved by an immense computer model. Suppose that we had computer power at least a million times better than the best currently available. All gases and volatile liquids entering the atmosphere could have been included. All of their known reactions were considered, and we had enough insight and inspiration to include the important unknown ones as well. Material transport through the atmosphere could have been calculated on a very fine three-dimensional grid that covered the entire globe. Chemical reaction and diffusion could have been integrated with radiation balance and circulation, and many of the arbitrary simplifying steps normally used in such modelling could have been avoided. Suppose then that we had devised such a model, and run it, and it had produced an output that matched the Antarctic phenomenon. In what sense would the model have provided an explanation?

We would know that the phenomenon could be accounted for by an interplay of the laws of conservation of energy, gravitation, chemical combination, ideal gas laws, and the full set of chemical inputs and reactions that had been incorporated. But that in itself would not seem satisfying as an explanation.

What we usually mean by an explanation, and require in an explanation, is an argument that can trace a chain of causality from underlying principles as causes, through a chain of intermediate steps, to the observed phenomena as effects.

Scientists who attempt to provide a detailed explanation of the Antarctic ozone phenomenon use concepts in air circulation like 'tropopause', 'Brewer-Dobson cell', 'polar vortex', as well as physical concepts like 'polar stratospheric cloud'. From among many atmospheric chemical species and reactions, they identify a particular small subset that is particularly influential on this phenomenon.

The huge model we have just envisaged can match outputs with the Antarctic phenomenon without having anything to say about any of these intermediate level concepts. Some of the intermediate level concepts would arise naturally and transparently within the model itself, and might be portrayed with a judicious choice of outputs; others may remain quite obscure, and be extremely difficult to evince from the model. In providing an excellent match of its outputs with observed phenomena, our huge model does not necessarily provide anything we find satisfactory as an 'explanation'.

On the other hand, if it is accepted that the model provides a good representation of the system, then it may be possible to use experimentation on and exploration of the model to come up with these intermediate level concepts to use in explanation. In some ways this will work better than exploration of the system itself because there is the possibility to run controlled experiments on the model that are simply not possible with the natural system.

The authors of the 'perpetual January' paper have been undertaking just such an exploration. They focus on a particular feature of the climate – the fifty-day oscillation – and check how the model performs at reproducing this one feature. 'Switching off' the progression of seasons in their model helps this focus. The oscillation can be more clearly discerned without seasonal interferences.

The advantage of studying the model, rather than the actual atmospheric system, then, is the availability of much greater experimental control. Inputs can be arbitrarily and individually varied, and the effects noted. The disadvantage is that extrapolation from the behaviour of the model to behaviour of the natural system can never be properly justified, and is therefore always risky.

In this sort of way, large computer models can become laboratories in their own right (Dowling, 1998), and give rise to publications like the perpetual January paper. But they also give rise to many epistemological pitfalls and difficulties. This is a new feature of late twentieth-century science, and deserves the serious attention of both scientists and philosophers.

A related philosophical issue that arises in conjunction with the sort of large scale simulation that I have just been describing, is the question of how the contributions of computer models are to be viewed as scientific knowledge. To take an example: we now have weather forecasting programmes that can produce a fairly accurate prediction of the state of future weather, for a period of four to five days ahead, over an area the size of a continent. To what extent does this, of itself, mean that we 'know' how the weather works? The simulation program is the embodiment mainly of fairly fundamental physical laws, and simple phenomena – coriolis forces, the earth's rotation, solar radiation, air/ocean energy transfer, the effects of topography on airflow, etc. In the case of weather forecasting, we do think that we 'know' what is going on. But weather forecasting was around as an art and an empirical science long before these computer models were developed. Many rough and ready rules were in place, some of which did not depend in any simple and obvious way on the underlying basic physical laws. As a result, we already had a whole string of terms and concepts at an intermediate level – cold fronts, prevailing winds, cyclones, upper atmosphere troughs, jet streams, and the like – to help trace a comprehensible chain of connection or causality from the physical laws to the observed weather. In another case, we may not be so well pre-equipped with the concepts and terms to provide the intermediate levels of explanation.

The deep question is: To what extent is that intermediate level a necessary part of the 'scientific knowledge' that forms the corpus of modern weather forecasting? Would it be enough simply to be able to demonstrate that a particular large computer model embodies the appropriate physical laws, and that that model was (moderately) successful in accurately predicting the weather for several days ahead? Suppose that we did not have all of the concepts and heuristics that apply at that intermediate level. If the connection could not be comprehended or verbalised, we could still produce the forecasts, but could we still say that we know how the weather systems work? Human curiosity would certainly drive us very strongly to look for pattern and connection at the intermediate level, either in the natural system, or in the model, or both. Being able to trace that chain of causality in a simple argument in natural language seems somehow important.

The main question, then, is whether such investigation forms a legitimate part of the scientific enterprise. In one sense, we are learning nothing new; we already know that the suite of physical laws incorporated into the large computer model account for the weather!

Even if we do accept that investigating the *natural system* for this intermediate level is legitimate, how can we justify investigating the *model*? Can the enterprise be 'scientific' when it actually turns its back on measurements of the natural system, to focus on tinkering with a computer package which allegedly describes its behaviour, but has no necessary connection with it? Remember that a guarantee that a model accurately represents a system is never available.

Computer models are now often used in science to predict the future behaviour of a system. Sometimes the focus is on exploitation of scientific knowledge in a technical way, as is the case with weather forecasting programmes from which forecasts are now obtained for several days ahead. But similar models are also often used in hybrid scientific/socio-political simulations. A model of a natural system of interest is constructed, and studied with different inputs representing various public policy options, or changes in human behaviour.

In all situations like this, there seems to be a tendency to give the evidence of the output of a model calculation undue weight. The fact that an output comes from a very complicated and sophisticated calculation can easily lend it a false authority when it is being evaluated as a piece of evidence. To have any validity at all, a model must fulfil several exacting requirements:

- The equations and effects that it takes into account must be correctly described, and accurately implemented.
- No important or relevant side effect or side cause may be overlooked.

- The input data on which the model is initialised must be sound, complete, and accurate.
- The model calculation algorithm must be accurate, and numerically stable (that is, minute differences in input values must not propagate to huge differences in outputs).

To repeat a well-worn cliché: what comes out of a model is only as good as what goes in.

In the stratospheric ozone story, there are at least three separate clear instances where computer models incorporating both social and scientific factors played a part. The first was in the model estimates of the likely current and continuing magnitude of ozone depletion in the Molina–Rowland scheme. The second was in developing scenarios for the possible effects of various policies of restriction on the use of CFCs and other inert chlorine compounds. And the third was in producing forecast outcomes for the likely timing of events under the regime that was adopted. In what year will the Antarctic ozone hole reach its largest extent? When will we start to see an actual decline in atmospheric levels of the various CFCs that have been phased out? When, if ever, will there no longer be formation of an Antarctic ozone hole? With these forecasts, a trend curve can be produced so that further action can be taken in the form of policy adjustments if the behaviour of the natural system starts to diverge too widely from the projections.

The period between Molina and Rowland's original paper in 1974, and the publication of AAOE papers in 1989, is a period of enormous advances of computer technology and capability. This is of great significance for the use of computer models in the developing story. Molina's original model estimation of the magnitude of chlorine-mediated ozone depletion, and the few which followed closely after it, gave fairly large values – around 7 per cent to 15 per cent. They were based on one-dimensional models which were then, according to Molina, state of the art. Two-dimensional calculations followed several years later, not because Molina and others had been simplistic, but because of improvements in computer capabilities. A few years had to pass before a two-dimensional model could be seen as a realistic calculation that would not be exorbitant in terms of memory or time. The cost of running a very large model has always been, and is still a major factor in planning a computer simulation as part of a scientific research project.

From about 1982 onward, the models tended to predict rather lower depletions, around 2 per cent to 4 per cent. A graph has been published to show how model estimates of ozone loss varied with the time of publication of the estimate (WMO, 1981; Schiff, 1983). Some of the data has been replotted in figure 13.1. Schiff comments as follows:

The results obtained have, however, been far from consistent; predictions of total ozone depletion made over the past decade resemble a stock market graph. Apparently atmospheric scientists are no better forecasters than are economists!

The final problem area that I wish to discuss in this chapter is also related to the rapid advances in computer technology, and to some extent it may be solved by those same advances. It is related to the vast amounts of data that can be generated by automatic measurement regimes.

One area where this makes a difference is with the problem of outliers. In any data collection exercise, occasional measurements will be made that fall well outside the expected range of values. There can be many reasons for this. Some, like transitory instrument malfunctions, or errors in result transcription, have occurred as a result of a form of corruption of the data. These are quite meaningless in any scientific analysis. Others might arise from a genuinely unusual disturbance of the natural system, and might have enormous significance, in spite of their transitory appearance. The problem, of course, is a problem of when and whether to ignore outliers. This has been much discussed over the years (e.g. Hon, 1989; Polanyi, 1946). My only contribution to the discussion in this context is to point out a major scale change. In traditional science, an outlier was a single anomalous point in an occasional experiment. But with intensive data collection, outliers become a regular feature of the landscape. In a modern experiment where the data consists of tens of millions to hundreds of millions of points, there are inevitably enough hiccups somewhere in the apparatus to produce numerous outliers. Instead of a single anomalous event, the experimenter must consider outliers in terms of a frequency. Typical outlier frequencies in a modern experiment involving extensive electronic data collection might range between about one point per million and one point per thousand. This may introduce new considerations into the debate. No longer does 'outlier' refer to a quirky individual result, but to a class of non-conforming results, even though they are an equally minute proportion of the total recorded observations.

The second problem area is one that may be seen in terms of either or both of two familiar metaphors: 'finding the needle in a haystack', or 'seeing the wood for the trees'. It relates to the activity of managing to discern the patterns and important features in data that might be presented as a million pages of numbers!

The problem is largely a technical one. Clever ways of plotting the data as graphs or maps may set it up so that the important features may be instantly discerned by the remarkable human faculty for visual pattern recognition.

But an underlying epistemological problem remains. The whole of the information content of our million pages of numbers cannot be presented

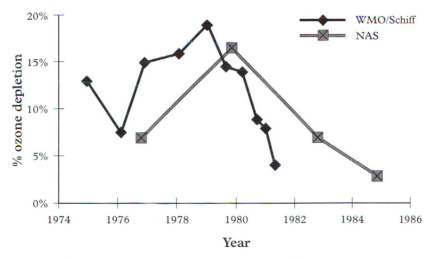

Figure 13.1 Predictions of long-term Cl-mediated ozone depletion (by date of the prediction). WMO/Schiff: Survey of computer models reported in primary literature. NAS: US National Academy of Sciences reports.

on a single page graphic, or even on a series of graphics on a manageable number of pages. So it is inevitable that in the translation from raw data to graphic, an artificial constraint is being placed on what will be found. By making the representation clear so that *some* types of pattern may be discerned, we are simultaneously guaranteeing that *other* types of pattern, if they exist, will be lost!

For example, in current satellite ozone measurements, 20 million readings per day are collected. The results are presented in the form of a global contour map. Production of the map from the data requires the making of averages of data collected near the same times and places, so as to produce a smooth picture without large local fluctuations that are regarded as 'noise'. This process inevitably makes us blind to any 'pattern' that might be present in those relatively large local fluctuations. Current theoretical understandings would regard the occurrence of such patterns as unlikely to the point of impossibility; nevertheless the data analysis has completely shut out such a possibility, which, if it were found, might lead to revolutionary science! There may be other cases where such a constriction in the data analysis is more plausibly important.

The third problem is probably a transitory problem, and to some extent an historical accident. In an earlier chapter we discussed the data backlog problem in connection with the Antarctic ozone hole discovery. At NASA in the early 1980s, automatic data collection software was apparently running several years ahead of automatic data analysis software. As a result, the satellite team did not notice the Antarctic ozone hole for several years after it became apparent in their data, simply because they had not taken a close look at the relevant part of the data! There was a severe, and historically crucial, analysis backlog.

In principle, the more data that is collected, the better base there is to work with in a scientific investigation. But there is an increased chance, when a very large data set is collected as a part of a scientific investigation, that the analysis will never find the unexpected. Humans working directly with the data set will, because of the size of the task they face, look at it from the point of view of the effect that they are expecting or hoping to discern. They are therefore likely to miss the unexpected pattern that, in a smaller data set, would 'hit them in the eye'. Not only that, but the sheer volume of the task of dealing with the data set may make them less likely to explore side-tracks in the data, or follow through with hunches. Computer workups of the data will be organised primarily with the expected or desired result in mind. The processing which helps to bring out one type of pattern, will directly obscure another!

NOTES

1 There is, of course, a debate among philosophers of science as to whether there is any real causality in the world explored by scientists, or whether they must merely seek regularity and correlation. I would argue that a quest for a causality deeper than mere regularity or correlation is an essential part of the modern scientific enterprise. If it were not, then the issue of gravitation theory would be a closed book, for example, because its phenomena and physical expression is precisely and accurately described by present theory, and the present drive to integrate its understanding with that of the other fundamental forces would be meaningless. To say that a quest for deeper causality is an essential part of modern science is not to say that such deeper causality exists, however.

14   The scientific consensus

> The only scientific consensus in existence [in 1978] regarded chlorofluorocarbons as a potentially serious, but as yet unconfirmed, danger.
> (Weiss, 1993)

In the ozone story we have a remarkable record of a series of changes in scientific consensus.

CFCs were initially regarded as the safest and best of chemicals. Then a finger of suspicion was pointed, and their use became a matter of some significant difference of opinion within the scientific community. Finally, some extra evidence came in, and they were slated for a complete phase-out, with the backing of overwhelming scientific opinion.

Molina and Rowland's warning about the possible role of chlorine compounds in stratospheric ozone depletion was initially taken very seriously by scientists. Then, as the evidence was not clearly seen in actual ozone levels, and as refinements of the models started to produce predictions of smaller depletions, the wider scientific community saw the issue less seriously as a problem. (This is not to deny that it was still widely regarded as a *potential* problem, nor that several groups of scientists continued to work on stratospheric chlorine chemistry.) But when the discovery of the Antarctic ozone hole made its impact, chlorine-mediated ozone depletion came once again to the fore as a significant scientific problem.

When the ozone hole was discovered, there were initially several quite diverse and incompatible attempts at explaining the unexpected phenomenon. Did the anomalous ozone depletion arise as the result of chemical destruction of ozone in reactions that could only be efficient in the particular local conditions at the time? Or was it rather the case that ozone was removed as unusual circulation patterns replaced the local atmosphere with ozone-poor air from elsewhere? The discovery also stimulated further investigative experimental and observational work. New results started to narrow the field of contending explanations. Then some more results quite rapidly swung the weight of scientific opinion behind a single broad approach, and finally helped in filling out the detail of an explanation that was generally accepted by nearly all of the atmospheric scientists.

What do we mean when we speak of a 'scientific consensus'? Why does it matter whether or not there is a scientific consensus on a particular issue? How is consensus established, and how can it be broken, and eventually revised?

My use of the term 'consensus', refers neither to a unanimity of scientific opinion on the one hand, nor to a simple majority vote, on the other. It refers rather to a scientific orthodoxy. Scientists who stand out against a consensual view, would not necessarily be straying beyond the bounds of scientific respectability. But they would be seen as taking an unusual or unorthodox approach, or at best, as members of an embattled minority. The onus would definitely be thrown onto them to justify their stand. By contrast, a scientific argument would typically use a consensual or orthodox view as a basis or starting point. This starting point will normally be conceded in its evaluation. Referees and critics will only check the evidence and the argument through the subsequent stages.

The notion of scientific consensus as a term which describes an orthodoxy, rather than a unanimity, does not agree with the way that some philosophers have used the term. Ziman (1978), for example, uses consensus in a sense which much more nearly connotes unanimity. Having done so, he runs into a measure of difficulty:

Even a complete consensus is seldom publicly determined or proclaimed; the best we may expect is an answer that is said to be the 'almost unanimous opinion of the experts', backed by what they would describe as 'the overwhelming weight of the evidence'.

For this reason, and others, my usage of the term to connote an orthodoxy will prove more helpful. Etymologically, 'consensus' and 'consent' are the same word. The shade of meaning in English ascribes a community connotation to 'consensus' as against an individual connotation for 'consent'. The community acquiescence implied in a consensus position is not a consent that that position is correct, but a consent that the position is the generally accepted one. Individual scientists, in wishing to oppose a consensus position, do not break down that community consent. Rather, the consensus consists in their recognition that the burden of proof has shifted in a manner unfavourable to their cause.

It is also important in any consideration of scientific consensus in a social and historical context, to draw a clear distinction between the consensus of the scientific community as scientists, and other areas and aspects of consensus that may have been influential – broad social consensus, political consensus, consensus of the policy-makers. A specifically scientific consensus is often not easy to delineate. There is not a clear-cut community of scientists, who have organised bodies that they have authorised to issue authoritative edicts on their behalf. There are bodies, though, that take on some of this role (the national Academies of Sciences of various countries, for example). Sometimes a senior and respected scientist has and expresses views as a private citizen that should be seen as distinct from professional views, and certainly as distinct from the scientific consensus. This can make for complications. But there is a very clear delineation of purpose. The scientific consensus is directed at establishing a corpus of scientific 'knowledge' which represents a description of how natural systems work, in the light of the best current theories and evidence.

There are other important forums for consensus on what are essentially scientific questions, in a variety of different communities – the public in general, the mass communication media, politicians, planning authorities. The orthodox view of scientists on the issue is always one of the inputs to any of these forums, but often not the determining one. As a result, there are sometimes clear cases where political action has been based on views which are out of step with current scientific assessments, even when there has been consultation with scientists, and goodwill on both sides.

There are a number of practical areas where it is important to understand the nature of a scientific consensus, and to be able to find what the scientific consensus is on a particular question.

The clearest case is that of a scientist working in a neighbouring discipline. In scientific research there are a lot of factors in experimental design and/or interpretation, that are outside the actual field of expertise of the investigator. The biologist needs to be able to use the results of chemical analyses of some of the materials in an experiment, for example. The prescribed analysis procedures need to be used with confidence. The accuracy, precision, and reliability of the method, and the detail of the way the analysis works, are matters for the analytical chemist. The biologist must simply take on trust the consensual view of analytical chemists. This view is normally expressed in a prescribed test method, which details experimental procedures and precautions, specifications of error limits, and caveats about possible interferences.

The referees may criticise the analytical chemistry only insofar as they find that the biologist has misinterpreted the consensus for the appropriate method, or as they find that the analysis was not correctly executed in accordance with the prescribed procedure. They do not present detailed criticisms of the analytical method in their critique of the paper – that is a separate issue to be taken up with the analytical chemists on another occasion!

A closely related situation arises when scientific findings impinge upon matters of public policy. It is very important in debates concerning possible policy changes, to know just where the weight of informed scientific opinion lies, and how strong the agreement is. It is usually in these situations that committees are convened under the auspices of a national Academy of Sciences or similar body to provide authoritative scientific guidance to the policy-makers.

We have seen this play an important role in several recent cases, for example issues concerning tobacco smoking and health, the banning of certain pesticides, and, more particularly relating to the material discussed in this volume, the need for controls over emissions of chlorinated compounds to the atmosphere, in the light of possible effects on the stratospheric ozone layer.

Issues of consensus are also important in actually determining the course of scientific investigation and effort. They influence the way that research funds are allocated, the likelihood of papers passing the peer review system and the balance in the agendas of scientific conferences. It is much harder to get unorthodox work published, for example! (Atkinson, 1994). The sorts of projects which are likely to prove fruitful, and worth pursuing, are effectively prejudged by these mechanisms. The fact that there is a feedback of the current consensus into the future development of the subject in this way produces a strong conservative ethos in science as a whole. This has already been widely discussed by philosophers (e.g. Polanyi, 1967).

It would be wrong, though, to underestimate the other influences which also impinge on the course of scientific effort. There is often direct and powerful political interference and direction, which forces work along lines that it would not normally take. The 'Star Wars' Strategic Defense Initiative, for example, involved an enormous injection of funds into a series of technological and scientific projects at a time when there was a balance of scientific opinion against their feasibility (*New Scientist*, 1986, 1993). The subversion of Soviet biology in the Lysenko affair is another widely quoted and discussed case.

Finally, it may be very useful to keep a finger on the pulse of the scientific consensus in an area: whether it exists, whether it is strengthening or weakening, whether details are being revised and modified. It can provide a very valuable tool, allowing the scientist or the historian of science to chart the course of adoption of new material into the corpus of 'scientific knowledge'.

The most comprehensive philosophical treatment of consensus in modern science is presented by Laudan (1984). In the first chapter of his book, he describes the essential tension and paradox of consensus in science. On the one hand there is a need for a high degree of consensus so that scientists can agree on the value of individual pieces of work, the current status of various theories, and the current state of knowledge onto which new work can build. On the other hand, disagreement and contention between rival approaches and theories is a necessary part of the driving force that produces problems for resolution, and drives observation and experiment in particular directions.

Laudan paints a picture of scientists being widely agreed on one explanation of a phenomenon, and then being able, quite rapidly, to revise their position, and become widely agreed on quite a different explanation, in the light of new developments.

The problem for philosophers is to account for this in terms of some sort of rational goal-setting and evaluation procedures on the part of scientists. On the face of it, it may seem more like a series of fickle enthusiasms, or following the whims of a rapidly changing fashion!

The key question, then, is the question of co-ordination. Why and how do scientists change their views almost simultaneously when a controversy is in the process of being settled, or when new evidence comes to light?

Laudan starts by outlining a classical hierarchical model which he sees as encompassing the views of those who had considered this problem before him. Scientists can easily and unanimously come to the same conclusions about the evidence from scientific investigations because they share a common methodological approach. Thus methodology provides a higher court for resolving any conflict over evaluation of facts. Any disputes over methodology are supposedly resolved by reference to a common set of aims and goals, and deciding which methodology is best suited to attain them. And the common set of aims and goals is somehow central to the scientific enterprise.

He is very critical of this model. For his own model he retains the same three-level framework (theories, methods, and aims), but introduces a more complete and egalitarian interaction between all three levels. He sees them as providing a network of mutual reference and support.

The view of consensus presented by Kuhn (1962) seems to centre more around a sort of tribalism among scientists – aligning their views and their work with a particular model approach or paradigm within their field. The consensus that he describes is a very local one, applying only to a particular discipline or sub-discipline at a particular time. This sort of consensus is broken only at times when a revolution is in progress within the particular sub-discipline – at times of paradigm shift. Questions of resolving disputes by reference to methodology or axiology seem very marginal to his view; he is more concerned with the notion that scientists from different 'tribes' or paradigms have great difficulty in establishing proper communication at all!

Kuhn associates consensus with periods of 'normal science', and concentrates more on the dissensus associated with scientific revolutions. Laudan (1984, pp. 17–18) is very critical of his failure to account for how consensus can ever be re-established after a period of dissensus:

Periods of revolutionary and normal science may each make a kind of sense in its own right, but Kuhn has no convincing story to tell about how science moves from one state to the other. Nor is it difficult to see why Kuhn lacks a theory of consensus formation: his account of dissensus requires such deep-rooted divergences and incommensurabilities between scientists that there remains no common foundation upon which to shape agreement anew.

But this criticism fails to appreciate part of Kuhn's position. The story that Kuhn tells, of course, does not involve reaching agreement, but 'conversion' or capitulation of scientists to the paradigm that will be adopted after the revolution. The opposition does not negotiate or compromise; it simply evaporates, or shrinks to a hard core of irrelevant diehards!

Presumably, to Kuhn, any notion of a broader scientific consensus which extends generally across the whole of science, and which defines a corpus of 'accepted scientific knowledge', is somewhat illusory. He does not seem to provide a satisfactory account of science in the broader sense of a body of knowledge extending across disciplinary boundaries.

Lugg (1986) discusses Laudan's approach to the problems of consensus, and finds that while it has broadened the discussion and clarified a lot of the discrepancy between philosophers' accounts and scientific practice, it has not really answered the key question. Lugg's conclusion is that:

To obtain a clear view of agreement and disagreement in science, we must step outside the framework of traditional epistemology and acknowledge that scientific investigation neither abides by nor needs a general philosophical theory of rationality. (Lugg 1986)

In the investigation of the Antarctic ozone hole, at least, we have a very clear picture of a situation where a theory was rapidly and almost universally abandoned, in a seemingly co-ordinated way, when its rival came to the fore. We have disagreement rapidly resolved and transformed to consensus. It is at least sometimes possible to account for rapid shifts in scientific view on the basis of surprising new observational evidence. It is not necessary in such cases to invoke appeals from theory to methodology and axiology to resolve disagreement, nor to depart from traditional epistemology to account in rational terms for the effects of the evidence on scientists.

There are three interconnected but different areas of disagreement and changing view in the story of chlorine-mediated depletion of stratospheric ozone. Each of them will be examined to see how consensus was formed, broken, and/or revised. The safety and wisdom of widespread use of CFCs is the first issue. The role of chlorine compounds in a global reduction of stratospheric ozone is the second. And the third issue is the scientific explanation of the causes of the Antarctic ozone hole.

When CFCs were first investigated and adopted as refrigerants, there were four main criteria that needed to be met. A refrigerant compound had to be stable, and not undergo chemical reactions under operating conditions, nor interact corrosively with its container. It had to have a volatility suitable to the purpose – condensation and evaporation needed to take place at a reasonable pressure at the operating temperature. These two criteria were the essential engineering requirements that allowed its use in the normal condensation-cycle refrigeration technology. In addition, there were two safety criteria. It was desirable that a refrigerant be non-flammable, and that it be non-toxic.

In the original paper advocating CFC refrigerants, Midgley and Henne (1930) tabulate eight commonly used or projected refrigerants. Of these, air cannot be used in condensation cycle technology (except at extremely low temperatures), and carbon dioxide and water are extremely marginal. Carbon dioxide must be compressed to several atmospheres pressure before it can be made to condense to a liquid; at lower pressures it goes directly from gas to solid. And water has a vapour pressure that is much too low to be of any practical value in a condensation cycle at normal refrigerator temperatures. Methyl chloride and methyl bromide are both quite toxic. They do not have strong odours, and so give no warning of any escape. Sulfur dioxide and ammonia are even more toxic, but these two compounds have a pair of significant advantages: they are both extremely pungent, and detectable by odour at very low concentrations. They thus give ample warning of their escape. They also both have a high affinity for water, and so minor escape incidents can be dealt with by hosing down. The remaining substance, butane, is non-toxic, but extremely flammable. Methyl chloride and methyl bromide are also flammable, but sulfur dioxide is not. Ammonia is very slightly flammable. It is not usually regarded as a fire hazard, but ammonia fires and explosions are not unknown.

It is thus clear that, from the outset, CFCs were filling a technological niche where no other substances were so suitable. In fact, on every one of the four criteria they were so good that they rapidly came to dominate the refrigeration industry, and also found application in other technologies that had requirements for similar materials. CFCs are particularly stable.

Table 14.1 *Refrigerant properties as seen in 1930*

Refrigerant	Stability	Volatility	Toxicity	Flammability
air	OK	cannot condense	OK	OK
carbon dioxide	OK	too high	OK	OK
water	OK	too low	OK	OK
ammonia	OK	OK	toxic, but gives warning	slightly flammable
sulfur dioxide	corrosive if wet	OK	toxic, but gives warning	OK
methyl chloride	OK	OK	toxic, no warning	flammable
methyl bromide	OK	low	toxic, no warning	flammable
butane	OK	OK	OK	highly flammable
CFCs	OK	OK	OK	OK

Source: (Adapted from table 1 of Midgeley & Henne, *Ind. & Eng. Chem*, **22**(1930), 542.)

They do not participate in chemical reactions even under quite severe conditions, let alone in typical environmental conditions. Because CFCs are a fairly large class of compounds rather than a single compound, a CFC or CFC mixture can be tailored to have any desired volatility. They do not react with oxygen, nor even with the more reactive oxidising species in the environment – ozone, atomic oxygen, or hydroxyl radicals. Far from being flammable, they are actually moderately effective fire suppressants. A 30 per cent mixture of butane in dichlorodifluoro-methane will not burn in air (Midgeley & Henne, 1930)!

The toxicity studies on dichlorodifluoromethane were bizarre, by today's standards. Dogs, monkeys, and guinea pigs were exposed to atmospheres containing 20 per cent and more of dichlorodifluoro-methane for days, and while they showed immediate respiratory and nervous symptoms, it proved very difficult to produce any ill-effects that persisted after the animals were removed to a normal atmosphere:

Results of this work completed to date have shown that exposure of guinea pigs to 80 per cent vapor in air which by dilution reduces the oxygen content to approximately 4 per cent causes the animals to fall to their sides and severe convulsions to occur almost immediately. Recovery from this condition is rapid and uneventful after a 15–minute exposure. An exposure of 20 to 30 minutes, however, causes death. The time of occurrence of death in these animals is markedly influenced by the low and fatal oxygen concentration. This is shown by the fact that 60 to 90 minutes are required to produce death when the animals are exposed to an atmosphere composed of 80 per cent dichlorodifluoromethane and 20 per cent oxygen. (Midgeley & Henne, 1930)

This is followed up with a table that compares the toxicities of ammonia, methyl chloride, carbon dioxide, and dichlorodifluoromethane. The first two materials are, of course, quite toxic. Carbon dioxide (normally regarded as only slightly toxic) is listed as fatal in the short term at 30 per cent, dangerous to life in 30 to 60 minutes at 6 to 8 per cent, and safe for several hours at up to 2 to 3 per cent. Short term fatality is listed unobtainable for dichlorodifluoromethane; an 80 per cent concentration is dangerous to life in 30 to 60 minutes, and mixtures up to 40 per cent are shown as safe for several hours!

The use of CFCs expanded into several new areas. The same set of properties that had made them uniquely suitable as refrigerants, also ensured that they were the best candidates for aerosol propellants, and foam blowing agents.

The early evidence was quite uncontroversial. An initial consensus, both scientific and regulatory, had built up, recognising these substances as particularly safe and suitable for a wide range of industrial applications.

This consensus remained unshaken until Molina and Rowland's paper appeared in 1974.

In the 1960s and early 1970s there had been a great increase in both scientific and public awareness of environmental and ecological issues. The role of trace levels of toxic chemicals had come very much to the fore: the build-up of background levels of organochlorine pesticide compounds, and an indication of possible effects on vertebrates, had led to the imposition of new controls on the use of DDT and similar compounds. Heavy metal pollution in several situations had also been an area of great concern. But none of this touched CFCs. All of the evidence was that these compounds were totally unreactive in the environment, and therefore were neither harmful in themselves, nor degraded to harmful products.

Lovelock's (1971) letter to *Nature* provided the initial stimulus to the work that questioned the general acceptance of CFCs. A measure of their then current status may be gleaned from his comment in that letter:

The presence of stable sulphur and carbon fluorides in the atmosphere is not in any sense a hazard, and their existence has only been detected by the very sensitive technique of gas phase electron absorption. The fluorides are, however, of special interest because they enter the atmosphere only from industrial and domestic sources, whereas other gaseous industrial emissions are also natural products . . .

From the results he reported, he suggested an atmospheric lifetime of about one year for CCl_3F.

It was this suggestion that provided the basis for Molina's post-doctoral project. CFCs were chemically inert. They were being produced at the rate of a million tons per year. A significant proportion of CFC production was escaping almost immediately to the atmosphere, and most of the balance was probably following it in the medium term. What was happening to it after that? There was evidence from Lovelock's measurements that it was largely accumulating in the atmosphere. But if his preliminary estimate for residence time of one year was anywhere near right then something else had to be happening to remove some of the material from the atmosphere. Actually, the estimate was wide of the mark. The residence time figure was soon revised to thirty–fifty years (Rowland, 1975[1] & 1996). Rowland's reminiscence is that:

The appearance in the atmosphere of a new man-made molecule provided a scientific chemical challenge: Was enough known about the physicochemical behavior under atmospheric conditions of molecules such as CCl_3F to allow prediction of its fate, once released into the environment? In 1973 I included in my yearly proposal to the U.S. Atomic Energy Commission (AEC), . . . a predictive study of the atmospheric chemistry of CCl_3F. (Rowland, 1996)

Before the consensus that CFCs were safe could evaporate, Molina and Rowland themselves had to become convinced that there was a serious problem. Molina and Rowland's argument clearly presents the evidence that had convinced them. It was sufficiently strong at least to constitute a prima facie case against the continued widespread use of CFCs.

When their paper was published, and they had backed up the publication with some extra publicity in several quarters,[2] it opened up a scientific debate. The previous consensus on the safety and appropriateness of CFC usage was replaced by an intense controversy:

The U.S. scientific community reacted to the 1974 theories by mounting a major research campaign, . . . The next several years were marked by intense professional and personal disputes within the scientific community. Although a series of laboratory and modelling studies resulting from these activities confirmed the validity of the chlorine-ozone linkage, they could not prove definitely that it described what was actually going on in the stratosphere. (Benedick, 1991, p. 11)

Reaction from the chemical industry was, as might have been anticipated, immediate and hostile. The industry had, at that stage, a strong vested interest in maintenance of the current CFC technology. There was also a very real awareness in industry that CFC products were much safer than their alternatives in terms of everyday operations. Ammonia refrigeration plants had been associated with some nasty industrial accidents over the years, and hydrocarbon aerosol cans occasionally turned into miniature flame throwers.

The response from industry moved the debate into the wider public and political arenas. The issue was already before the US congress as early as 1974.

The international chemical industry vigorously denied any connection between the condition of the ozone layer and the increasing sales of CFCs. Industry forces quickly mobilized their own research and public relations efforts to cast doubt on the theories. (Benedick, 1991, p. 12)

In a relatively short period of time, half a year or so, the consensus on all levels had been shattered.

An examination of the argument in Molina and Rowland's paper shows that, in this instance, it was *not new observational nor experimental evidence* that had led to the change of views among the scientific community. It was rather a *new insight*, based on the linking of several strands of observational evidence that had, for the most part, been around for some time before.

There was no doubt, for example, that CFC molecules, otherwise so unreactive, would break up when exposed to short wavelength UV light. Rowland (1996) puts it very succinctly in his Nobel lecture:

All multiatom compounds are capable of absorbing UV radiation if the wavelength is short enough, and almost all will decompose after absorbing the radiation.

The reactions of chlorine compounds in the stratosphere could readily be inferred from reaction systems that had been studied in the laboratory, coupled with modelling studies. The chlorine catalytic cycle was known. It is directly analogous to the nitric oxide cycle, which had played a large part in the SST debate just a few years previously. Rowland had become impressed with this analogy after attending lectures by Johnston on nitric oxide chemistry in the stratosphere (Rowland, 1994 & 1996; Johnston, 1992).

What did arise from new observations was the evidence that CFCs had accumulated in the atmosphere and had long atmospheric lifetimes. But with hindsight it can be seen that their very inertness was likely to mean an absence of other sinks, and accumulation in the atmosphere.

The actual measurements of HCl and CFCs in the stratosphere, which provided some of the direct evidence for Molina and Rowland's theory, were not obtained until well after their original paper was published.

Once the original scientific consensus had gone, and there was a considerable body of scientific opinion that continuing releases of CFCs and similar compounds to the atmosphere would be damaging to the ozone layer, the consensus to limit their use eventually followed. But this was a political and public policy consensus.

The way was shown in the United States, where legislation imposed on the administrator of the Environmental Protection Agency the responsibility to regulate:

any substance . . . which in his judgment may reasonably be anticipated to affect the stratosphere, especially ozone in the stratosphere, if such effect may reasonably be anticipated to endanger public health or welfare(August 1977 amendment to the US Clean Air Act, as cited by Benedick, 1991, p. 23).

In practice, this set a policy standard where action could be taken, and was taken, long before any scientific debate was concluded. The potential danger was so serious that prudence required action to be taken against CFCs on reasonable suspicion only. In subsequent international negotiations, this same standard for policy action eventually prevailed.

Scientific controversy and further investigation followed for many years. The case against CFCs was actually looking rather weak in 1984 (S. Solomon, 1988), the year when international negotiations were reaching their most critical stages, and the year immediately prior to the announcement of the discovery of the Antarctic ozone hole.

There is thus a clear distinction and lack of parallel between the scientific and political/public policy assessments of the CFC problem at that stage.

The second area where changes in the point of view of scientists can be traced, is in the importance of chlorine chemistry in stratospheric ozone depletion. The issue was whether emissions of CFCs and similar compounds were causing significant depletion of ozone, or were likely to do so in the near future.

The main theses of Molina and Rowland's paper were that the chlorine-based catalytic cycle for ozone removal was a significant factor in stratospheric chemistry, and that anthropogenic inputs of inert chlorine-containing compounds at the earth's surface had led, and were leading, to increasing stratospheric levels of active chlorine compounds. This opened a very protracted debate. There were several shifts in the tide of opinion. But right from the time of Molina and Rowland's initial paper through the discovery of the ozone hole to the time of the AAOE, there was no real scientific consensus on the central question.

This is not to say that there were not areas of consensus within the debate. It would be fair to say, for instance, that all agreed that the chlorine catalytic chain reactions were a real mechanism that could play a part in stratospheric chemistry, and that all agreed that CFCs would dissociate to produce chlorine atoms if exposed to short wavelength UV light. One area of disagreement was whether or not the extent of chlorine-mediated depletion would be significant – say 3 per cent or more – or minor – less than 2 per cent. There was also disagreement as to the extent of the influence of CFC releases on stratospheric chlorine levels. At a later stage, when the Antarctic phenomenon was recognised, there was disagreement both as to whether chlorine chemistry was responsible, and as to whether the phenomenon would remain purely local, or was a harbinger of some more serious global problem.

In the years immediately following Molina and Rowland's paper, the tide ran largely in support of their hypothesis. Others were able to confirm the soundness of their general scheme, and produce models which indicated ozone depletions of similar magnitude to, or slightly larger than Molina's model had. Chlorine-containing species were measured in the stratosphere – first hydrogen chloride (Lazrus *et al.*, 1975; Farmer *et al.*, 1976), and later CFCs themselves (1975 publications by Schmeltekopf *et al.* and Heidt *et al.*, as cited in Rowland, 1996). These measurements were very much in line with predictions that could be evinced from Molina and Rowland's hypothesis.

But from about 1979 onwards, the balance of scientific opinion started to swing in the other direction. The failure of any significant ozone depletion to become manifest was an increasing problem. Recognition of the chemical role of chlorine nitrate in the stratosphere, and the incorporation of chlorine nitrate chemistry into the modelling greatly reduced the amount of ozone depletion predicted. And computer technology had advanced to the point where it became feasible to consider the ozone depletion problem with realistic two-dimensional models. These also tended to produce smaller ozone depletions.

Some indication of the climate can be obtained in the figures for ozone depletion provided in a series of reports by the US National Academy of Sciences. Estimates of global ozone depletion (for late twenty-first century if 1973 CFC production figures were maintained) rose from 7 per cent in 1976 to 16.5 per cent in 1979, and then fell back down to between 5 and 9 per cent in 1982, and between 2 and 4 per cent in 1984.

The balance of opinion in the scientific community by 1985 was that chlorine-mediated ozone depletion was a minor and relatively unimportant effect. But that was the year when the whole issue was re-opened by the announcement of the discovery of the Antarctic ozone hole.

It must be made clear that re-opening the debate is all that the ozone hole announcement did; it certainly did not decide the issue in the other direction. Firstly, although its discoverers had attributed the Antarctic spring ozone depletion to chlorine chemistry, the evidence was far from convincing, and there were other possible explanations that did not involve chlorine chemistry. Secondly, even granted that the Antarctic phenomenon was due to chlorine chemistry, it was not clear that it bore any relationship to a global ozone depletion. The Antarctic phenomenon, dramatic as it was, affected only a very small part of the earth's surface, over a very short period of time each year. It did not amount to much when averaged out globally, and there was at that time no evidence of the phenomenon affecting ozone levels at other times or places. This particular debate had still not really concluded when, in 1988, the report of the Ozone Trends Panel produced a careful analysis which showed for the first time that global ozone loss was a real effect. There was marginal statistical significance in the comparison between 1976–86 data and 1965–75 data for column ozone measured at ground stations in the Northern temperate zone. The level of the depletion was about 2 per cent for the decade.

In May 1987, immediately prior to the AAOE, a panel of six atmospheric scientists testified to the US Senate Committee on Public Works and Environment. The result is described by Weiss (1993) in the following terms:

When asked if, based on the existing evidence, the theory of global ozone depletion (the theory that CFCs would drastically reduce global ozone) was valid, only Susan Solomon and David Hoffmann said yes; the rest of the panel said they did not know. Half the panel (S. Solomon, Hoffmann, and Farmer) thought that there was, or would soon be a consensus on the existence of global reductions in stratospheric ozone, and all except Dr. Tung agreed that if such depletion could be found, it was more likely than not that chlorofluorocarbons and halons were the cause.

This seems a very convincing demonstration of a lack of consensus that prevailed at least until that date. Previously, Rowland and Watson had testified to the same hearings:

Sherwood Rowland admitted that great uncertainty still existed in attempting to project future global ozone depletion, and NASA's Dr Robert T. Watson said he was unsure of the [Antarctic ozone] hole's global significance. (Weiss, 1993)

In 1994, the statistics showed greater depletions at all latitudes, but this could largely be attributed to the eruption of Pinatubo, which produced particularly low values at the end of the study period. The panel recommended extreme caution in the interpretation, as it is not possible to separate an underlying pattern from the significant depletion caused by a single major event at the end of the period (WMO, 1994, pp. 1.12–22).

It is therefore not at all clear that there is even today a scientific consensus about whether global chlorine-mediated ozone depletion (as opposed to the Antarctic phenomenon) is a significant and serious problem. There probably is a consensus that the monitoring programmes have got the size of this ozone depletion about right – somewhere in the 2–6 per cent level globally (total since 1965), with practically no depletion at the equator, and increasing to higher latitudes. The action that has been taken against continued CFC emissions to the atmosphere should, if it continues to be effective, ensure that the depletion gets no worse.

The picture of the scientific consensus painted for this particular aspect of the problem is quite different from that connected with the fate of the CFCs. In this case, a clear consensus seems to have been incapable of forming while the observational evidence for actual ozone depletion was uncertain. This illustrates a marked difference from the consensus that needs to be achieved by the policy-makers. Unlike the scientists, they cannot afford to remain uncertain for long.

Finally, scientific consensus can be examined as it formed around the chlorine theory of the Antarctic ozone hole. There has already been detailed discussion of the chlorine monoxide measurement in the AAOE as a crucial experiment in achieving this consensus. An elegant and eloquent presentation of experimental results effected the rapid achievement of a consensus that chlorine chemistry was responsible for the phenomenon, where there had been vigorous disputation between rival theories beforehand.

In this particular instance, the stress must be placed on the weight of the observational evidence in its own right. There is no question, for example, of a factual dispute being resolved at a methodological level (as might be expected following Laudan or his predecessors) – it was simply resolved by the presentation of telling new evidence. The methods of the chemists and the meteorologists both in observation and in theory generation were, and remained very different. There was little disputing by either group the efficacy or appropriateness of the other's methods. The meteorologists did throw back at the chemists their own original admission that some of the mechanisms they were proposing were 'speculative'. This seems to be the nearest anyone came to a methodological debate!

The consensus that did form around the chlorine theory of the Antarctic ozone depletion ought not to be seen as a rout by the chemists of the meteorologists' position. While it became accepted that the latter had got much of the circulation story diametrically wrong (observations and models eventually showed persistent descent rather than upwelling in the Antarctic vortex, even at the springtime break-up), it was also accepted that it was primarily the very special conditions brought about by Antarctic circulation patterns that had made the new reactions introduced into the chemists' scheme reasonable and appropriate rather than speculative and exotic! This is stressed, for example, in the report by Kerr (1987).

The main point that comes out of the examination of scientific consensus in the three aspects of the ozone investigations is the primacy of the actual observational evidence. I would suggest that any account of scientific consensus that loses sight of this is likely to falter.

But the first issue – the case of CFCs – also shows that the observational evidence on its own may have little power to convince. It must be assembled and presented to make a case. On at least some occasions the evidence needs to be coupled with a new and convincing theoretical *insight* to have any power to influence scientific opinion. The evidence that Molina and Rowland used to formulate a case against CFCs was, by and large, not new. But it had no influence until the various strands were drawn together from different corners of the scientific edifice, and new implications drawn from their conjunction. Apart from model calculations of the likely extent of any chlorine-mediated ozone depletion, there was nothing in the evidence on which they based their argument that had not already appeared in the primary scientific literature. But it was assembled from very diverse sources, associated with different sub-disciplines of science. It required the guidance of a strong new theoretical insight to pick out the relevant evidence and put it together.

This part of the story forms a marked contrast with the 'smoking gun' result of the AAOE. A particular set of measurements was made, where ozone and chlorine monoxide radicals were simultaneously measured. On one day in twelve, a special set of conditions arose where there was an exact and detailed match between abnormally high chlorine monoxide levels and abnormally low ozone levels. According to current theories, chlorine monoxide levels match the *rate of ozone removal*, which is quite a different thing to *extent of ozone loss*. Only for a short period in the spring season would removal rate parallel extent of loss. And on one day during that critical period, the air on the edge of the Antarctic vortex had a laminar structure so that the flight encountered a succession of patches of anomalous polar air on the edge of the vortex. The result was the 'smoking gun' plot, which showed a succession of rapid changes in the mixing ratios of both ozone and chlorine monoxide radicals, with an exact match between the changes in the two species. But once those particular measurements had been made, there was no need to assemble other evidence, nor room for further argument. An intelligent lay person with a minimal background briefing can immediately determine that the close correlation between chlorine monoxide and ozone mixing ratios must mean that the ozone depletion is based on chlorine chemistry.

When there is a crucial experiment, it forms a particularly clear-cut basis for a scientific consensus. I have already argued that crucial experiments are much more diverse than has generally been recognised.

The view that is promoted by scientists and scientific publications is that scientific consensus arises out of a rational weighing of the evidence, following a healthy and vigorous scientific debate. This may or may not be somewhat naive as an historical or sociological account of what actually takes place. But there does not seem to be anything in the ozone story that indicates that the consensus or uncertainty at the various stages of the investigation was epistemically inconsistent with a reasonable weighing of the currently available evidence.

An examination of dissenting positions

The consensus view of the Antarctic phenomenon, as outlined in the previous chapters, is by no means universally accepted. There has been a significant body of opinion, particularly in the United States, that the debate has been manipulated and subverted by a part of the scientific community, and that the evidence does not really support the published conclusions. On the one hand, these dissenters have made accusations against the scientists involved in publicising the threat to the ozone layer. Charges have included bias in evaluating the evidence, manipulating conference agendas and the peer review system, and having a hidden agenda connected with the extreme environmental lobby. They see the ozone depletion story as part of an industry concerned with stirring public feelings about forthcoming environmental doom. On the other hand, the scientists from the mainstream position tend to regard the dissenters as having inadequate technical background and understanding of the particular areas of science involved, and as not 'playing fair' by the rules of scientific discussion. They see the dissenting views as coming from beyond the pale of legitimate scientific debate.

Although atmospheric scientists generally regard the scientific investigation and debate as having reached a clear conclusion, and do not take this dissenting position seriously, the publicity achieved by the dissenting group has been sufficiently effective that many people believe that the scientific debate is not yet decided.

Most of the arguments brought up by dissenters are mustered in a book by Maduro and Schauerhammer (1992). This is widely recognised as the leading work from the dissenting camp. According to one review:

This book is extremely important since it is probably the best known and most widely quoted text aimed at debunking the concept of ozone depletion and the deleterious effects of CFCs and other so-called ozone-depleting chemicals. The book has been used as a primary reference by Dixy Lee Ray, Rush Limbaugh, and others who dispute the reality of ozone depletion and the effects of CFCs. (Newton, 1995, p. 155)

In another passage from the same source, the book is described as:

The book that appears to have been the single most influential document in the 1990s among critics of the CFC-ozone hole hypothesis. (p. 88)

On the basis of such recommendations as these, it seems to be a good candidate for closer examination as a dissenting source.

The earlier chapters of the book present the main theses:

1. Chlorinated fluorocarbons and related compounds cannot, it is claimed, be important as sources of any chlorine responsible for ozone depletion in the stratosphere, and for the Antarctic ozone depletion in particular, since natural sources of chlorine are so much greater than anthropogenic sources.
2. The Antarctic phenomenon is a natural phenomenon which is not new, not accurately described by the atmospheric scientists involved in the 'ozone scare', and not caused by chlorine chemistry.
3. There is no evidence that the Antarctic ozone hole really matters, in terms of increased ultraviolet radiation.

In the later chapters of the book the authors discuss an alleged conspiracy involving environmentalists, large chemical companies, and atmospheric scientists, in the promotion of disaster scenarios. They conclude by outlining a series of technological and engineering projects which they claim could greatly enhance quality of life for the people of the earth. These are presented to 'give readers who are angry about environmental hoaxes a positive alternative to fight for'.

It is clear from the outset, then, that this is an attack on the orthodox view on all possible fronts. It is quite a different matter from the debate that is normally conducted within an area of a scientific discipline. It would be typical for a dissenting contribution to a scientific debate to challenge a single aspect of the basis of the theory under attack. In most cases this challenge would be backed either with new evidence from an experimental study, or a new insight that comes from a novel development or articulation of part of a rival theory. Maduro and Schauerhammer's book is not presenting a challenge of this sort. If it is a contribution to a scientific debate, it is clearly a revolutionary one.

This book draws no new observational data into the discussion. All of the authors' argument is based on published sources or private communications with scientists; there is no new material arising from their own experiments, nor any detailed presentation of significant experimental results that have failed to get into print. At most their claim can be that some of the sources they cite have been 'overlooked' by the mainstream atmospheric scientists. The crucial question, of course, is whether this oversight is accidental, arises from different perceptions of what data are relevant to the question, or is part of a conspiracy to suppress alternative views.

It could be that this book ought to be judged non-scientific, or even anti-scientific. Its presentation suggests that the conclusion – a conviction that the story of chlorine-mediated ozone depletion must be wrong – has preceded the evidence. When an analysis is driven by the desire to reach a particular conclusion, there is a major danger that it will step outside the rules of scientific debate. Typically, evidence may be considered selectively and out of context. A large number of arguments, of very variable quality, may be mustered to refute the unwanted theory, in the hope and belief that at least some of them will stick. The invocation of a conspiracy theory is another typical and worrying symptom.

It is important to remember, though, that there is not necessarily anything wrong with the conclusion preceding the evidence per se. Mendeléev was so convinced of the correctness of his periodic law that he felt free to tamper with accepted values of atomic weights, and postulate new, unknown chemical elements, on what was really the flimsiest of evidence (Brock, 1994).

It would be quite wrong to dismiss either the arguments against the orthodox view of stratospheric ozone depletion, or even the conspiracy theory, on these grounds alone. To find that the work has certain similarities in structure with some pseudo-scientific and anti-scientific works, is not to find it scientifically invalid. That would be a form of 'guilt by association'. The arguments that are put forward must be examined in detail, and judged on the evidence. Because the arguments are numerous, and, in many cases, unconnected, the only way to make a final judgement is by working laboriously through them one at a time. A single valid counterargument might, in principle, undermine the orthodox view of the situation, even if it were hidden among tens of faulty ones.

This task will not be undertaken here. We will merely look in a broader fashion at some of the main lines of dissent, as presented in the first six chapters.

The political arguments and allegations of conspiracy which follow are both outside the scope of this work, and extremely difficult to evaluate. Conspirators usually seek to avoid leaving much evidence of their activities, and such evidence as there is is often highly ambiguous. The final chapter on great global projects seems totally irrelevant both to their argument and to my analysis.

The first major strand of Maduro and Schauerhammer's argument is that the release of CFCs and similar compounds to the atmosphere is a very minor fraction of the total chlorine release, mostly from natural sources. Their figures are generally in accord with those published elsewhere, though there are significant differences in detail.

But figures for the release of chlorine compounds to the atmosphere at ground level do not necessarily parallel those for the origin of stratospheric hydrogen chloride and chlorine nitrate. The crucial question is the efficiency with which chlorine from each of these sources is delivered to the stratosphere. The argument put forward by Rowland and Molina, and accepted as part of the mainstream scientific view, is that CFCs are delivered to the stratosphere with considerable delay, but with almost 100 per cent efficiency, while the chlorine compounds associated with the other emissions are delivered with much lower efficiency. Maduro and Schauerhammer address some of these aspects of the situation, but fail to do so in an accurate or systematic way.

Firstly, their table 1.1 and figure 1.1 contain a single extra entry among the 'Atmospheric Sources of Chlorine'. This is described as 'Chlorine theoretically released by the alleged breakup of CFCs', and is set at 1 per cent of the total annual chlorine release from CFCs. But as soon as an isolated entry like this occurs, the table is no longer inviting us to compare like with like. What is really needed is a second table which contains this entry along with estimates of the amount of chlorine released from each of the other sources that finds its way to the stratosphere. What proportion of the particulate sodium chloride dust formed by evaporation of sea spray eventually arrives in the stratosphere, for example? Nothing is said in the text, other than that tropical storms are capable of carrying sodium chloride particles into the stratosphere. But is this the fate of 1 per cent of salt spray, or 1 part per million, or 1 part per trillion? In either of the last cases, salt spray becomes an insignificant contributor to stratospheric chlorine, as claimed by the atmospheric scientists. This would be so in spite of the fact that it might account for one thousand times as much chlorine release to the lower atmosphere as CFCs. The efficiency of transfer of volcanic hydrogen chloride is discussed, but not in quantitative terms.

There is also a very serious error in this table entry. It is produced by fallacious reasoning, and in effect produces a 1 per cent transfer efficiency for CFCs to the stratosphere, compared with the generally accepted figure of 80–100 per cent. The argument runs as follows:

According to the theory, approximately only 1 percent of the CFCs produced on Earth is broken up in the stratosphere every year. (The reason is that CFCs, because they are chemically inert, have lifetimes of more than 100 years in the atmosphere). Therefore a year's production of CFCs would contribute *at most* 7500 tons of chlorine to the atmosphere. (Maduro & Schauerhammer, 1992, p. 12)

But this completely misrepresents the situation. Certainly only 1 per cent of this year's CFC production can break up this year, but so can 1 per cent of the remainder of the production of every previous year. Nothing can happen to the 99 per cent of this year's production that is not broken up this year; it simply accumulates in the atmosphere awaiting some future year when it will rise to the stratosphere and be broken up. In a steady state situation, if the world production of CFCs had been constant for a century or more, a figure equal to the whole of this year's production would decay this year, even though only 1 per cent of it would actually be CFCs from this year's production. Because the world production of CFCs had, until recently, been rapidly building up from a zero level sixty years ago, and because the efficiency of CFC transfer may be a little less than 100 per cent in the long term, a current figure around 30 per cent of annual CFC production would seem appropriate for this table entry. That is a figure thirty times higher than the one shown.[3]

In the text accompanying the figure and table in the book, another source of atmospheric chlorine is mentioned:

In addition, untold numbers of tons of chlorine enter the earth from outer space, a result of meteorite [sic] showers and cosmic dust burning up as they enter the atmosphere. (Maduro & Schauerhammer, 1992, p. 12)

Why, one might ask, are the numbers of tons untold? A statement like this has no place in a scientific work, where the rules are that if something cannot be referenced and quantified, it should not be mentioned in this way. In effect, it is nothing but innuendo. Perhaps the numbers of tons of chlorine are untold simply because they are insignificantly small. If the proposal is a serious one, an estimate of the required number could readily be obtained by combining estimates of rate of influx of meteoric debris to the earth/atmosphere system with typical chlorine concentrations in meteors of various types.

From a general consideration of chlorine emissions into the atmosphere, the text moves to the question of accumulation of chlorine in the Antarctic:

Therefore, the propagandists conclude, CFCs are arriving at the South Pole in great concentrations, and are being broken down by ultraviolet radiation, releasing the killer chlorine molecules that then poke a hole in the ozone layer. (Maduro & Schauerhammer, 1992, p. 13)

But as we have seen, the atmospheric scientists are saying no such thing. Maduro and Schauerhammer are setting up 'straw men'. The two vital factors that are not properly mentioned and included in the analysis are the relative isolation of tropospheric and stratospheric air masses from

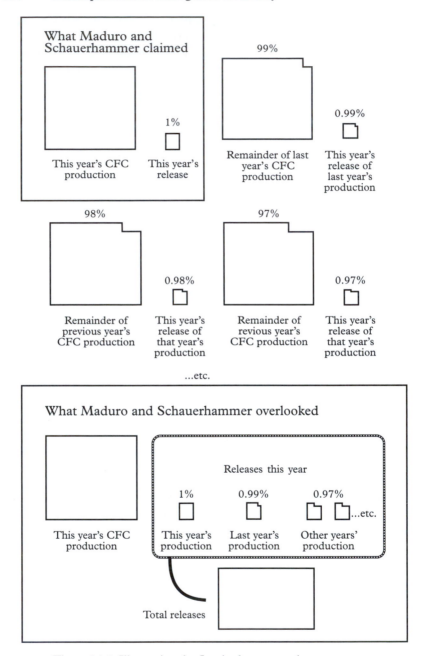

Figure 14.1 Illustrating the flaw in the ozone release argument.

one another, and the detail of the particular chemical form in which chlorine is present at various stages of the process.

The conventional scientific view differs drastically from the caricaturisation in the quotation above. To summarise once more: CFCs are slowly entering the stratosphere near the equator. They break up as they rise in the tropical stratosphere and encounter strong ultraviolet irradiation. After a series of reactions, the chlorine that they contain is stored in the reservoir species hydrogen chloride and chlorine nitrate. In these relatively unreactive forms, chlorine is transferred through the stratosphere to higher latitudes and lower altitudes. If clouds are present in the polar stratosphere when these reservoir molecules arrive there, further chemical reactions occur on ice crystal surfaces, forming the precursors molecular chlorine and hypochlorous acid, which can break down in visible light – ultraviolet is not necessary – to produce the atomic chlorine and chlorine monoxide free radical species, that can effectively remove ozone.

Notice particularly that, according to the orthodox view, any CFCs that arrive near the South Pole are not involved in any ozone depletion. CFC molecules themselves are totally unreactive. Polar spring ultraviolet levels are too low to break them up into reactive chlorine-containing species. And there is negligible upward transport from the polar troposphere to the stratosphere, nor, indeed within the polar stratosphere. The caricaturisation bears no resemblance to the actual claims of the mainstream atmospheric scientists.

But Maduro and Schauerhammer point out the impossibility of sufficient upward transport of CFCs from the polar troposphere, as if it were an argument against the story of Antarctic ozone depletion due to CFCs. There is no claim in the conventional story that CFCs break up anywhere near the polar regions.

The discussion moves on to volcanic sources of chlorine, examining particularly the possible role of Mount Erebus, a large volcano on the edge of the Antarctic continent. Maduro and Schauerhammer (1992, pp. 14–17) point out that Mount Erebus has been in a state of continuous eruption since 1972. They argue that:

- eruption of Mount Erebus injects 1000 tons/day of active chlorine compounds into the atmosphere;
- because of the extreme dryness of the Antarctic troposphere, the atmospheric lifetimes of these active chlorine compounds are much greater than those quoted as typical for such compounds;
- McMurdo Sound, where the NOZE investigations took place, is just 10 km downwind of Mount Erebus, and so readings of ozone and/or chlorine compounds taken at this base are grossly distorted because of local effects of the volcanic plume;

- the implication is then drawn that, in the Antarctic, the chlorine from Mount Erebus is much more abundant than active chlorine compounds from anthropogenic sources such as CFCs could possibly be.

The claimed input of chlorine compounds from Mount Erebus may or may not be correct; it certainly can not be deduced from the article cited as the authority without making other assumptions. It is not an unreasonable value, but how it was obtained is not at all clear.

The next problem is that the eruptions of Mount Erebus are continuous and gentle. This is not, by all accounts, the type of volcano that explosively spews ejecta into the stratosphere. Any hydrogen chloride plume from Mount Erebus is unlikely to reach more than a few kilometres altitude in the first instance, and in the polar winter it will be held at low altitude by the strong descent in the polar vortex. The very same arguments that the authors used irrelevantly against polar CFCs ascending into the stratosphere, is a very pertinent argument against a chloride plume from Mount Erebus making a similar ascent.

The third problem is that although the NOZE experiments were indeed based at McMurdo, most of the measurements were relevant to stratospheric processes and concentrations rather than surface ones. Even for the instruments that were ground based, the scientists were at least claiming, according to the normal usage of such instruments and interpretation of their results, to provide a vertical profile of the distribution of ozone and of chlorine compounds. Low level hydrogen chloride, and even the presence of other chlorine compounds at low levels in the atmosphere simply would not interfere with the measurements. Thus, for example, some of the scientists involved could refer to NOZE results in these terms:

Our 1986 measurements of chlorine monoxide showed a strong layer in the vicinity of 20 km [altitude], with a peak mixing ratio of the order of 10^2 times that predicted for this altitude range by normal stratospheric chemistry. (de Zaffra *et al.*, 1989)

More importantly, many of the critical data were not collected at McMurdo. The picture put together by the atmospheric scientists relied on data collected from at least four widely separated Antarctic ground stations, from satellite observations, from balloon and rocket-based measurements, and from the AAOE flights which sampled directly in the polar stratosphere. Cross-checking to ensure that a consistent pattern had been obtained between all of these sources of data was an important aspect of the scientific investigation.

Having raised the issue of Mount Erebus, Maduro and Schauerhammer turn their attention to volcanoes more generally. Their claim is that volcanic inputs of chlorine compounds directly into the stratosphere are much greater than anthropogenic inputs. Their argument to support this claim runs roughly as follows:

- the amount of chlorine released to the atmosphere by volcanoes is very difficult to measure directly;
- in the late 1970s a vulcanologist made some chlorine determinations which he interpreted as meaning that previous estimates of chlorine emissions may have been too low, possibly by as much as a factor of 20 to 40;
- large individual eruptions involve the ejection of very large amounts of material. Material from such eruptions is sometimes injected directly into the stratosphere.

The next few pages of their book describe the dramatic effects of some volcanic explosions. Nothing resembling a calculation of the proportion of volcanic chlorine reaching the stratosphere, or even a reference to such a calculation is presented. In discussing the Tambora explosion, the authors get sidetracked onto the later parts of their thesis – chlorine chemistry and radiation issues:

Now if the ozone-depletion-by-chlorine theory were true, such a catastrophic release of chlorine in 1815 should have wiped out the ozone layer completely, flooding the earth with so-called cancer causing ultraviolet rays. Every single man, woman, and child on earth should have suffered from skin cancer (Maduro & Schauerhammer, 1992, p. 19).

Note the innuendo in the last clause of the first sentence: are they seriously arguing that ultraviolet rays do not cause cancer? But the more serious problem with this, is that they have refuted their own argument with what they have said a few paragraphs earlier:

. . . injecting enormous amounts of ash and debris directly into the stratosphere. The volcanic cloud *reduced the amount of sunlight reaching the surface of the Earth* [my emphasis], lowering temperatures.

An aerosol of volcanic ash is very effective at blocking those ultraviolet rays!

The next group of arguments concern salt spray from the oceans. Assertions that a very large amount of chlorine enters the atmosphere as particulate sodium chloride from the evaporation of salt spray, and that some of this salt makes its way to the stratosphere are uncontroversial. But the proportion of sodium chloride that finds its way to the stratosphere from ocean spray residues is minute, according to the consensus of scientific wisdom. Any estimation of this proportion is completely missing from the argument.

Instead, we are presented with an improper comparison – sodium chloride release to the *atmosphere* (as a whole) is compared with CFC break-up in the *stratosphere*! The figure used for the latter quantity is in any case a factor of 30 too low, because it was obtained from the miscalculation discussed earlier. The figure that is desperately needed for a proper comparison is the size of the sodium chloride injection into the *stratosphere*, and that figure is not produced.

Those who hold CFCs responsible for a significant increase in chlorine-mediated stratospheric ozone depletion *do not need to* claim that none of the sodium chloride from salt spray finds its way to the stratosphere; only that the contribution from this chlorine is smaller than that from CFCs – perhaps half as much or less.

Maduro and Schauerhammer (1992, p. 26) complain that 'the ozone doomsday papers' do not refer to the natural presence of chlorine compounds in the stratosphere prior to the manufacture of CFCs, nor do they refer to chlorine from the oceans.

Their claim is largely, but not entirely true. This does not mean that their complaint is justified. There is an obvious reason why the origins of pre-CFC chlorine, or chlorine from the oceans, are not referred to. It is a simple question of relevance. Research papers are required to be concise and focused. The currently accepted views on salt spray, and on the amounts and origins of natural chlorine in the stratosphere were not being challenged. They were part of the underlying corpus of scientific knowledge that was being used as a basis in these papers, and were therefore 'taken as read'. The journal editors would probably have been very unsympathetic to the inclusion of discussion of this sort of material in the papers, in the unlikely event that the authors had seen a need to do so. It is not particularly difficult to find discussions both of ocean salt and of natural stratospheric chlorine in the mainstream atmospheric science literature.

Maduro and Schauerhammer review a paper which they feel supports their case (Delaney *et al.*, 1974). They claim that it conclusively shows that 'vast amounts' of oceanic chlorine reach the stratosphere.

What they do not pick up on is that this paper actually provides them with some information about just how much! Chlorine analyses were done on particles collected in balloon flights at 16 and 18 km, in the very lowest part of the stratosphere (as well as at several heights through the troposphere). The measurement was thus specifically of chlorine in particles; gas phase chlorine compounds in the stratosphere were not measured. Mass mixing ratios for chlorine in particles at 16 to 18 km altitude are plotted between 0.03 and 0.11 ppbw. Data for hydrogen chloride gas levels in the stratosphere range from about 0.4 ppbv at the bottom of the stratosphere (16 km altitude) to about 3 ppbv at the top (Warneck, 1988, p. 119). Translating from volume to mass fraction would provide 0.5

ppbw and 4 ppbw respectively. The only conclusion that can be drawn is that salt spray contributes at most 20 per cent (i.e. 0.1 ppbw/0.5 ppbw) of the total chlorine present in the lower stratosphere. (The sodium imbalance the authors refer to indicates that it is probably only half as much!). It is also worth noting that this chlorine is in a particulate form, where it cannot contribute to the Molina–Rowland scheme, and even its participation in the Antarctic phenomenon may be problematic.

The types of actual particles collected in the study cited do not seem to have been investigated. In a much later paper dealing with the volcanic cloud from the explosive eruption of El Chichón in 1982, Woods *et al.* (1985) comment that the techniques they used

... revealed the presence of NaCl particles (halites), which are rarely if ever seen at these altitudes [i.e. 18–21 km]

Any sea spray residues would, in the absence of further chemical processing, be in the form of halites.

Maduro and Schauerhammer's next arguments deal with exchange of material between troposphere and stratosphere. The discussion seems relatively uncontroversial and only marginally relevant, since there is no denial in any quarter that such material exchange does occur. One suggestion that does seem a little bizarre is that 'many scientists' believe that downward transport of stratospheric ozone is the main source of tropospheric ozone, and might even be responsible for smog alerts. No source is cited for this particular speculation. A significant amount of ozone does reach the upper troposphere by downward transport. Seldom does ozone which enters the troposphere by this mechanism penetrate downward to ground level. The origin of ozone in smog from the interaction between hydrocarbons and oxides of nitrogen is very well established, and not a matter of controversy.

The discussion of methyl chloride from biomass burning is based on data which come largely from interviews and conversations with named scientists. The information might be sound, but it has not passed the filter of peer review.

Although it is not directly relevant, an aside dealing with carbon dioxide in this section illustrates some of the problems with the style of argument these authors use when they do attempt to be quantitative. In an interview, a Brazilian scientist provides a figure of 540 million tons for annual carbon dioxide emissions from burning in the Amazon rain forest. An American scientist, in a private conversation with the authors, suggests that the figure might be more like 4 billion tons, when other sources of carbon dioxide emission associated with deforestation are included. It is then pointed out that the Amazon represents less than half of global forest burning. A comparison is invited with an alleged figure of 5 billion tons for the global industrial release of carbon dioxide. The reader is indirectly led to conclude that biomass burning (8 billion tons is implied but not stated) contributes more carbon dioxide to the atmosphere than industrial activity (5 billion tons).

But the figure of 5 billion tons, which is not referenced, is fairly easily found. It is widely quoted in many articles and textbooks dealing with the global carbon cycle, as the *carbon content* of the carbon dioxide released (e.g. Wayne, 1991, p. 18). But only 27.3 per cent of the mass of carbon dioxide is carbon. Five billion tons of carbon means just over 18 billion tons of carbon dioxide as the annual global industrial output. If the 4 billion tons figure for Amazon forest burning and associated soil release is taken seriously, that might lead to a global figure for biomass burning of 10 billion tons at most. But the figure may equally well be as low as 1 billion tons or so, if the Brazilian scientist's calculations are more accurate! Instead of being larger than the industrial emissions, the carbon dioxide from biomass burning lies somewhere between about one twentieth and one half of the industrial output, if the authors' sources are taken at face value, and the calculations done properly.

The chlorine figures are treated in similar cavalier fashion. A paper by Crutzen and others is cited as providing a figure of 420,000 tonne for chlorine release as methyl chloride from biomass burning. But Maduro and Schauerhammer choose to multiply this figure by at least ten because of alleged satellite surveys that show Crutzen's estimates of rates of deforestation to have been much too low. No source is cited. A figure of 4.2 million tons is submitted as the appropriate figure for annual chlorine release from tropical biomass burning. This figure is then doubled again to arrive at 8.4 million tons because of a rather vague suggestion that wildfires in developed countries in the temperate zone might contribute as much again.

On the balance of the evidence presented, it would probably be fair to concede that somewhere between 420,000 tonne[4] and 8.4 million tons of chlorine are released annually to the atmosphere, largely as methyl chloride, from biomass burning.

The 1994 report of the Intergovernmental Panel on Climate Change provides relevant data that can help to put this methyl chloride release on a more accurate and realistic basis.[5] The figure they provide for total atmospheric content of methyl chloride is 5.0 million tonne, and the atmospheric lifetime is given as 1.5 years. This corresponds to a total annual input of 3.3 million tonne of methyl chloride, or 2.3 million tonne of chlorine as methyl chloride (since methyl chloride is only 70 per cent chlorine). This 2.3 million tonne must include both the biomass burning source – estimated in Maduro's book as 8.4 million tons – and the 'seaweed' source discussed in the following section – estimated in the book as 5 million tons.

The current orthodox view of atmospheric scientists is that CFCs are a major source of stratospheric chlorine compounds, and the dominant source of the increase in stratospheric hydrogen chloride and chlorine nitrate that has led to development of the Antarctic ozone hole.

A careful analysis of the arguments presented by Maduro and Schauerhammer has shown that they are not effective in rationally under-mining that view. On the other hand, they contain numerous clear errors, that in every case lead either to drastic underestimation of CFC contributions to the chlorine burden of the stratosphere, or significant over-estimation of one or more of the natural sources. The authors' own position on the issue looks quite unsound.

Not only is the authors' position unsound, but their arguments on this part of the question must be judged unscientific. Each one is either dogged by vagueness, or flawed by demonstrable error or misinterpretation. None ought to have passed a scientific peer review process.

Maduro and Schauerhammer write at length about the possibility of CFCs being removed from the atmosphere otherwise than in the stratosphere. They describe possibilities of bacterial degradation, absorption in leaves, deposition in the oceans. The description is all in qualitative terms. No attempt is made, either by Maduro and Schauerhammer themselves, or in references to the publications that they cite, to extrapolate any of the findings to provide an estimated size for a global sink.

There is a very simple reason for this. Rowland (1994) summed up the results of CFC monitoring in the lower atmosphere as follows:

By the mid-1980s, CFC increases were large enough to show that the corresponding atmospheric lifetimes must clearly be very long – 50 to 100 years – and no undiscovered tropospheric sinks existed.

To elaborate this a little: the rate of build-up of CFC content of the lower atmosphere was large enough, when compared to the known production figures for CFCs, that it could be ascertained that at most 1 per cent to 2 per cent of the total CFC content of the atmosphere was being removed each year by all sinks (and this can be deduced without any knowledge of what the sinks are). Decomposition by UV light in the stratosphere was by then a thoroughly investigated sink. It was 'known' to be removing 1 per cent of the total CFC content of the atmosphere each year. Therefore all other sinks, whatever they may be, are only removing between 0 per cent and 1 per cent of the total atmospheric CFC content annually; that is they must be responsible for only between 0 and 50 per cent of total CFC removal, while the stratospheric sink accounts for between 50 per cent and 100 per cent.

What, then, was the basis of the claimed knowledge of the rate of removal of CFCs from the stratosphere? The main evidence came from stratospheric measurements of CFC levels, which showed fairly constant mixing ratios up to a height of 25 km, and then a very rapid decrease with increasing height (Rowland, 1996, p. 1790). No physical circulation process can account for this. It can only be due to decomposition in UV light. The rate of CFC removal represented by the altitude profile can be deduced from the known rates of material transfer in atmospheric circulation.

The evidence that other sinks for atmospheric CFCs are relatively minor can thus stand quite apart from any study of the alleged sinks themselves.

Rowland (and others among the mainstream atmospheric scientists) leaves an opening for an attack on the ground of alternative CFC sinks, in saying that there are none – as in the quoted passage above. All that the evidence supports, and all that needs to be said for the ozone depletion theories to be valid, is that other CFC sinks, if they exist, and whatever they may be, are very minor contributors to CFC removal, compared to the stratospheric sink.

The second string of Maduro and Schauerhammer's attack on the orthodox view of Antarctic ozone depletion is a questioning of the reality of the phenomenon itself, or at least of the way it is typically described by the atmospheric scientists.

Maduro and Schauerhammer's message in introducing their discussion of the Antarctic ozone hole is confused and self-contradictory. Thus we are told on page 120 of their book that Dobson's Southern anomaly is the same thing as the ozone hole, and on page 121 that it is not. Claims of prior discovery of the ozone hole at Dumont d'Urville in 1958 and at Syowa in 1984 have already been discussed in Chapter 6 of this volume. The former is certainly important to the general thrust of Maduro and Schauerhammer's arguments, but it is difficult to see any effect that transferring credit for the discovery from the British Antarctic group to the Japanese would have on their case.

From the introduction to their chapter, where the reader is tacitly invited to regard the ozone hole as much the same thing as Dobson's Southern anomaly, through the early part of the discussion, where the suggestion is that there was an ozone hole in 1958 which disappeared for many years, only to return in the late 1970s, the authors come to the next issue they want to discuss, with another change in position. They seem to concede that the ozone hole is new, or at least more serious than it formerly was. They turn to arguing that it is not man-made, and that chlorine compounds have little or nothing to do with it.

Some discussion of natural cycles and other factors that influence ozone levels is presented. It leads to a pronouncement that the ozone hole is a natural and ephemeral phenomenon. In one sentence (Maduro & Schauerhammer, 1992, p. 127), the data are alleged to 'suggest' it. In the next they prove conclusively that the hole was there decades ago.

The evidence and argument to support such a contention simply is not there. At best, there might be some support for it if the 1958 Dumont d'Urville reinterpretation were taken as solid and incontestable fact. But even in that case, a single anomaly of that type might rather provoke a search for unusual antecedents relating to that particular occasion, rather than an induction that the phenomenon is 'ephemeral' in a more general sense!

The logical slide from an allegation of error to an allegation of fraud, without presentation of supporting evidence, ought also not be left unmarked.

The rest of this chapter of their book is devoted to possible alternatives to the chlorine account of Antarctic ozone depletion. Various material is presented from the standpoint of the circulation and solar cycle theories. No mention of the AAOE or its results, nor citation of any literature more recent than the AAOE is included. This may be only marginally excusable in a volume published four and a half years after the AAOE, and two and a half years after the full and final publication of its results. Needless to say, the AAOE results themselves completely disarm these arguments, to the point where their main protagonists, Mahlman, Fels, Schoeberl, *et al.*, abandoned them in favour of the chlorine theory.

Having already concluded that chlorine chemistry is not the cause of the Antarctic ozone depletion, and that the chlorine that is not causing the phenomenon is not coming from CFCs, Maduro and Schauerhammer devote their final chapter of 'scientific' analysis to whether or not the Antarctic ozone hole really matters.

The central issue that they address is the danger of increased skin cancer incidence. This is implied in the connections drawn by mainstream scientists between decreases in ozone and increases in surface ultraviolet irradiation, and between increased surface ultraviolet radiation and increased incidence of skin cancers. Other alleged effects of increased radiation arising from ozone thinning are also discussed.

The first claim that Maduro and Schauerhammer make is that there is no evidence that the amount of damaging UV-B radiation reaching the earth's surface has increased. They cite data collected at a series of US field stations during 1974–85, which show a clear decrease in the total amount of surface solar UV-B radiation through the period.

Their argument is that if ozone levels really decreased by 3 per cent, and if UV-B irradiation increases by 2 per cent for each 1 per cent ozone decrease, UV-B levels ought to have increased by 6 per cent or so. But it is quite apparent that this is based on a simplistic misrepresentation of the atmospheric scientists' position. The claim for a 3 per cent ozone depletion represents an underlying figure for the chlorine-mediated contribution, which is part of an overall pattern of ozone presence which involves variations with the solar cycle, the quasi-biennial oscillation, and other factors. By the same token, ozone levels are only one of several factors that influence surface UV radiation. Average cloud cover, and general 'haziness' (that is, the amount and type of tropospheric aerosol present) can obviously also affect surface ultraviolet levels to a much greater extent than a small variation in stratospheric ozone. Perhaps more important in this case, though, is the question of stratospheric aerosols. Major eruptions of Mount St. Helens and El Chichón in 1982, followed a relatively quiet period for volcanoes in the 1970s. El Chichón, in particular, injected a large amount of material directly into the stratosphere, which had a significant effect on incoming solar radiation, for two to three years following the eruption (Mankin & Coffey, 1984).

More recent data from New Zealand (McKenzie, 1996), show both a significant increase in surface UV-B, and a strong correlation of surface UV-B with ozone levels during the period 1982–90. The influence of any volcanic aerosol on these figures has not been factored out; it may be fortuitously absent, since the El Chichón cloud probably did not extend so far South, and the next major eruption, that of Pinatubo, occurred in 1991.

Maduro and Schauerhammer then proceed to point out the relatively small scale of the UV-B dose increase that might be associated with a moderate depletion of stratospheric ozone, with the very large variations of UV-B reaching the earth's surface at locations at different latitudes, or at different altitudes. They compare the increased risk for an individual with that of moving address a few hundred kilometres closer to the equator.

They briefly dismiss the other point that is sometimes raised – ecological damage because plants and animals may have difficulty adapting to increased UV at any fixed location – by pointing out the versatility of various crop plants in adapting to conditions over a wide latitude range. The latitude range over which a crop species can grow efficiently typically would span a range of UV radiation levels greater than any radiation change brought about by moderate ozone depletion. One part of this debate that they have not addressed is the issue of some of the specialised ecologies in the Antarctic and sub-Antarctic. There, species that may be important in the food chain have had to face very different UV-B levels in the Antarctic ozone hole, from the extremely low ones they have evolved to cope with (Silver & de Fries, 1990, pp. 113–14).

Finally, the authors turn to a claim that UV-B radiation is not as damaging as has been supposed. Their first claim is that, while other skin cancers do show some epidemiological correlation with total UV dosage, malignant melanomas do not. Their playing down of the importance of other forms of skin cancer is a rather bizarre overstatement. Their claim about melanomas is somewhat out of date, and does not tell the whole story of a very complicated connection that is only starting to be clearly understood (Armstrong, 1996).

They conclude the chapter with a review of a number of claimed beneficial effects of UV-B radiation exposure: both generally accepted ones, and some contentious ones. Making a great deal of the fact that UV-B kills certain bacteria seems a little of a two-edged sword; on the one hand it may indicate a means of removing these organisms if they are not wanted; on the other it seems indicative of a general injuriousness of UV-B to living things![6]

Overall, then, the finding of this analysis must be that, while Maduro and Schauerhammer (1992) adopt (in places) the language and forms of a contribution to a scientific debate, that is not how it should be viewed or classified.

No serious attempt is made to provide any new observational nor experimental evidence nor new theoretical insight that might be effective as scientific argument. The arguments put forward lack any real substance. In most cases they contain errors of logic or mathematics, or avoid quantitative detail, or both.

It is unfortunate that a book published in 1992 avoids discussion of the results of the AAOE series of experiments in 1987, particularly when they played such a crucial role in swinging the scientific consensus firmly behind the chlorine-based theories of the Antarctic ozone hole. This failing is compounded by producing old arguments from the standpoint of the solar cycle and circulation-based theories, when the protagonists of these outdated theories had long since abandoned them in the light of new evidence.

The book is *not* a contribution to a scientific debate. It does not present a serious challenge to the current scientific consensus on chlorine-mediated ozone depletion.

But that does not mean that Maduro and Schauerhammer's work is not an effective and influential one at other levels. The arguments are presented with a political rhetoric that is very convincing for the uninformed reader, the careless casual reader, or the reader who is predisposed to a view similar to theirs. It has played a role in influencing debate at levels other than the scientific: the political debate in the US congress, and the public debate in the mass media outlets.

Rowland's evaluation is dismissive: he claims that the book is 'a good job of collecting all the bad papers in one place' (Taubes, 1993, quoting from Rowland's presidential address to the AAAS). This is an unfortunate suggestion. *Some* of the papers quoted by Maduro and Schauerhammer should not be seen as 'bad' in any sense. It is rather the case that they are cited in a way that is out of context, or they represent out of date work which was good at the time, but has since been refuted.

But the atmospheric scientists have found that they cannot afford to be so dismissive in public forums, even if they continue to ignore Maduro and others arguing in a similar way in the strictly scientific forums. And even this latter step lends credence to accusations of a conspiracy by atmospheric scientists to silence their critics, and suppress work that does not fit in with their favoured theories.

One atmospheric scientist suggests that the scientist trying to contribute to a public debate is:

. . . caught between the exaggerations of the advocates, the exploitations of political interests, the media's penchant to turn everything into a boxing match, and your own colleagues saying we should be above this dirty business, and stick to the bench. (S. Schneider, as quoted by Taubes, 1993)

Some recent secondary commentators have seen the scientific debate on chlorine-mediated ozone depletion as not yet settled, and cited Maduro and Schauerhammer's book as an important document for the minority view.[7]

I cannot accept that their book is a part of a scientific debate, for the reasons that have emerged in this discussion. A more appropriate view is that the scientific debate is now closed, with a clear consensus behind the orthodox views of the ozone hole, and chlorine-mediated global ozone depletion. A public and political debate continues in some quarters, based largely on the same flawed and outdated arguments that Maduro and Schauerhammer present (see, e.g. Clarkson *et al.*, 1994).

Conclusions about the scientific consensus

In the analysis in this chapter, and, indeed, throughout this volume, we have seen how a body of scientific evidence accumulated in the primary literature, and how it shaped various aspects of the debate and eventual consensus about several aspects of the investigation of the ozone layer.

It could not be said that what we have found is a science that is based on a solid and rational ontology or epistemology as might be demanded by philosophical purists. Either models like Popper's are too narrow and rigid to provide a realistic description of science, or this area of science has not yet qualified as sound and mature science, and is unlikely to do so in the near future. Clearly, I prefer the former characterisation.

On the other hand, what we have seen is a science that has made pragmatic and sensible use of such evidence as there is. In most cases the scientific consensus has been backed by proof that would be likely to stand in a court of law as 'beyond reasonable doubt', and in all cases by proof rather stronger than 'the balance of probabilities'.

The caricaturisation of science as a monolithic conspiracy, manipulated by an elite, motivated by issues of research funding and political power, does not fit well with the healthy and vigorous debate that can be seen to have taken place. The way that that debate was settled, and the relationship of the settlement to the evidence is clearly recorded in the primary scientific literature. It can easily be audited by informed outsiders – say other scientists from a neighbouring discipline. In this instance at least there seems to be little ground for complaint.

This is not to say that political and sociological issues are unimportant. There is little doubt that the way scientific institutions and infrastructure are organised produces a strong conservative bias. There may well be instances where personal ambition has managed to distort parts of the scientific edifice to a greater or lesser extent. The dynamics of human social interactions affect bodies like national academies of science or the Ozone Trends Panel no less than they do other similar institutions. But conspiracy allegations are implausible. As an example, the Ozone Trends Panel includes, and has always included prominent scientists who were major players on both sides of a vigorous debate between chlorine and circulation theories of anomalous Antarctic ozone depletion. When such a body arrives at a consensus position in accord with one of these views, and in contradiction of the other, in the light of new evidence, it must be taken seriously. This is even more the case when the new evidence is clearly and publicly presented in a form accessible to anyone who can take the trouble to learn enough background material to follow the more technical side of the argument.

At the end of the twentieth century, there is a firm but provisional consensus about the science of the ozone layer. The investigations that we have explored in this volume have been thorough, and the conclusions appear to be well grounded in and firmly justified by the experimental and observational evidence. I believe that here we have a modern instance of good science.

The status of the evidence on which the scientific consensus is built in this case cannot be seen as providing firm epistemological justification in a global sense. There is nothing that would disarm the thorough-going sceptic. But there is justification quite sufficient for an auditor who is prepared to go along with the general thrust of current scientific belief to accept the detail of the consensus that has been reached about these phenomena, and to admit it into the general scientific corpus. Good science of the type represented by these investigations can thus be seen as a valid and worthwhile pursuit.

NOTES

1 In this article Rowland claims that Lovelock, and Wilkniss *et al.* had established a current background of about 1 part in 10^{10}. The one-year residence time was based on the figure of 1 part in 10^{11} given in Lovelock's earlier letter.
2 Molina, M.J., Public Lecture, University of Melbourne, 4 December 1996. In reply to a question from the audience, Prof. Molina stated that he and Rowland had realised from very early that their work had important public policy implications. They took what action they could, within the bounds of professional propriety, to ensure that their work was widely noticed.
3 J.R.Christie, private communication. A very simple spreadsheet calculation was set up. CFC production was assumed to increase linearly from zero in 1934 to its 1975 level, and then to hold that same level from 1975 to 1990. Each year 1 per cent of total CFCs was assumed lost to the stratosphere, and 0.25 per cent lost to all other sinks. These conditions correspond to an atmospheric lifetime of eighty years, and an 80 per cent efficiency for transfer to the stratosphere. The total 1990 transfer to the stratosphere was a figure equal to 28.9 per cent of the 1990 production. Leaving the rate of stratospheric transfer fixed at 1 per cent, the total transfer rose to 30.2 per cent at 100 per cent transfer efficiency, and fell to 25.4 per cent at 50 per cent transfer efficiency.
4 The usage of ton and tonne in this passage may seem a little confusing. In essence, the American authors follow local practice and work in imperial tons. The scientific sources, and the author of this volume, prefer to work in tonne, or metric tons of 1000 kg. An imperial ton is just over 1016 kg. The difference in size between the two units is trivial for most purposes, and certainly for the purposes of the discussion in this chapter.
5 1994 IPCC Interim Report, Radiative Forcing of Climate Change 1994. As cited in WMO Report, 'Scientific Assessment of Ozone Depletion: 1994', Table 2–1, p. 2.4.
6 A well known story concerns a minister of religion working with a group of homeless alcoholics. He is supposed to have poured out a small puddle of whisky, and placed a small worm in it. The worm wriggled briefly, and died within a half minute or so. 'Alcohol is a poison!' he thundered, 'What does that experiment show you?' 'If I drink plenty of whisky, I won't get worms,' came the reply from one of his audience.
7 Newton, D.E., *The Ozone Dilemma*, ABC-CLIO, Santa Barbara, 1995. The conclusion to a chapter entitled 'Ozone layer depletion: myth or reality?' is that 'The debate concerning ozone depletion is far from over'. (p. 22.)

References

AAOE. (1989). The planning details and results of the AAOE are published in a series of papers in two special issues of the *Journal of Geophysical Research*: 94, D9, pp. 11181–737, and D14, pp. 16437–854.

AES (1998). *Guide to the WMO/GAW World Ozone Data Centre*. (Version 1.0 Draft). Toronto: Environment Canada.

Anderson, J.G., Brune, W.H., & Proffitt, M.H. (1989). Ozone destruction by chlorine radicals within the Antarctic vortex: the spatial and temporal evolution of ClO/O_3 anticorrelation based on in situ ER-2 data. *Journal of Geophysical Research* **94**, 11465–479.

Armstrong, B. (1997). UV effects on human health. In *Proceedings of the First SPARC General Assembly*. Publication WCRP-99. 2, pp. 505–8. Geneva: World Climate Research Programme.

Atkinson, M. (1994). Regulation of science by 'peer review'. *Studies in History and Philosophy of Science* **25**, 147–58.

Austin, J., Jones, R.L., Palmer, T.N., & Tuck, A.F. (1987). Circulation changes and chemistry: implications for the destruction of ozone in Antarctica. *Unpublished paper.*

Benedick, R.E. (1991). *Ozone Diplomacy*. Cambridge, Mass.: Harvard University Press.

Brady, J.E. (1975). *General Chemistry*. 5th Ed, 1990. p. 5. New York: Wiley.

Brillouin, L. (1956). *Science and Information Theory*. 2nd Ed, 1962. New York: Academic Press.

Brock, W.H. (1994). *The Fontana History of Chemistry*, pp. 314–26. Glasgow: Fontana.

Brush, S.G. (1989). Prediction and theory evaluation: the case of light bending. *Science* **246**, 1124–9.

Brush, S.G. (1994). Dynamics of theory change: the role of predictions. In Hull, D., Forbes, M., & Burian, R., Eds. *PSA 1994: Proceedings of the 1994 Biennial Meeting of the Philosophy of Science Association*, Volume 2, pp. 133–45. East Lansing, Mich.: PSA.

Bunce, N.J. (1995). *Introduction to Environmental Chemistry*. Winnipeg: Wuerz.

Callis, L.B., & Natarajan, M. (1986). The Antarctic ozone minimum: Relationship to odd nitrogen, odd chlorine, the final warming, and the 11-year solar cycle. *Journal of Geophysical Research* **91**, 10771–796.

Chapman, S. (1930a). On ozone and atomic oxygen in the upper atmosphere. *Philosophical Magazine and Science Journal* **10**, 369–83.

Chapman, S. (1930b). A theory of upper-atmosphere ozone. *Memoirs of the Royal Meteorological Society* **3**, 103–25.

Chubachi, S. & Kajiwara, R. (1986). Total ozone variations at Syowa, Antarctica. *Geophysical Research Letters* **13**, 1197–8.

Chubachi, S. (1984). Preliminary result of ozone observation at Syowa Station from February 1982 to January 1983. *Memoirs of the National Institute Polar Research* Special Issue **34**, 13–19.

Clark, I.D. (1974). Expert advice in the controversy about Supersonic Transport in the United States. *Minerva.* **12**, 416–32.

Clarkson, T., Matthews, A., & McKenzie, R. (1994). *Christchurch Press*, April 14, 1994. p. 11.

Crutzen, P.J., & Arnold, F. (1986). Nitric acid cloud formation in the cold Antarctic atmosphere. *Nature* **324**, 651–5.

Crutzen, P.J. (1970). The influence of nitrogen oxides on the atmospheric ozone content. *Quarterly Journal of the Royal Meteorological Society* **96**, 320–5.

Crutzen, P.J. (1971). Ozone production rates in an Oxygen-Hydrogen-Nitrogen oxide atmosphere. *Journal of Geophysical Research* **76**, 7311–27.

Cunnold, D.M., Fraser, P.J., Weiss, R.F., Prinn, R.G., Simmons, P.G., Miller, B.R., Alyea, F.N., & Crawford, A.J. (1994). Global trends and annual release of CCl_3F and CF_2Cl_2, estimated from ALE/GAGE and other measurements from July 1978 to June 1991. *Journal of Geophysical Research* **99**, 1107–26.

Delaney, A.C., Sheldovsky, J.P., & Pollock, W.H. (1974). Stratospheric aerosol: the contribution from the troposphere. *Journal of Geophysical Research* **79**, 5646–50.

Dobson, G.M.B. & Harrison D.N. (1926). Measurement of the amount of ozone in the earth's atmosphere, and its relation to other geophysical conditions. *Proceedings of the Royal Society* **A110**, 660–93.

Dobson, G.M.B. (1968a). *Exploring the Atmosphere.* London: Oxford University Press.

Dobson, G.M.B. (1968b). Forty years of atmospheric ozone at Oxford: a history. *Applied Optics* **7**, 387–405.

Dowling, D. (1998). *Experiments on Theories: The Construction of Scientific Computer Simulation.* Ph.D. thesis, University of Melbourne.

Fabry, C. & Buisson, H. (1913). L'absorption de l'ultraviolet par l'ozone et la limite du spectre solaire. *Journal de Physique* **3**(Série 5), 196.

Fabry, C. & Buisson, H. (1921). Étude de l'extremité ultra-violette du spectre solaire. *Journal de Physique,* **2**(Série 6), 197.

Farman, J.C., Gardiner, B.G., & Shanklin, J.D. (1985). Large losses of total ozone reveal seasonal ClO_x/NO_x interaction. *Nature* **315**, 207–10.

Farman. J.C. (1977). Ozone measurements at British Antarctic Survey Stations. *Philosophical Transactions of the Royal Society of London* **B279**, 261–71.

Farman. J.C., & Hamilton, R.A. (1975). Measurements of atmospheric ozone at the Argentine Islands and Halley Bay, 1957–72. *British Antarctic Survey Scientific Report* no. 90 (40 pp.).

Farmer, C.B., Raper, O.F., Norton, R.H. (1976). Spectroscopic detection and vertical distribution of HCl in the troposphere and stratosphere. *Geophysical Research Letters* **3**, 13–16.

Ferry, G.V., Neish, E., Schultz, M., & Pueschel, R.F. (1989). Concentrations and size distributions of Antarctic stratospheric aerosols. *Journal of Geophysical Research* **94**, 16459–74.

Fleck, L. (1946). Problems of the science of science. In Cohen, R.S. & Schnelle, T., Eds. *Cognition and Fact.* pp. 113–28. Boston: Reidel, 1986.

Franklin, A.D. (1981). What makes a 'good' experiment. *British Journal for the Philosophy of Science* **32**, 367–79.

Gilbert, G.N., & Mulkay, M. (1984). Experiments are the key: Participants' histories and historians' histories of science. *Isis* **75**, 105–25.

Gillespie, R.J., Humphreys. D.A., Baird, N.C., & Robinson, E.A. (1986). *Chemistry.* p. 91. Boston: Allyn & Bacon.

Goldsmith, P., Tuck, A.F., Foot, J.S., Simmons, E.L., & Newson, R.L. (1973). Nitrogen oxides, nuclear weapons testing, Concorde, and stratospheric ozone. *Nature* **244**, 545–51.

Gribble, G.W. (1994). *Chemistry & Industry.* 6 June 1994, p. 390.

Grünbaum, A. (1976). Is falsifiability the touchstone of scientific reality? Karl Popper vs. inductivism. In Cohen, R. S., Feyerabend, P. K., & Wartofsky, M. W., Eds. *Essays in Memory of Imre Lakatos.* pp. 213–52. Dordrecht: Reidel.

Hacking, I. (1983). *Representing and Intervening.* Cambridge University Press.

Hadfield, (1994). . . . as Japan seeks last-minute opt-out from ban. *New Scientist* 19 March 1994, p. 6.

Hampson, J.F. (1964). Photochemical behaviour of the ozone layer. *CARDE Technical Note 1627/64.* Valcartier, Quebec: Canadian Armament Research and Development Establishment.

Hampson, J.F. (1966). *CARDE Technical Note 1738/66.* Valcartier, Quebec: Canadian Armament Research and Development Establishment.

Harrison, H. (1970). Stratospheric ozone with added water vapour: Influence of high altitude aircraft. *Science* **170**, 734–6.

Heidt, L.E., Vedder, J.F., Pollock, W.H., Lubb. R.A., & Henry, B.E. (1989). Trace gases in the Antarctic atmosphere. *Journal of Geophysical Research* **94**, 11599–611.

Hon, G. (1989). Towards a typology of experimental errors: an epistemological view. *Studies in History and Philosophy of Science* **20**, 469–504.

Hunt, B.G. (1966a). The need for a modified photochemical theory of the ozonosphere. *Journal of Atmospheric Science* **23**, 88–95.

Hunt, B.G. (1966b). Photochemistry of ozone in a moist atmosphere. *Journal of Geophysical Research* **71**, 1385–98.

Johnston, H.S. (1971). Reduction of stratospheric ozone by nitrogen oxide catalysts from supersonic transport exhaust. *Science* **173**, 517–22.

Johnston, H.S. (1972). Newly recognized vital nitrogen cycle. *Proceedings of the National Academy of Sciences of the USA.* **69**, 2369–72.

Johnston, H.S. (1992). Atmospheric ozone. *Annual Reviews of Physical Chemistry.* **43**, 1–32.

Kerr, R.A. (1987). Winds, pollutants drive ozone hole. *Science* **238**, 156–8.

Komhyr, W.D., Grass, R.D., & Leonard, R.K. (1986). Total ozone decrease at South Pole Antarctica. *Geophysical Research Letters* **13**, 1248–51.

Kuhn, T.S. (1962). *The Structure of Scientific Revolutions*, 2nd Ed. 1970. University of Chicago Press.

Lakatos, I. (1974). The role of crucial experiments in science. *Studies in History and Philosophy of Science* **4**, 309–25.

Laudan, L. (1984). *Science & Values*. Berkeley: University of California Press.

Lazrus, A.L., Gandrud, B.W., Woodard, C.N., & Sedlacek, W.A. (1975). Stratospheric halogen measurements. *Geophysical Research Letters* **2**, 439–41.

Le Grand, H.E. (1988). *Drifting Continents & Shifting Theories*. Cambridge University Press.

Le Grand, H.E. (1990). Is a picture worth a thousand experiments. In H.E. Le Grand, Ed. *Experimental Enquiries*. pp. 241–70. Amsterdam: Kluwer.

Leeuwenhoek, A. van (1677). The observations of Leeuwenhoek on animalcules engendered in semen. As reproduced in Cole, F.J. *Early Theories of Sexual Generation*. Oxford University Press. 1930.

Leovy C.B. (1969). Atmospheric ozone: An analytic model for photochemistry in the presence of water vapour. *Journal of Geophysical Research* **74**, 417–26.

Litfin, K.T. (1994). *Ozone Discourses*. New York: Columbia University Press.

Loewenstein M., Podolske, J.R., Chan, K.R., & Strahan, S.E. (1989). Nitrous oxide as a dynamical tracer in the 1987 Airborne Antarctic Ozone Experiment. *Journal of Geophysical Research* **94**, 11589–98.

Lovelock, J.E. (1971). Atmospheric fluorine compounds as indicators of air movements. *Nature* **230**, 379.

Lugg, A. (1986). An alternative to the traditional model? Laudan on disagreement and consensus in science. *Philosophy of Science* **53**, 419–24.

Maduro, R.A., & Schauerhammer, R. (1992). *The Holes in the Ozone Scare*. Washington: 21st Century Science Associates.

Mahlman, J.D., & Fels, S.B. (1986). Antarctic ozone decreases: A dynamical cause? *Geophysical Research Letters* **13**, 1316–19.

Mankin, W.G., & Coffey, M.T. (1984). Increased stratospheric hydrogen chloride in the El Chichón cloud. *Science* **226**, 170–2.

McElroy, M.B., Salawitch, R.J., Wofsey, S.C., and Logan, J.A. (1986). Reductions of Antarctic ozone due to synergistic interactions of chlorine and bromine. *Nature* **321**, 759–62.

McKenzie, D. (1994). Loophole opens up black market in CFCs. *New Scientist.* 14 March 1994, p. 6.

McKenzie, R. (1996). Ozone depletion and UV radiation: A health risk for New Zealanders? *New Zealand Public Health Report* **3**, 10. pp. 75–7.

McKenzie, R.L. & Johnston, P.V. (1984). Springtime stratospheric NO_2 in Antarctica. *Geophysical Research Letters* **11**, 73–5.

McPeters, R. (1997). Private email, as reproduced in Christie, M. (1997). *Chlorine and Stratospheric Ozone: Philosophical Studies of a Scientific Investigation*. Ph.D. thesis, University of Melbourne.

Meyer, E. (1903). Über die Absorption der ultravioletten Strahlung in Ozon. *Annalen der Physik* **12**(Folge 4), 849–59.

Midgley, T., & Henne, A.L. (1930). Organic fluorides as refrigerants. *Industrial & Engineering Chemistry* **22**, 542–5.

Midgley, T. (1937). From the periodic table to production. *Industrial & Engineering Chemistry* **29**, 241–5.

Mill, J.S. (1843). *System of Logic*. Book 3, Chapter 8. 1967 Reprint of 1906 Edition. pp. 213–52. London: Longmans.

Molina M.J., Tso, T-L., Molina L.T., & Wang, F.C-Y. (1987). Antarctic stratospheric chemistry of chlorine nitrate, hydrogen chloride, and ice: Release of active chlorine. *Science* **238**, 1253–7.

Molina, L.T., & Molina, M.J. (1986). Production of Cl_2O_2 by the self reaction of the ClO radical. *Journal of Physical Chemistry* **91**, 433–6.

Molina, M.J., & Rowland, F.S. (1974). Stratospheric sink for chlorofluoromethanes: chlorine atom catalysed destruction of ozone. *Nature* **249**, 810–12.

Molina, M.J. (1996). Polar ozone depletion. (1995 Nobel Lecture). *Angewandte Chemie International Edition in English* **35**, 1778–85.

NASA (1988). *Present State of Knowledge of the Upper Atmosphere 1988: An Assessment Report*. NASA Reference Publication 1208. Washington: NASA.

New Scientist (1986). Scientists line up to oppose research into SDI. 30 October 1986, p. 16.

New Scientist (1993). Features on the U.S. strategic defense initiative. 20 March 1993, pp. 24–33.

Newell, R.E. (1970). Water vapour pollution in the stratosphere by the supersonic transporter? *Nature* **226**, 70.

Newman, P.A. (1994). Antarctic total ozone in 1958. *Science* 264, 543–6.

Newton, D.E. (1995). *The Ozone Dilemma: A Reference Handbook*. Santa Barbara: ABC-CLIO.

Pitcher, E.J. & Geisler, J.E. (1987). The 40 to 50 day oscillation in a perpetual January simulation with a global circulation model. *Journal of Geophysical Research* **92**, 11971–8.

Polanyi, M. (1946). *Science, Faith and Society*. Republished 1964. University of Chicago Press.

Polanyi, M. (1967). The growth of science in society. *Minerva* **5**, 533–45.

Popper, K. (1959). *The Logic of Scientific Discovery*. Reprinted 1992. London: Routledge.

Pukelsheim, F. (1990). Robustness of statistical gossip and the Antarctic ozone hole. *Institute of Mathematical Statistics Bulletin* **19**, 540–2.

Roan, S. (1989). *Ozone Crisis*. New York: Wiley.

Rowland, F.S. (1975). Chlorofluoromethanes and stratospheric ozone – A scientific status report. *New Scientist* **68**, 2 October 1975, pp. 6–11.

Rowland, F.S. (1988). Chlorofluorocarbons, stratospheric ozone, and the Antarctic 'ozone hole'. *Environmental Conservation* **15**, 101–15.

Rowland, F.S. (1994). *Chemical & Engineering News* August 15, 1994, pp. 8–13.

Rowland, F.S. (1996). Stratospheric ozone depletion by chlorofluorocarbons (1995 Nobel Lecture). *Angewandte Chemie International Edition in English* **35**, 1786–98.

Schiff, H.I.(1983). Ups and downs in ozone prediction. *Nature* **304**, 471.

Silver, C.S., & de Fries, R.S. (1990). *One Earth, One Future.* pp. 103–15. Washington: National Academy of Sciences.

Solla Price, D.J. de. (1963). *Little Science, Big Science.* New York: Columbia University Press.

Solomon, P., Connor, B., Zaffra, R.L. de, Parrish, A., Barrett, J., & Jaramillo, M. (1987). High concentrations of chlorine monoxide at low altitudes in the Antarctic spring stratosphere: Secular variation. *Nature* **328**, 411–13.

Solomon, S. (1988). The mystery of the Antarctic ozone 'hole'. *Reviews of Geophysics* **26**, 131–48.

Solomon, S., Garcia, R.R., Rowland, F.S. and Wuebbles, D.J. (1986). On depletion of Antarctic ozone. *Nature* **321**, 755–8.

Solomon, S., Mount, G., Sanders, R.W., & Schmeltekopf, A. (1987). Visible spectroscopy at McMurdo station, Antarctica: Two observations of OClO. *Journal of Geophysical Research* **92**, 8329–38.

Stephenson, J.A.E. & Scourfield, M.W.J. (1991). Importance of energetic solar protons in ozone depletion. *Nature* **352**, 137–9.

Stolarski, R.S. & Cicerone, R.J. (1974). Stratospheric chlorine: a possible sink for ozone. *Canadian Journal of Chemistry* **52**, 1610–15.

Stolarski, R.S. & Schoeberl, M.R. (1986). Further interpretation of satellite measurements of Antarctic total ozone. *Geophysical Research Letters* **13**, 1210–12.

Stolarski, R.S., Kruger, A.J., Schoeberl, M.R., McPeters, R.B., Newman, P.A. & Alpert, J.C. (1986). Nimbus-7 satellite measurements of the springtime Antarctic ozone decrease. *Nature* **322**, 808–11.

Taubes, G. (1993). The ozone backlash. *Science* **260**, 1580–3.

Thomason, N. (1994). Was Feyerabend's Galileo a closet rationalist? *British Journal for the Philosophy of Science* **45**, 255–64.

Tiles, J.E. (1993). Experiment as intervention. *British Journal for the Philosophy of Science* **44**, 463–75.

Tuck, A.F., Watson, R.T., Condon, E.P., Margitan, J.J., & Toon, O.B. (1989). The planning and execution of ER-2 and DC-8 aircraft flights over Antarctica, August and September, 1987. *Journal of Geophysical Research* **94**, 11181–222.

Tung, K.K, Ko, M.K.W., Rodriguez, J.M., & Sze, N.D. (1986). Are large Antarctic ozone variations a manifestation of dynamics or chemistry? *Nature* **322**, 311–4.

Stratospheric Ozone Review Group, U.K. (1988). *Stratospheric Ozone 1988.* London: HMSO.

Warneck, P. (1989). *Chemistry of the Natural Atmosphere.* San Diego: Academic Press.

Wayne, R.D. (1991). *Chemistry of Atmospheres.* 2nd Ed. Oxford: Clarendon Press.

Weiss, A. (1993). Causal stories, scientific information, and the ozone depletion controversy. In Brante, T., Fuller, S., & Lynch, W., Eds. *Controversial Science.* pp. 225–40. Albany, NY: SUNY Press.

WMO (1994): *Scientific Assessment of Ozone Depletion: 1994.* WMO Global Ozone Research and Monitoring Project – Report No. 37. Geneva: WMO.

Woods, D.C., Chuan, R.L., & Rose, W.I. (1985). Halite particles injected into the stratosphere by the 1992 El Chichón eruption. *Science* **230**, 170.

Zaffra, R.L. de, Jaramillo, M., Parrish, A., Solomon, P.M., Connor, B., & Barrett, J. (1987). Observation of abnormally high concentrations of chlorine monoxide at low altitudes in the Antarctic spring stratosphere, I: Diurnal Variation. *Nature* **328**, 408–11.

Zaffra, R.L. de, Jaramillo, M., Barrett, J., Emmons, L.K., Solomon, P.M., & Parrish, A. (1989). New observation of a large concentration of ClO in the springtime lower stratosphere over Antarctica, and its implications for ozone-depleting chemistry. *Journal of Geophysical Research* **94**, 11423.

Ziman, J. (1978). *Reliable Knowledge*. 1991 edition. Cambridge University Press.

Index

Airborne Antarctic Ozone Expedition
    (AAOE), 60–5, 66–9, 90, 97, 99, 105,
    108–18, 125–7, 130, 136, 139–40, 150,
    165, 180–4, 192, 199, 201
aircraft exhaust, 24–7, 36, 39, 120, 154
Amundsen-Scott (South Pole) station
    (US), 43, 45
Anderson, J., 62–4, 115, 141
anomalous data points, *see* outliers
anomaly, 12–13, 16, 28, 43–7, 49–50, 53,
    57, 67, 83, 90, 95, 96–8, 99, 101, 115,
    123, 124, 127, 131, 133–4, 140, 155,
    162, 169, 198, 199, 203
Antarctic, 6, 10, 12, 21, 38–65, 68, 83,
    85–100, 103, 106–11, 115, 120, 123,
    124, 126, 127, 130–8, 140–8, 150, 151,
    155, 161, 162, 165, 167, 169, 174, 175,
    180–6, 189, 191, 192, 195–201, 203
Antarctic ozone hole, *see* ozone, Antarctic
    depletion phenomenon
antithesis, 129–32, 141–4, 146
arched hypotheses, 144–7
Argentine Islands station (Britain), 41
asymmetry, *see* symmetry
Atmospheric Environment Service
    (Canada), 12, 42
Atomic Energy Commission (US), 29,
    178

Bacon, Sir Francis, 94
Bayesian analysis, 123, 144, 146, 147
Benedick, Richard, 35, 36, 44, 58, 178,
    179, 180
biomass burning, 195–6
British Antarctic Survey (BAS), 38, 43, 46,
    50–1
Brush, Stephen, 75–7
Buisson, H., 9

Canadian Meteorological Service, *see*
    Atmospheric Environment Service
catalytic chain reaction, 25, 26, 30, 34, 37,
    78, 117, 119, 135, 137, 154, 180

causality, 1, 10, 32, 34, 41, 54, 56, 67, 79,
    90–1, 93–5, 98, 100, 121, 122, 124,
    130, 133, 134, 137–8, 141, 150, 155,
    160, 162–4, 168, 169–70, 182, 193,
    198–9
ceteris paribus,
CFC-12 (dichlorodifluoromethane), 19,
    20, 29, 127, 176, 177
Chapman, S., 12–16, 25–8, 31, 92, 149,
    153
chlorinated fluorocarbons (CFCs), 5, 18,
    21–2, 29–32, 35–6, 40, 53–4, 57–8, 68,
    77–85, 87, 89–90, 102, 127, 153, 154,
    165, 169, 175–99, 204
chlorine monoxide, 30, 34, 53–5, 59–65,
    98–106, 108–21, 125–7, 131–2, 134–8,
    145, 147, 183, 184, 191, 192
chlorine theory, *see* theory of Antarctic
    phenomenon, chlorine-based
chlorine nitrate, 34, 64, 83, 155, 181, 188,
    191, 197
chlorine, atomic, 30–2, 53, 62, 63, 78, 100,
    191
Chubachi, S., 49–50
Cicerone, R., 36, 44
circulation theory, *see* theory of Antarctic
    phenomenon, circulation
Clark, Ian, 26
clouds, polar stratospheric, 64, 100, 111,
    116, 148, 155–6, 161, 162
computer algorithms, 44, 165
confirmation, 41, 43, 59, 60, 64, 66, 84,
    90, 103–5, 108, 111–13, 122–32, 141,
    143–7
consensus, scientific, 6, 15, 35, 48, 66,
    103, 108, 127, 134, 169–85, 193,
    201–4
conspiracy theories, 111, 120, 186, 187,
    202, 203
Copernican theory, 144
Cornu, A., 9
correlation, 10, 11, 33, 53, 54, 57, 61,
    63, 101, 109, 113–17, 120, 121, 124,